BUILDING A
NEW EUROPE

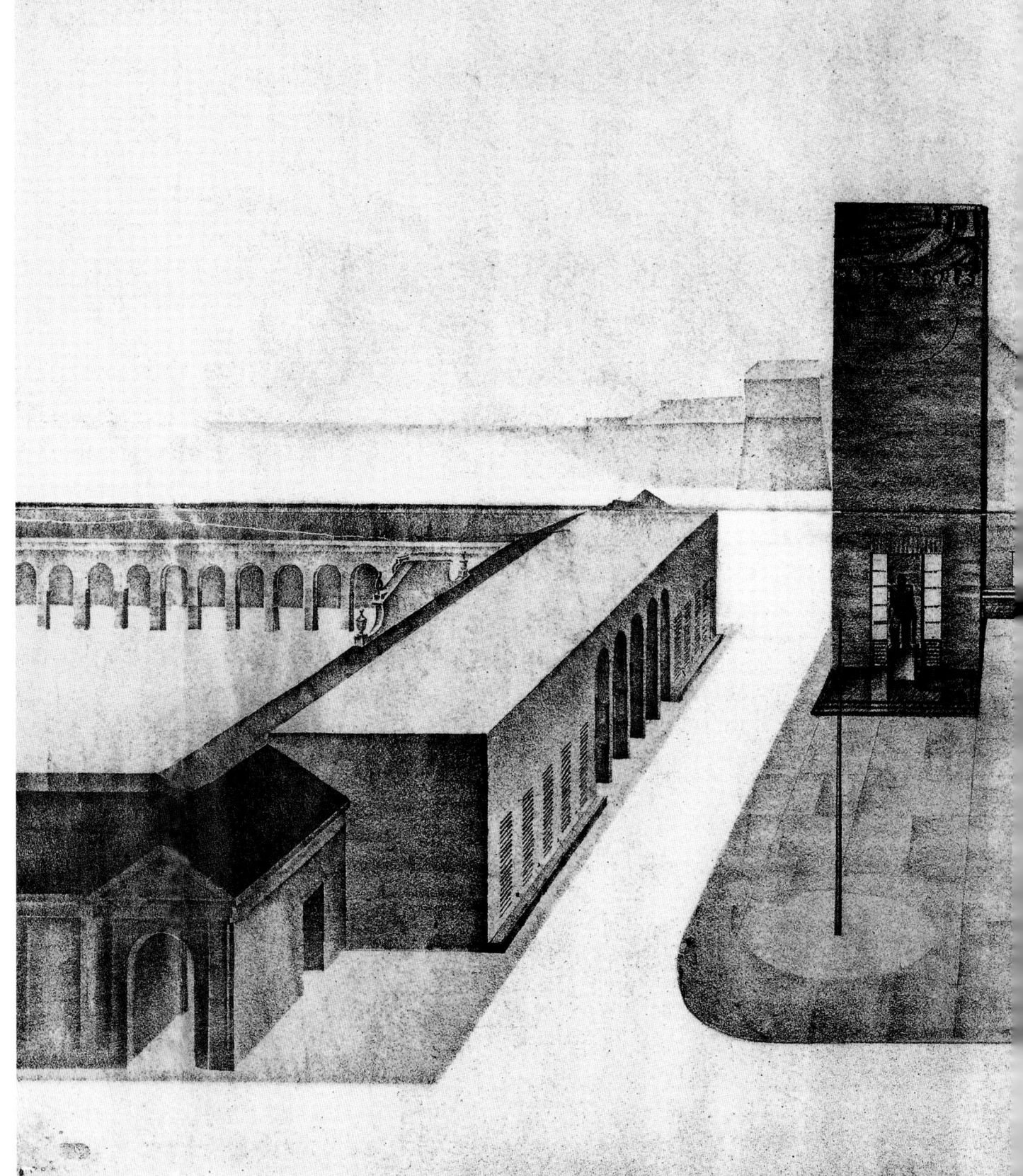

BUILDING A NEW EUROPE

PORTRAITS OF MODERN ARCHITECTS

ESSAYS BY
GEORGE NELSON
1935–1936

INTRODUCTION BY
KURT W. FORSTER

FOREWORD BY
ROBERT A. M. STERN

YALE UNIVERSITY PRESS NEW HAVEN AND LONDON
IN ASSOCIATION WITH THE YALE UNIVERSITY SCHOOL OF ARCHITECTURE

Published with assistance from Herman Miller, Inc., and from Vitra AG, Basel, Switzerland. Copyright © 2007 by Yale University. All rights reserved.

This book may not be reproduced, in whole or in part, including illustrations, in any form (beyond that copying permitted by Sections 107 and 108 of the U.S. Copyright Law and except by reviewers for the public press), without written permission from the publishers.

Publications Director, Yale School of Architecture: Nina Rappaport
Editorial Assistant and Image Editor: Hannah Purdy

Designed by Jena Sher and Michael Bierut, Pentagram

Set in Lmvdr, Bodoni Twelve ITC, and Gotham by Jena Sher

Printed in China
by Kwong Fat Offset

Library of Congress Cataloging-in-Publication Data
Nelson, George, 1908–1986.
Building a new Europe: portraits of modern architects: essays by George Nelson, 1935–1936
George Nelson; introduction by Kurt W. Forster; foreword by Robert A. M. Stern.
p. cm. Includes index.
ISBN: 978-0-300-11565-9
(cloth : alk. paper)
1. Architects–Europe–History–20th century. 2. Architecture–Europe–20th century.
I. Yale University. School of Architecture. II. Pencil Points. III. Title.
NA958.N45 2007
720.92′2–dc22 [B] 2006038462
A catalogue record for this book is available from the British Library.

The paper in this book meets the guidelines for permanence and durability of the Committee on Production Guidelines for Book Longevity of the Council on Library Resources.
10 9 8 7 6 5 4 3 2 1

CONTENTS

Foreword by Robert A. M. Stern *vii*

Introduction by Kurt W. Forster *1*
An American in Rome: George Nelson Talks with European Architects

Portraits
Marcello Piacentini *29*
Bent Helweg-Moeller *39*
Luckhardt Brothers *47*
Gio Ponti *57*
Le Corbusier *69*
Mies van der Rohe *81*
Ivar Tengbom *93*
Giuseppe Vaccaro *107*
Eugène Beaudouin *115*
Raymond McGrath *125*
Walter Gropius *137*
Tecton *147*

Architect Biographies *161*

Notes *165*

Index *171*

Illustration Credits *174*

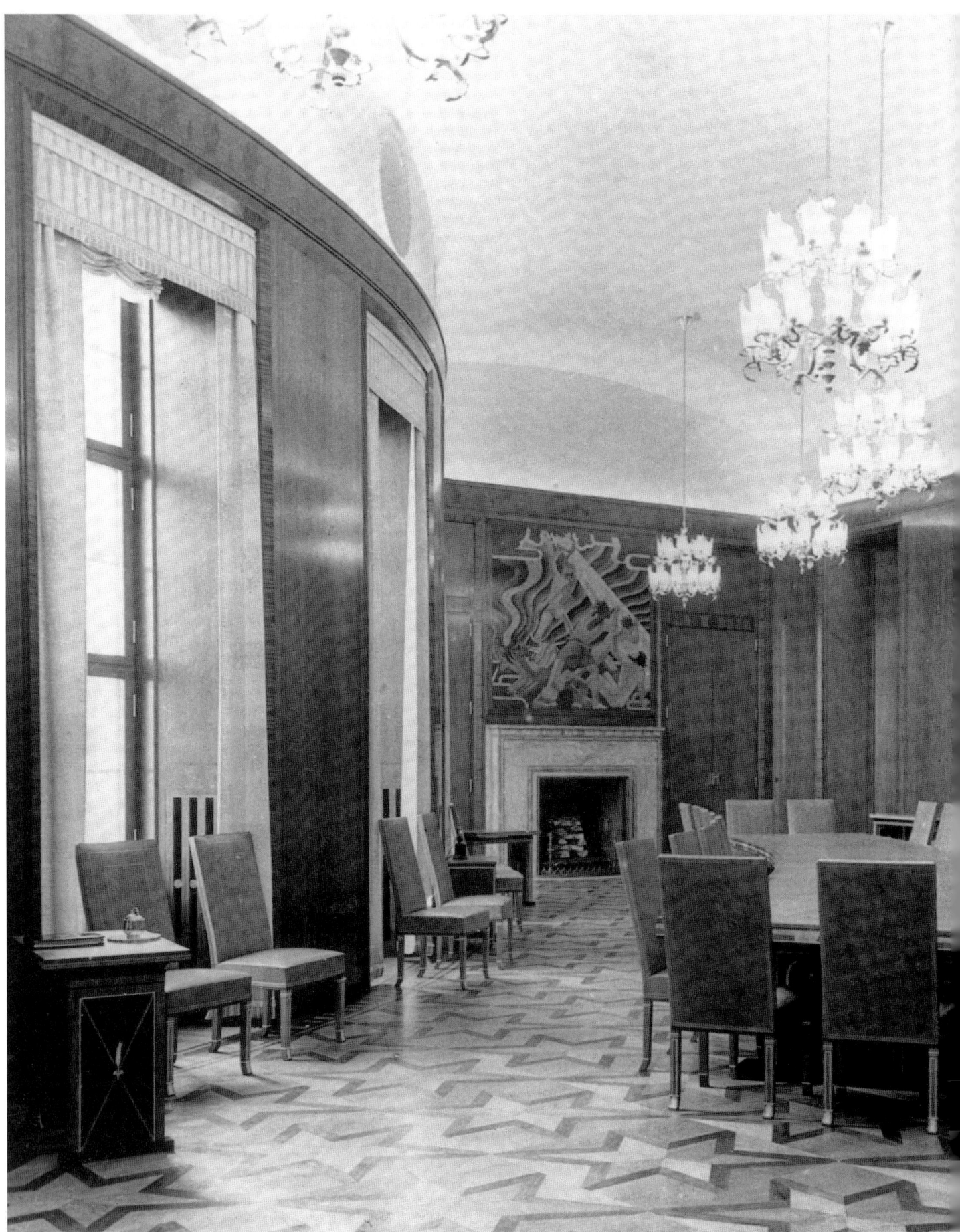

FOREWORD

ROBERT A. M. STERN

Best known as a furniture designer, George Nelson (1908–1986) was also an architect and design journalist. Nelson graduated from Yale College (B.A. 1928) and Yale School of Fine Arts (B. Arch. 1931), before going on to Rome as a Fellow of the American Academy (1932–34). While in Rome, in addition to following the usual program of exploring in detail the city's historic buildings, streets, and landscapes, Nelson embarked on a remarkable project interviewing leading Modern European architects. Not bounded by ideology, Nelson cast a wide net, interviewing modern classicists as well as International Style Modernists. The inclusiveness of his approach reflects the transitional nature of 1930s architecture, of which he was probably first made aware at Yale, where the influence of Otto Faelton's Modern Gothic was counterbalanced by Raymond Hood's enthusiasm for Le Corbusier's architecture and urbanism. In 1977, at a speech delivered at the International Design Conference in Aspen, Nelson recalled his time at Rome:

In the early thirties there was a great deal of controversy whether modern architecture was here to stay or not. Back home, there was considerable doubt about it. Architects were still covering their buildings with pilasters and columns and arches and all that, which, I must say, look better today than they did when we were in rebellion against them. But in Rome the extraordinary thing I learned was that everything was modern. You would be walking down a street past a fifteenth-century palazzo and sticking out of the wall of the palazzo would be a ruin of an arch; the palazzo was built around the ruin centuries older than the palazzo. Then because business wasn't good in Rome either, a corner of this palace had been remodeled and somebody had put in an ultramodern candy shop. So there were these three epochs coexisting in one building. And suddenly you realized the obvious, that everything that is worth anything is always modern because it can't be anything else, and therefore there are no flags to wave, no manifestoes, you just do the only thing you can honestly do now.

Nelson's interviews formed the basis of twelve profiles that were published in *Pencil Points* soon after he returned to the United States. The series presented the work of architects practicing in seven countries: Denmark, England, France, Germany, Ireland, Italy, and Sweden. The range of the architects was as diverse as their geography–including extreme Modernists, like Le Corbusier, Mies van der Rohe, and Walter Gropius, as well as conservative Modern traditionalists like Eugène Beaudouin, Marcello Piacentini, and Ivar Tengbom.

Pencil Points was founded in 1920 to cater to the interests of draftsmen in large offices. By the mid-1930s the magazine was in the process of reinventing itself to meet the changing interests of a profession reeling under the one-two punch of the Depression and the rising impact of stylistic Modernism. *Pencil Points'* search for a new identity culminated in 1943 when it was transmogrified into *Progressive Architecture*.

Nelson became an associate editor (1935–43) and then a consulting editor (1944–49) of *Architectural Forum*. He also maintained an active architectural practice. Working with William Hamby, Nelson produced his first significant building, the eminently Corbusian Sherman Fairchild townhouse on East 65th

Street in New York (1941), now sadly renovated beyond all recognition. In the 1950s, working with Gordon Chadwick, Nelson produced a number of important weekend houses, including Otto Spaeth's shingle-clad residence (1956) in East Hampton, New York. In its way it is a critical work, offering a scholarly and inventive reinterpretation of McKim, Mead, and White's Low House (1887), Bristol, Rhode Island, which was demolished in the 1950s.

It was as a furniture designer that Nelson made his most enduring contribution, beginning in 1945 with a modular storage unit called Storagewall. This led to a long association with the Herman Miller furniture company, where, as designer and design director, he worked closely with Charles and Ray Eames, Isamu Noguchi, and others. Nelson's own work in furniture design for Herman Miller included such mid-twentieth-century standards as the marshmallow sofa and the swagged-leg chair, as well as clocks and various other items of industrial design which he undertook for other firms. Nelson and his firm George Nelson and Associates were also responsible for graphic design and exhibition displays, most notably the American National Exhibition in Moscow (1959), scene of the famous "kitchen debate" between Nikita S. Khruschev and Vice President Richard M. Nixon.

The *Pencil Points* essays are notable not only for Nelson's inclusive selection of architects, but also for his consideration of the various political backgrounds within which the architects were operating. Nelson's sensitivity to local nuance led him to explore as few others of his time did the way architecture was being politicized, especially by the totalitarian regimes. Nelson's unblinkered inclusiveness should also be contrasted with the increasingly narrow focus of such leading Modern architecture polemicists of the day as Walter Gropius, Sigfried Giedion, Henry-Russell Hitchcock, and Philip Johnson. Nelson's Modern pantheon contained architects whose work lay outside that of the Bauhaus and the so-called International Style. Today, as a new generation of architects and historians looks back to the heritage of twentieth-century Modern architecture, discovering for themselves long marginalized figures and movements, the wisdom of Nelson's approach can be appreciated all the more.

This book would not have been possible without the generous support of Brian Walker, president and CEO of Herman Miller, and of Rolf Fehlbaum, the president of Vitra AG. I want also to thank Kurt W. Forster, the Vincent Scully Visiting Professor of Architectural History at Yale, for so generously agreeing to help place Nelson's essays in the context of 1930s European architecture, politics, and culture. Nina Rappaport, publications director at the Yale School of Architecture, saw the project through to its publication, and Hannah Purdy, an architect and recent graduate of Yale, undertook to recover archival images and resource materials to illustrate the text, locating the images that Nelson had used in almost all cases and finding appropriate substitutions where necessary.

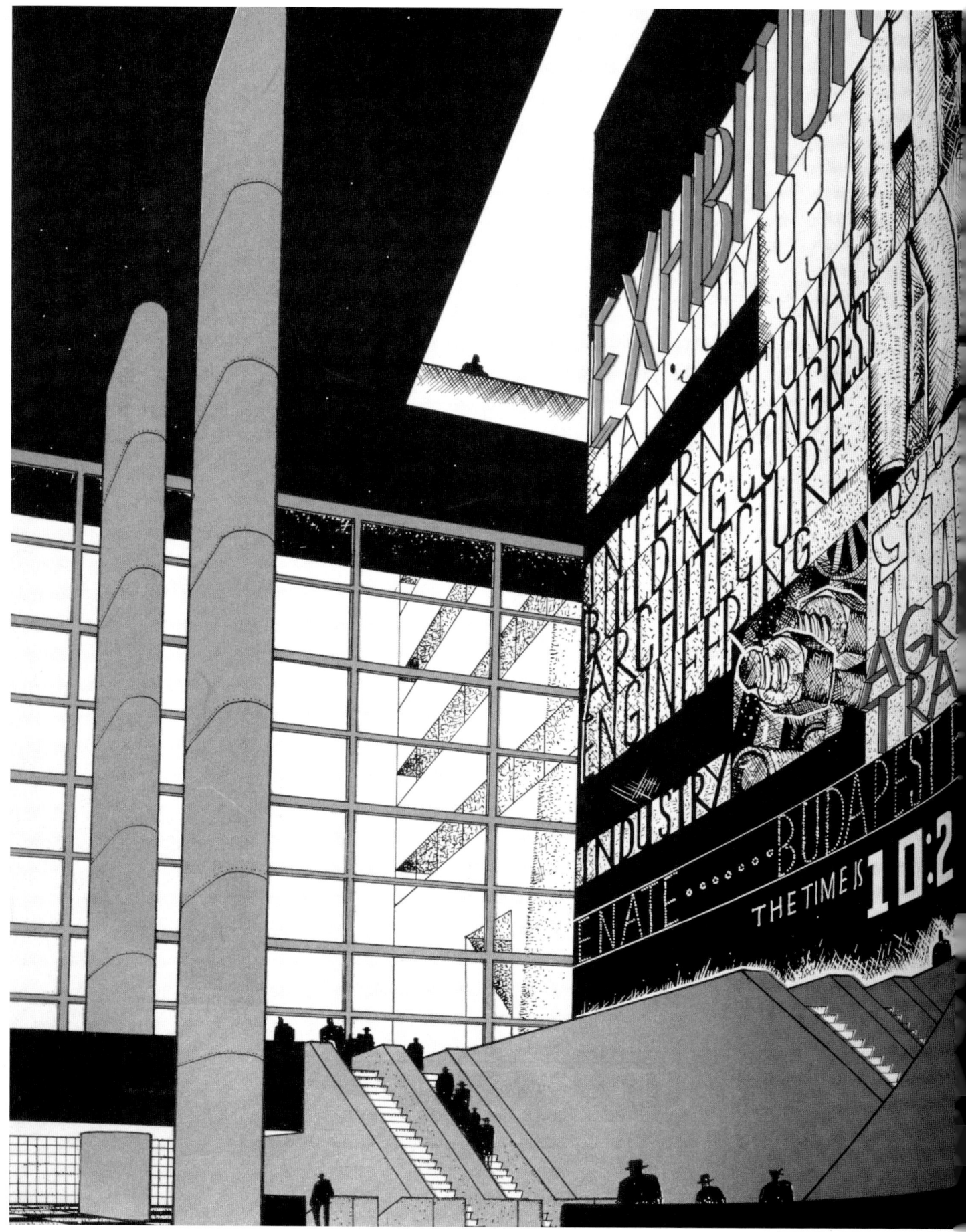

AN AMERICAN IN ROME
GEORGE NELSON TALKS WITH EUROPEAN ARCHITECTS

KURT W. FORSTER

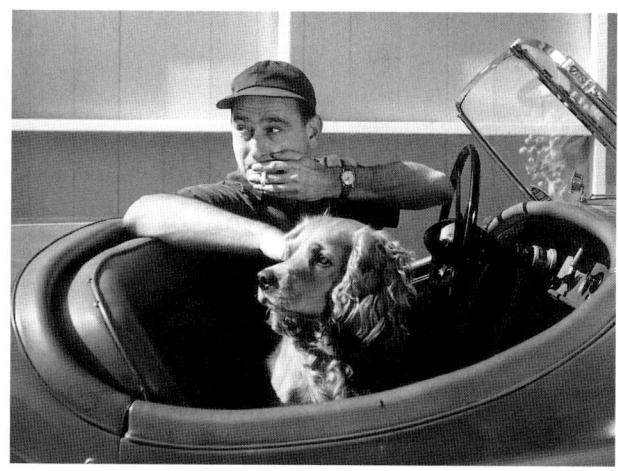

A photograph shows George Nelson (1908-1986) in the cockpit of his Jaguar, turning back as if to wave goodbye while taking a drag on his cigarette. Nelson, rarely without a cigarette and its bluish haze, is wearing a baseball cap and a short-sleeved sports shirt, looking more like Humphrey Bogart than a designer of the 1950s. In fact, the Sherman Fairchild House on 65th Street in New York, which he designed in 1941, would make a perfect location for a film that might turn noir, or soon brighten into Technicolor.[1] The latter is what indeed happened, as Nelson went on to design brilliantly colored objects such as sofas, chairs, cabinets, lamps, and clocks—all conceived to fill the interiors created by "home-builders" of the postwar years.[2]

When Nelson wrote about architecture he almost sounded like Bogart, too, delivering pithy observations and clipped pronouncements pared down to the cryptically obvious: "There was no ballyhoo about it," he said of a Danish architect's work. "He did his work and that was all there was to it."[3] Nelson had a knack for incisive characterization, deftly daubing anecdotes into the broader picture of the times. He reported that when Mies van der Rohe lowered his heavy frame into a comfortable chair during a visit to the Tugendhat house, he faced an onyx-clad partition and exclaimed, "Now there is a *wall!*"[4] Nelson's writing talent carried him across cultural and generational gaps long before he achieved anything equivalent in design. Such a perfect match of persona and product is a hallmark of the second third of the twentieth century, when grapefruit juice, linoleum flooring, GE kitchen appliances, and shiny Chevrolets promised a seamless transition to modernity.[5] How Nelson arrived at that point is of no concern here, but his youthful exploration of European and American architecture is.

That the portrait of the designer as (still) a young man should depict him in a snazzy convertible, and with his four-legged companion, adds a tinge of Tintin to a character always on the move and after things only his keen nose could detect. When in Europe during the early 1930s Nelson did not rest on his academic laurels. Instead of seeking refuge in American émigré circles like those of Florence, where Bernard Berenson held court, or Paris, where Gertrude Stein and her coterie had long favored the new, Nelson immediately reacted to the urgency of renewal and the resurgence of authoritarianism that had begun to stir throughout Europe. What is more, he sensed an insidious affinity, or at least a tension, between modernization and totalitarianism. He traveled to Scandinavia and Germany to see for himself, and he sought more information from the plethora of publications in circulation at the time, and from the frequent trips architects used to take to such meetings as the CIAM conferences (Congres International d'Architecture Moderne)—onboard ship in 1933 and in England in 1934. Nelson was in Europe while Christopher Isherwood sat out the gathering storm in Germany and chronicled it in his *Berlin Stories*, and while Ernest Hemingway moved between plumbing the pagan mystery of Spanish bullfights and playing ex-

opposite:
George Nelson in his car with his cocker spaniel, c. 1950.

below:
George Nelson and William Hamby, Sherman Fairchild House, New York (1941) (Architectural Forum, April 1943).

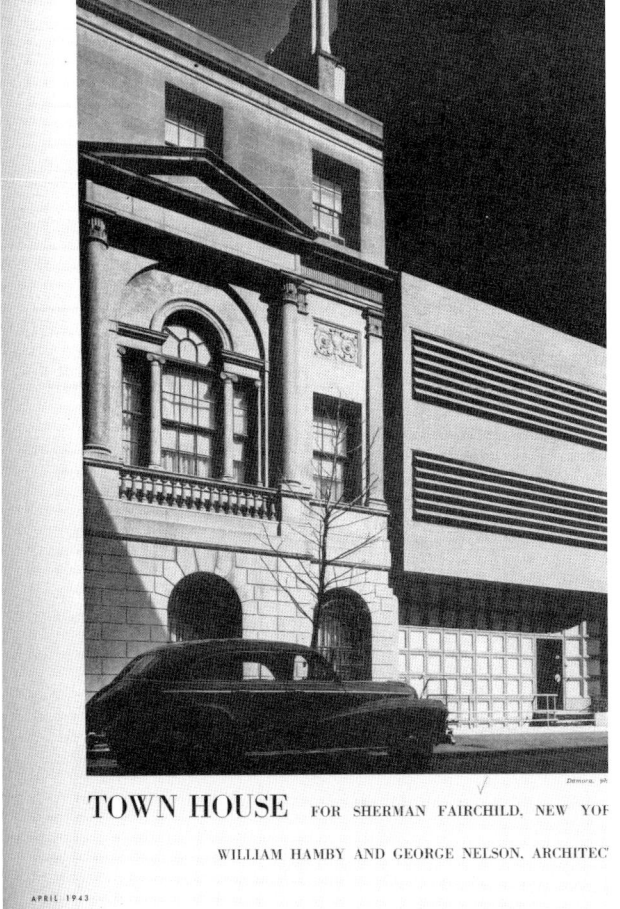

patriate in Paris, where one intellectual after another sought a first refuge on the flight from Nazism.

In the early 1930s, designers and architects from many countries crisscrossed Europe, some of them soon to be on their way overseas, others without premonition of the political turbulence and personal travails that awaited them. A young sophomore from St. Louis, Charles Eames, traveled through northern Europe in 1929, allegedly paying special attention to new architecture but dutifully sketching mainly the old.[6] Many years later Eames recalled the effect that such pilgrimage sites as the Weissenhof Siedlung in Stuttgart had on him, comparing it to "having a cold hose turned on you."[7] Philip Johnson and Henry-Russell Hitchcock motored through central Europe in search of the latest architecture to be included in their show at the Museum of Modern Art.[8] Unbeknownst to Nelson, we presume, Saul Steinberg had arrived from his native Romania in 1933 to study architecture at the Milan Polytechnic just as such Jewish architects as Erich Mendelsohn and Konrad Wachsmann were beginning to leave Germany. Wachsmann moved down to Rome, where he found opportunities as an expert in the technology of concrete.[9] Italy, always a magnet for foreigners, continued to attract Germans—Jews and gentiles alike—who sought friendly umbrage in the country that offered a temporary haven for northerners who cherished a romantic view of the south.[10]

Having graduated from Yale University with a bachelor of arts degree in 1928 and a bachelor of fine arts

INTRODUCTION

below:
Dust jacket from George Nelson and Henry Wright, Tomorrow's House: A Complete Guide for the Home-Builder *(1945).*

opposite:
McKim, Mead, and White, American Academy in Rome, principal façade.

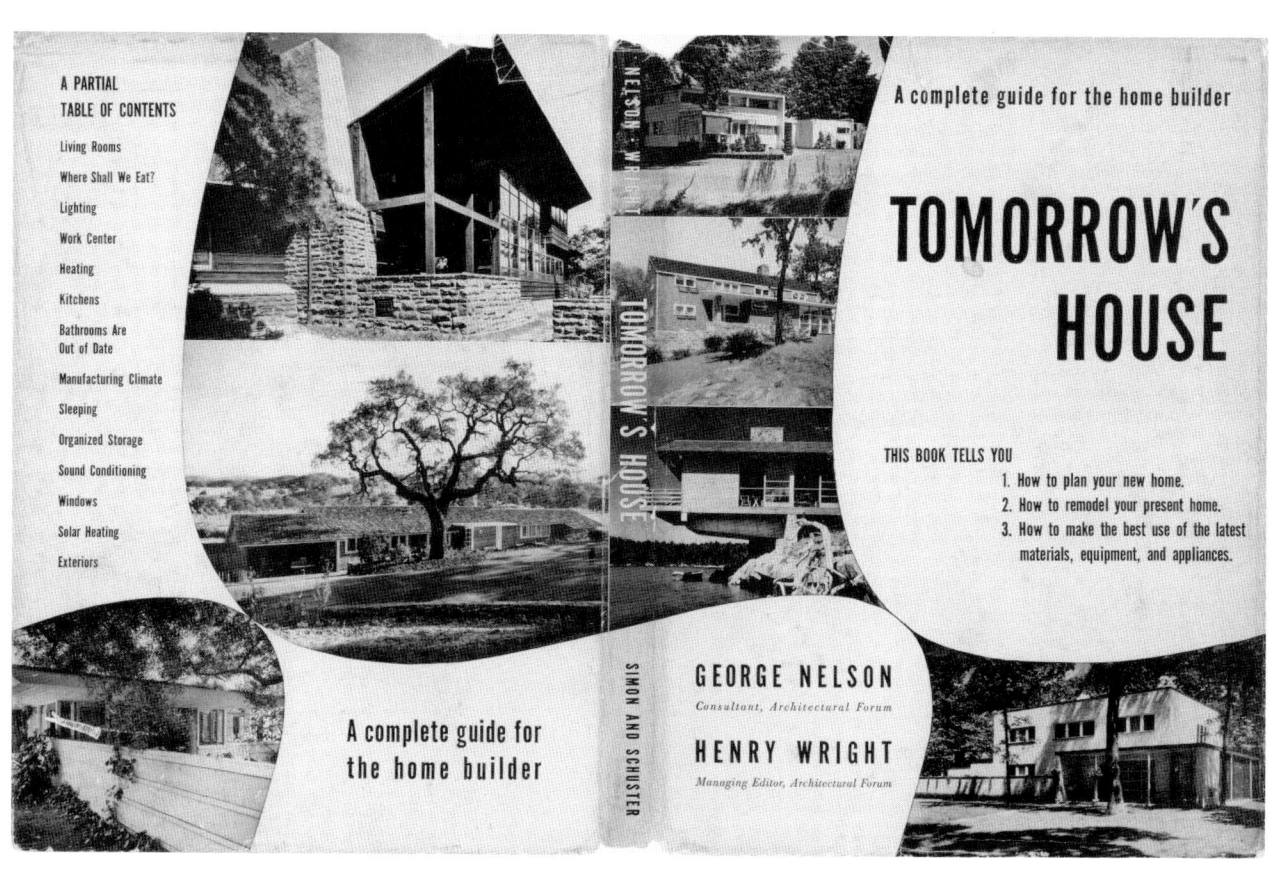

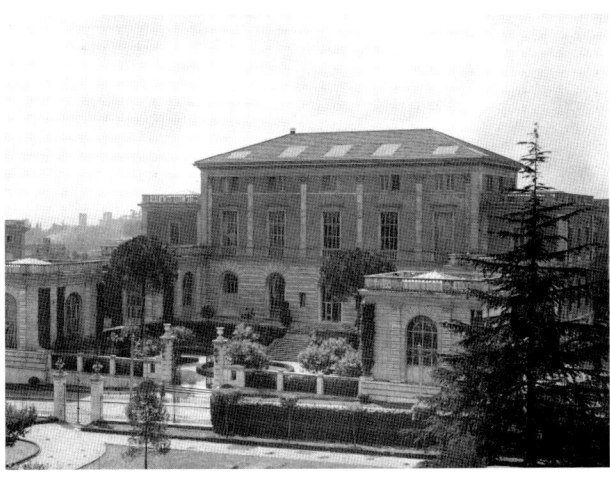

degree in 1931, George Nelson won the Rome Prize of the American Academy in 1932. At that time he was an architecture student at the Catholic University in Washington, D.C.[11] He may have moved to that school hoping to increase his chances for the Paris Prize, on which he worked for the better part of the year. After losing by a narrow margin he dove straight into the Rome Prize competition and lucked out. The Rome Prize was what Yale graduates coveted the most. Nelson's winning entry, a somewhat pedestrian design for an auditorium, foursquare and topped by a dome, vaguely recalled the Rotunda at the University of Virginia. McKim, Mead, and White had redone the interior of the Rotunda, and the connection is likely to have helped Nelson's proposal before a jury known to favor Yalies and the legacy of an architect, McKim, whose pride had been the establishment of an American Academy in Rome.[12]

Only twenty-four years old when he sailed for Italy, Nelson left a country in the grip of the Depression and headed for one celebrating the tenth year of its Fascist resurgence.[13] He enjoyed residence at the American Academy, a massive neo-Renaissance palazzo, and proximity to the Villa Aurelia and the expansive gardens on the Gianicolo hill. These were framed in the splendor of a setting as Henry James might have described it, overlooking a city in the throes of political transformation. The Academy was only one of numerous foreign institutions that had been established in recognition of the city's erstwhile preeminence as the repository of a millenary European culture. One traveled to Rome in the wake of eighteenth- and nineteenth-century cognoscenti in order to explore the past and commemorate its achievements, and perhaps to imagine ways of recovering some of its qualities—or at least some of its trophies. Such expectations were built into the very fabric of the palazzo the Academy occupied: its stately vestibule and hallowed halls breathed the grandeur of which American industrialists had grown fond, making McKim, Mead, and White rich as they designed similar palaces for New York clubs and Newport mansions. The solemn architecture of the American Academy was a perfect instance of carrying owls to Athens, or, more precisely, palazzi to Rome, producing that slightly disturbing effect of a look-alike claiming a seat at the banqueting table.[14] However, one must not overlook the fact that Italians had already been doing much the same thing, lining the newly opened avenues of Rome with ministerial monoliths and heavy-set apartment buildings.

ROME REFORMED

By 1932 the city of Rome no longer beckoned visitors only with its warren of medieval streets, princely residences for papal families, and grand spoils of imperial times, but also impressed them with starkly modern manifestations: the dowdy Palazzo delle Esposizioni was temporarily wrapped in blank façades and sported metal pylons in the guise of giant fasces. These emblems of the new regime were everywhere, and Mussolini made frequent personal appearances amid the black

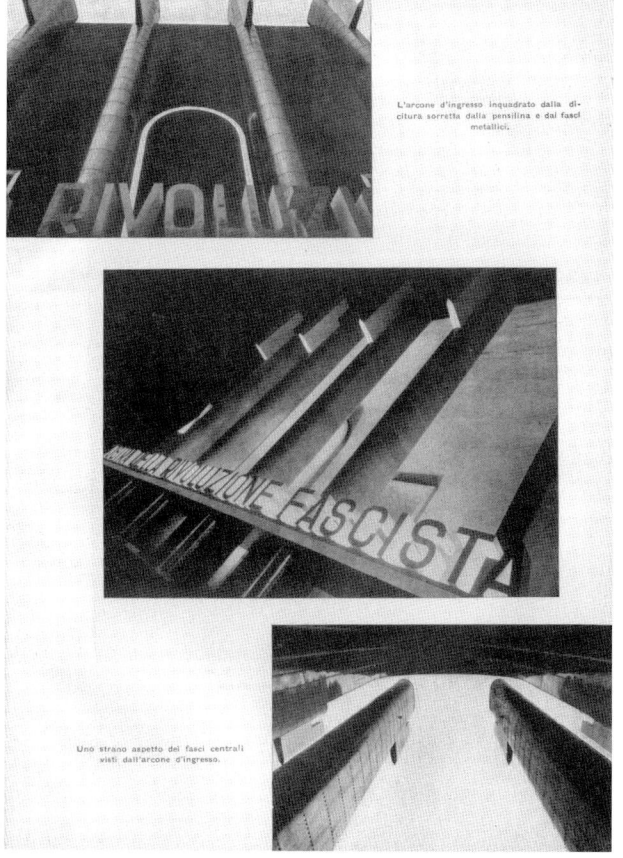

Adalberto Libera, façade of the Palazzo delle Esposizioni, Rome, for the Mostra della Rivoluzione Fascista (1932), and Giuseppe Terragni, Sala O (documenting the year 1922), illustrated in the catalogue of the Deciennale exhibition, ed. Dino Alfieri and Luigi Freddi (Rome, 1933).

shirts and the youth of the Balilla.[15] At the Città universitaria, a complex of contemporary buildings began to take shape under the direction of Marcello Piacentini and involving the Milanese architect Gio Ponti, both of them subjects of Nelson's reports, while the pickaxe had begun to open breaches in the carcass of the city, altering the topography of key areas: the Largo Argentina and the wide Via delle Botteghe Oscure leading to the Capitoline Hill, as well as the Via Barberini with its new hotels, cinemas, and shops, sprang from Piacentini's new *piano regolatore* for the capital city, which had been adopted in 1931.[16] Among the most trenchant changes in the Roman townscape was the demolition of the entire quartiere Alessandrino and removal of the Velia hill between 1924 and 1932, when Mussolini inaugurated a triumphal avenue, linking Palazzo Venezia (the Duce's preferred seat of office) with the Colosseum. In May 1936 the avenue was renamed Via dell'Impero to mark the conclusion of the Italo-Ethiopian war. Something not so funny happened on the way to grandeur, as the ancient fora never met their modern counterparts in the shape of a giant Palazzo littorio.[17] Size and ambition far overreached time and resources, leaving only a forlorn runway through the ruins to this day. Other so-called *sventramenti*, or eviscerations of the city, were more successful: an entire wedge of the Vatican City was hauled away and the area around the Mausoleum of Augustus cleared of century-old accretions. At the western outskirts the arenas and buildings of the Foro Italico were nearing

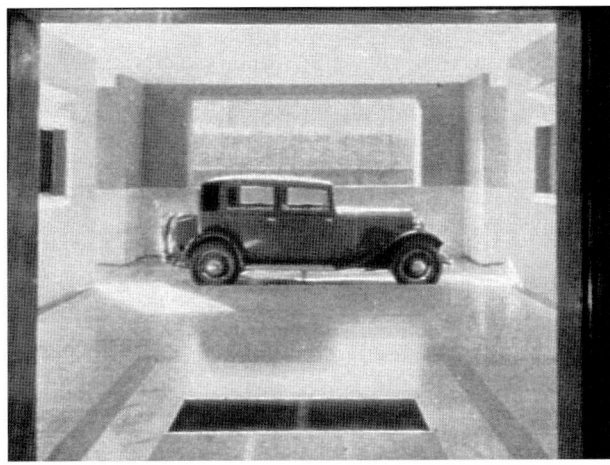

New car in the gleaming atrium of a Roman residence (early 1930s).

completion in 1932. Sleek modern cars circulated in the streets, and elegantly dressed men and women put a bright face on a city whose thick layers of dust were being blown into the air. Like many of his Italian contemporaries, Nelson was taken with the "spectacle of fast cars going down the street, past the ruins," for speed, he added, "only increases, if anything, the sense of their magnificence and power."[18] One is reminded of an observation that the Berlin architect Karl Friedrich Schinkel made in 1803, extolling with nearly identical words the "splendid and powerful effect" that Venetian palaces make along the Grand Canal "as one rides past them."[19] In a word, things were beginning to move, and even the immobile colossus of Rome was caught up in the excitement of the modern metropolis.

When Nelson arrived at the Academy in 1932, Rome was not only festooned for a year of political pomp but it also had enterprising and intelligent people in government, attracted such writers as Luigi Pirandello, Alberto Moravia, Massimo Bontempelli, Emilio Cecchi, and Curzio Malaparte, and produced journals of architecture and literature that have remained landmarks of their kind.[20] In the Academy's library Nelson's attention was certainly drawn to *Casabella, Quadrante,* and *Domus,* journals that regularly featured architecture from many countries. By virtue of their typography and layout alone these journals would have attracted a discerning eye like Nelson's. *Casabella* allotted space to new architecture and design under its rubric "Dalla stampa di tutto il mondo" (From the press around the world), conveniently grouped by country and publication. Nelson considered it "in many ways the most interesting in Italy," but he also held the founding editor of *Domus,* Gio Ponti, in high esteem.[21] He kept up with the latest developments and even beat the press with such notices as Ponti having won the competition for a new building at the University of Padua.[22]

It is perhaps impossible to say just how much Nelson knew first-hand of the emerging Third Rome, as it came to be known, but there is every indication he was aware of its potential and its protagonists. In fact, when he decided to cast his impressions in written form, he inaugurated his articles with a portrait of Marcello Piacentini, the kingpin of Roman planning and architecture, whose administration building at the Città universitaria had just been completed when Nelson arrived. During his sojourn in Rome, Italian life assumed a more aggressive edge, and the Duce's expansionist plans, leading to the Italo-Ethiopian war, cast a lengthening shadow over what might have been viewed as improvements at home, were it not for such alarm signals as house arrest and exile for writers and journalists, including Curzio Malaparte (1898-1957), Francesco Nitti (1868-1953), and numerous others.

By the time the Polish novelist Witold Gombrowicz (1904-1969) gave himself a brief "Roman holiday" after Nelson had already left, the tensions and lulls in an atmosphere of growing fear were widely observed by perceptive foreigners: "I warmed myself in the sun in the gardens of the Villa Borghese," Gombrowicz

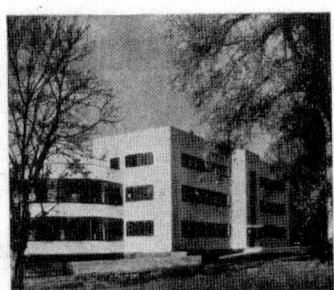

LA CONSTRUCTION MODERNE
Ospedale a Berna, arch. Salvisberg.

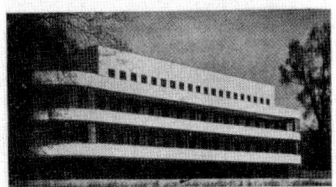

LA CONSTRUCTION MODERNE
Ospedale a Berna, arch. Salvisberg.

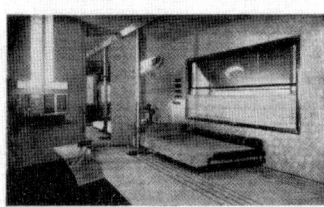

LA CONSTRUCTION MODERNE
Arredamento al Salone d'autunno.

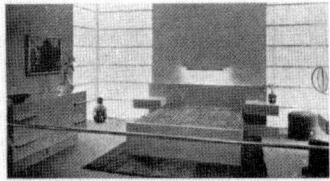

L'ARCHITECTURE
Arredamento al Salone d'autunno.

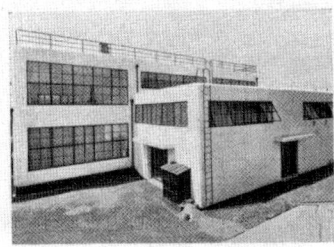

DIE FORM - Istituto tecnico a Kioto.

l'abitazione « minimum » e l'« apartmenthouse » illustrato da progetti degli architetti russi M. Barsc e V. Vladimirov.

DANIMARCA

Arkitekten Maanedshaefte, Vingaardsstr. 21, Copenaghen - novembre 1930.

Tutto il fascicolo è dedicato alla commemorazione dell'architetto danese del settecento Philip de Lange, le cui opere vengono estesamente riprodotte.

FINLANDIA

Arkkitehti, Dagmarinkatu 6, Helsingfors - dicembre 1930.

Interessante la riproduzione del padiglione finnico all'esposizione di Anversa costruito dall'architetto Erik Bryggman, padiglione che presenta un simpatico aspetto moderno.
Seguono i progetti premiati nel concorso per una nuova chiesa a Helsingfors, che mostrano tutti notevoli qualità artistiche.

FRANCIA

L'Architecture d'Aujourd'hui, 5, Rue Bartholdi, Boulogne sur Seine - dicembre 1930.

Questo ricchissimo numero contiene una esposizione di dati assai varia. Quanto a nuove costruzioni e progetti segnaliamo in prima linea la graziosissima villa Savoye a Poissy recentissima opera di Le Corbusier ed il suo progetto per un rifugio dell'esercito della salute a Parigi. Vi sono inoltre illustrati un ponte in cemento armato costruito a Brest dall'ing. Freyssinet ed il grande stabilimento da bagno della spiaggia di Wannsee nei dintorni di Berlino. È pure riprodotto un casamento di abitazioni eleganti al Quai d'Orsay a Parigi dell'arch. Roux-Spitz.
Inoltre, vi sono delle relazioni sull'esposizione di Stoccolma e su quella del « Salon d'Automne » a Parigi. Proseguono anche le risposte alle inchieste della rivista sui materiali moderni e sulle finestre; di queste risposte segnaliamo in modo speciale quelle degli architetti Auguste Perret e M. Guévrekian. Ricordiamo infine un gran numero di articoli interessanti e soprattutto quello sull'architettura scritto da Adolf Loos, propugnatore dell'architettura moderna. Un altro articolo si occupa dell'espressionismo nell'architettura basandosi specialmente sulle recenti costruzioni russe. Charles Siclis, l'architetto del teatro Pigalle a Parigi, parla della relazione fra architettura e scena.

La Construction Moderne, 13, Rue de l'Odeon, Parigi - 4 gennaio 1931.

Vi si dà un largo resoconto sulle realizzazioni ed i progetti architettonici esposti al

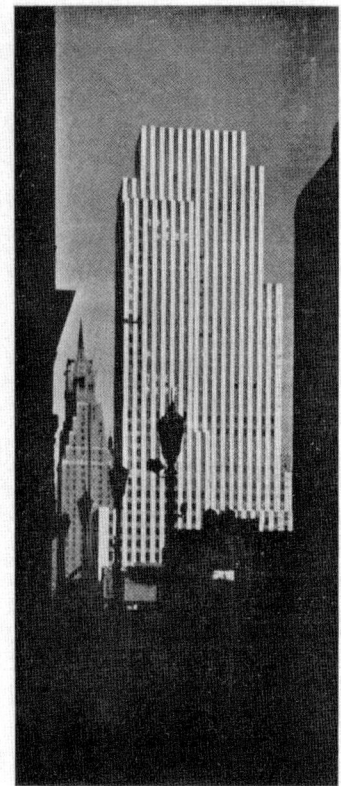

L'ARCHITECTURE D'AUJOURD'HUI
The News Building, Nuova York, arch. Howells e Hood.

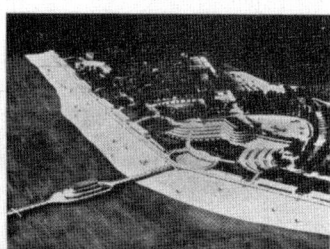

L'ARCHITECTURE D'AUJOURD'HUI
Stabilimento da bagno a Wannsee.

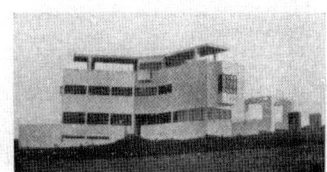

BAUWELT - Villa in Inghilterra.

"Dalla stampa di tutto il mondo" (Casabella, November 1931).

recalled. "I went to the sea at Ostia, and spent more time wandering about... than fulfilling the duties of a tourist in the museums and churches." But the bell jar of the carefree Roman atmosphere was cracked. "In that air and against that noble landscape there was also something turbid and monstrous, a spectre as if from a nightmare. The newspapers carried shrill praise of the Berlin-Rome Axis, and the stench of blackmail and betrayal – for me, the conspiracy between Italy and Germany meant the betrayal of Europe – dominated the streets, Mussolini's speeches, the fascist songs, and even the soldier games played by the brats in front of the Villa Borghese."[23] Playtime in Italy was over, the grand projects ground to a halt, and the news about buildings suddenly gave way to saber rattling. By the time Nelson's articles were published, the inexorable descent of Europe into totalitarianism had begun to be felt everywhere.

WORD PORTRAITS

It is certainly a tribute to Nelson's acute eye and deft pen that the political travails of Europe seeped into his accounts, terse as they are, of people and places. He tried his hand at a genre that as yet had little literary definition or journalistic form. Essays based on visits to artists or close readings of their work began to proliferate in the later nineteenth century, as writers and scholars "drew" cameo portraits of their contemporaries. Guillaume Apollinaire had famously composed word pictures of Cubist painters, and Gertrude Stein took up where he left off with verbal portraits of her friends.[24] The desire to draw such portraits in words, or even set them to music, transformed living subjects into characters.[25] If the genre was literary and experimental in its beginnings, it soon became popular with journalists. It opened a welcome margin between literature and entertainment, allowing scholars to address contemporary issues and journalists to dabble in scholarship, but, most of all, it kindled the curiosity of an ever wider public. While the former dared to leave their ivory towers, the latter strayed into literature and history, brandishing "verbatim evidence" rather than mere gossip and colportage.[26]

A year before Nelson sailed for Europe, Edmund Wilson published *Axel's Castle,* an intriguing array of studies not unlike those Ernst Robert Curtius had produced a few years earlier under the title *Die literarischen Wegbereiter des neuen Frankreich,* followed by *Französischer Geist im neuen Europa,* touching on some of the writers Wilson discussed in his book.[27] In Italy, Giacomo Debenedetti began to publish literary studies focusing likewise on Proust and other contemporaries.[28] Although Curtius and Debenedetti were literary historians of classical training and discipline, they adopted the French model of the "essai," pioneered by such historians of culture as Hippolyte Taine, the Goncourt brothers, and Paul Valéry. Whatever the level of literary performance, the task remained much the same: to sketch the portrait of an individual, not only for its own sake but also as an exemplar of his times and of the art he practices. To impart liveliness to likeness, writers needed to cull character from the works, to grasp an author's peculiar way of spinning the strands of experience and weaving them into the fabric of his work. Attentive unraveling rendered the work more accessible, owing to the elucidation of its cultural context, while assuring greater depth of understanding and suggesting wider significance. Characteristically, these efforts entailed "translation" of one kind or another—for example, when Curtius reflected on contemporary writers from a country that was decried as Germany's archenemy only a couple of years earlier. Interpreters were needed for works of literature that appeared increasingly strange or even incomprehensible, and whose forbidding traits cried out for elucidation. Not that the enigmatic sides of a work would thereby disappear, but the attempt to address them posed a challenge to the reader's mind which prompted future reflection. Portraits of artists, writers, and politicians always retain hidden aspects. Personal acquaintance may help explain puzzling or dismaying traits, yet unless the subject's life is over, much remains open and unpredictable. Such "portraits" as Nelson drew of the architects he met are not merely put together from a kit of characteristics but rather depend on intuition about a person's past, his motivations, and the possible consequences of his professional life.

A German writer who turned his talent for word portraits of eminent political figures and artists into a genre of its own was Maximilian Harden.[29] There are striking similarities between Harden's handling of biographical sketches and Nelson's, as unlikely as that might at first appear. Harden overreached at times, and his rhetoric could be sorely overblown, but he also knew how to play his cards to great effect, as when he delivered this cameo on Lenin: "'He never,' murmur his enemies to the left, 'was a Communist, and his writings, strong only controversially, will not last as long as his embalmed body.' It is possible. There will still remain his practical-tactful genius, his extraordinary personality, which could attack the problem, be the Paul of Socialism: there would remain the solitary great man."[30]

George Nelson opens his article on Mies van der Rohe with a comparably tight and equally incisive reflection. He barely sets the scene, says tantalizingly little about the man but much about his impact on the world. Nelson perfectly encapsulates the enigma of Mies when he writes: "On the top floor of a rather dowdy old house in Berlin there lives a man who, in spite of having built little, spoken less, and written not at all, has somehow come to be considered one of the greatest architects of his time. Such is the power of personality and an idea."[31] Facing an architectural sphinx who posed the fundamental questions and exposed the inadequacy of facile answers, Nelson hits on a typically modern conundrum: Mies is famous because others constantly speak and write about his work. His ideas are heard, and his buildings, few as they are, have gained an astounding media presence. Nelson is in a position to compare Mies in this regard with other architects he interviewed: Le Corbusier comes across as a traveling salesman of his ideas, moving from town to town delivering exhortatory lectures and leaving a trail of articles and pamphlets in his wake.[32] Walter Gropius, by contrast, commands the respect of his clients because his bearing and manner suggest that he is their social equal. He is an old-fashioned "expert" of the professorial kind, versed in dealing with institutions and public administrators. As a *Geschäftsmann,* Gropius has chosen the widest possible field of activity, "the street, town, region, [and] nation."[33] These are the dimensions that, according to Nelson, best illustrate his career.

PHOTOGRAPHS AND FIGURES

Fueled by entrepreneurial ambition, Gropius recognized the paramount importance of images. For this reason he published a picture book as the inaugural volume of the *Bauhaus Bücher.* It was followed in 1928 by another compendium of plates by the stylish photographer F. R. Yerbury, and, in the year of Nelson's arrival in Rome, by an encyclopedic collection of photographs by the Italian architect Alberto Sartoris.[34] Pictures were not only the slabs that paved the way to the perception of contemporary architecture, but they were the very medium of its distinctively modern qualities. Photography began to matter more than ever, for it alone captured the qualities of the materials that came to prominence with modern buildings—glass, steel, aluminum, electric lighting—and conveyed their desired atmospheric effects. Nelson quickly caught on and paid special attention to the work of a young architect in London who stood out precisely for his ability to evoke those effects. When Nelson shaped his presentation of Raymond McGrath for publication he would rely on splendid photography, almost all interior views and details. Nelson was intrigued by some insidious parallels between the trajectory of the young Australian art student (and lifelong painter), who had come to London on a traveling fellowship, and his own biography as a young American with a degree in fine arts and a fellowship at the Academy in Rome. He was also fascinated by McGrath's subtle work at a country house and his design for the new studios of the BBC.[35] Of McGrath's first work, the transformation of a Victorian into a modern house, Nelson said that the "aluminum foil, pink plaster, indirect lighting, cut-glass fountain, and so on, were not intended to be the ultimate expressions of any fixed ideas, but rather a searching for an atmosphere more in harmony with present-day living."[36] When highly reflective or dull materials and lighting are combined to create a suffused atmosphere that oscillates between hush and gloss, only photography can render them adequately. The client for this job immediately recognized the role of photography in capturing these evanescent qualities when he wrote in a letter of appreciation to the architect that "the photos, somehow, seem to clinch your wondrous achievement."[37]

Nelson was very young when he traveled to Europe,

little more than a college kid, but his naiveté carried him through many rough spots and allowed him to seem astonishingly confident in the eyes of several of his interlocutors. A keen professional interest on his part undoubtedly helped him gain that confidence. He proudly reports how a big fish, Le Corbusier, joined him in a Roman café with an avuncular greeting: "Alors, vous faîtes ce sacré métier d'architecte?"[38] Nelson caught up with the *sacré monstre* in the city's most famous haunt of artists since the late eighteenth century, and while not dropping the name (it was the Caffe Greco near the Spanish Steps), he refers to the famous writers and artists who used to gather there. Nelson's clever opener establishes two points with one stroke: he makes it instantly clear that we are dealing with a "historic figure" whose every word will ultimately insert itself into the discourse of architecture across time, and also that we are listening to a man of "devastating sincerity." Nelson went so far as to admire Le Corbusier's will to forge irrefutable arguments, even if they plunged him into fatal "reductio ad absurdum."

As Nelson relates them, Le Corbusier's pronouncements often take the form of articles of faith. To the extent that the architect's goal may be shared by many listeners and readers whether or not they have any knowledge of architecture or agree with its prophet, Le Corbusier's views make a compelling case. Combining as he does logic with prophesy, he sounds at times like Buckminster Fuller and at others like a fulsome evangelist. Favoring air-conditioned apartments, Le Corbusier declares that the "lives of the tenants have been transformed, literally transformed."[39] The claim is no more ludicrous than it is technically accurate, although what is true about it may just be disagreeable. But it takes a Nelson to follow this quotation with the subtle observation that, "as [Le Corbusier] spoke, his own face underwent a sort of transformation. Architecture, to this man, is not a series of monuments to the architect. It is a means of attaining a way of living."[40] And since this way of living is Le Corbusier's, it surely had to work its effect on him in the first place.

LIVES AND LIFESTYLES

Nelson nourished no literary ambitions per se; he did not seek to impress his teachers or popularize his subjects. He opted for the casual tone of reportage rather than a more elevated one. Nonetheless, his insights can be as keen as his asides are trenchant or amusing. He took a realistic view of life as he found it in Rome and elsewhere, recognizing flaws as well as talents among his subjects. He kept an eye on the larger canvas, inquiring into the conditions under which architecture was being practiced and wondering about the advantages and drawbacks in comparison with the situation in his own country. He was unapologetic about life as he found it in Italy, Germany, Scandinavia, and England. Not one to dish out mere generalities, Nelson let the atmosphere of the country color his impressions and suggest clues for further probing. Of the Town Hall in Stockholm he remarked that "this prodigious monument, which has already taken on a character of agelessness, is, as much as any organized collection of sticks and stones can be, the complete summing-up of a culture."[41] Nelson sought to offer such a summing-up of the works he went to see and of the architects he met, gauging not only their standing in the profession but also their impact on the culture at large. He detected the strands that link a building with the powers that brought it into being. When he writes that "Mussolini will leave his Rome in red stucco instead of marble [as did Emperor Augustus]," Nelson considered it "beside the point," for the "new style fits admirably into the program of his party and goes well with his highly advertised predilection for youth."[42] In England, the young men of diverse national origin and training who had teamed up to form the studio Tecton, the only true collective among all the offices Nelson visited, impressed him and no doubt inspired a "brotherly" feeling, as their average age was under thirty.

Nelson pressed for answers, inquiring into private motivations as well as the entanglement of individuals in public institutions. While clients were of less concern, he sought to understand what prompted architects to explore their ideas, even under adverse circumstances. Not without some exasperation he asks, "What makes a modern architect? Those readers who have been irritated by the series of buildings which have illustrated this series"– and there were quite a few of them – might consider a "combination of knavery and imbecility as the most likely qualities."[43] He wasn't turning a blind eye to conditions in his native country, either. To counterbalance potshots at social housing in France, he admonished readers that a "Westchester suburb is probably the most pretentiously hideous sight in the world."[44] Did he know, or studiously overlook, that the editorial advisor whose voice was gaining weight in the offices of *Pencil Points,* Ralph Walker, lived in New York's Westchester County?[45] Walker, for his part, rather smugly held up the suburb as the ultimate refuge from the city, writing in spring 1936 that "when you get even a little removed from Forty second Street and Fifth Avenue [that is, from the editorial offices of *Pencil Points*] as the little valley of Westchester where I live, the crescendo of the city should have no meaning."[46] Little did he know that the city was going to catch up within his lifetime and spoil the bucolic setting cluttered by so many hackneyed buildings.

Architects as individuals never ceased to fascinate Nelson, all the more so, perhaps, because he didn't yet possess an identity of his own as an architect. In his article on Giuseppe Vaccaro, Nelson even includes childhood sketches among the illustrations, recognizing the power of talent and vocation even when later work may not bear out youthful promise. Other architects he admired for their ability to forge a life of dedication and exuberance. He almost envied Eugène Beaudouin's restless pursuit of interests that drove him as far as Persia and prompted him to travel to the United States at a time when only a few (most prominently Richard

Neutra and Erich Mendelsohn) had done so with positive results. Beaudouin has "certain peculiarities," he admits. "He likes exercise, is interested in sanitation, wears no hat, approves of America, and lives all year round on a houseboat on the Seine."[47] What may at first sight strike one as a flippant characterization bordering on caricature turns out, on second thought, to be a deft sketch in which every stroke counts. Exercise and sanitation go hand in hand, allowing you to throw other cares (along with your hat) to the wind. One so unfettered by convention is also at liberty to like what may not be fashionable or opportune. That Beaudouin admitted to liking America, and even traveled there to see with his own eyes, finds its counterpart in his decision to inhabit a houseboat, an apt metaphor for modern man's precarious accommodation in the metropolis. Everyone else would have mentioned Le Corbusier's floating asylum, but Nelson speaks of Beaudouin's boat.

The laconic Mies van der Rohe living in solitude, the doctrinaire Le Corbusier on yet another of his evangelical missions, and the shy McGrath in the hushed studios of the BBC spring to life in these memorable vignettes. It is precisely the element of reportage, of catching people and ideas on the fly, that made Nelson's articles not only good reads but also valuable documents. Language was occasionally a hurdle, but Nelson mostly managed to clear it – even if he felt at times, as when he interviewed Mies, that he should have brought along a grammar to learn his "gehabt haben's" in a hurry.[48]

Nelson chose a different "key" for each of the three Italians he interviewed, bringing out a specific resonance with each: he is sympathetic in his appreciation of Ponti as an artist; somewhat distant, if analytical, in his account of Vaccaro; and guardedly caustic in his rendering of Marcello Piacentini, who wears his "unique position of power and eminence" like a badge of honor in recognition of lethal battles won.[49] In the case of Vaccaro, Nelson may have been impressed with the coverage this prolific architect, and sometime collaborator of Piacentini, enjoyed at the time.[50] Gio Ponti, on the other hand, exemplified precisely the quality Nelson was to achieve in his own life: a capacity for joyous and manifold work in a striking graphic vein. Inventive, quick, and articulate, Ponti possessed a youthful inquisitiveness and talent for decorative invention, as well as a curiosity for engineering. Among the few who considered housing a "problem of civilization" rather than an economic calamity to be countered by rigorous industrialization, he chose the title *Domus* for the journal he inaugurated in 1928.[51] I suspect that Ponti, along with such fugitive figures as McGrath, appealed to Nelson precisely because they had achieved a blend of artistic invention and professional performance under circumstances that could only be called trying. As a momentary alter ego, Ponti may have sustained Nelson's desire to subsume architecture under the panoply of design rather than channel his talents into straight and narrow practice. Italian architects of the interwar years, more than others, explored the byways of a profession that was in the process of tightening its own definition. Little surprise then that Nelson emerged after the war as a designer of a cast that made him appear fraternal to Italian colleagues. When the Italian designer Ettore Sottsass, Jr., befriended Nelson after the war, he conceded that his American colleague "knew the Italian intellectual game very well, he knew about the Italian crafty ways, he knew about Italian conceits and sins, the courage, patience, sophistication, and secrets."[52]

BOOKS AND JOURNALS, HERE AND OVER THERE

Before Nelson embarked on his Roman fellowship, a number of books were published that proved of lasting value for his future work as editor and author. These books fall into distinct groups: those that could be said to have helped Nelson to plan his exploration of new European architecture from afar, and those that served him as a map for navigating the old world. Henry-Russell Hitchcock's *Modern Architecture: Romanticism and Reintegration* (1929) may have opened Nelson's eyes to a speculative if quirky picture of how modern concepts of building have emerged in an unpredictable fashion since the eighteenth century. For *The International Style,* the catalogue that accompanied the famous exhibition, Hitchcock momentarily pitched his thinking at the latest manifestations of what appeared to him a halting but definite evolution. Another publication, advocating a more generous view of modern architecture, had appeared between *Modern Architecture* and *The International Style:* Sheldon Cheney's popular, wide-ranging, and well-illustrated *New World Architecture* (1930).

Cheney embraces both American and European architecture, singles out skyscrapers as the central manifestation of the collective will, but also recognizes the "classicizing tendencies" that remained strong even among modern architects. He explained that "the Moderns turn to this architecture of the Greeks" when they seek "inspiration, for renewal of their belief in the simple, the direct, the logical thing as the beautiful thing—for confirmation of their faith that expressive form will flower where the passionate artist bases his designing on function and material and honest thinking."[53] Nelson certainly shared Cheney's conviction that the straight path to understanding architecture led first to the architect before entering the maze of general issues and the tangle of doctrines. He would most likely have agreed with Cheney's emphasis on the "passionate artist" who speaks through the "audacity of the massive building, the long naked line, the sheer wall"—the "sheer wall" of which Mies was so proud at the Tugendhat house, and the "massive buildings" Gropius designed for workers' housing.[54] Cheney devoted ample space to Frank Lloyd Wright, who was then sinking toward the nadir of his entire career, and cleverly juxtaposed American and European developments in such a manner as to lend them the same degree of authenticity and quality as when he matched up

Erich Mendelsohn's famous Ufa-Palast in Berlin with the far more modest but equally original interior that Frederick Kiesler designed for the Film Guild Cinema in New York.[55] Surely the most comprehensive—and if for that very reason also the most diffuse and heterogeneous—compendium of photographs became available just as Nelson arrived in Rome: Alberto Sartoris' *Gli elemeni dell'architettura funzionale.* Some of the architects Nelson interviewed were themselves authors of books that must have held interest for him because they did not simply retail familiar views or advocate accepted values. Marcello Piacentini's polemical *Architettura d'oggi* (1930) and his editorials for the journal *L'architettura* articulated strenuous resistance to the tendencies widely sustained in northern Europe at the time. Italians, it became clearer every day as Nelson beat the pavement of the capital, were not only touching base with ancient Rome but lusting after its grandiloquence and the public symbolism of its buildings. Though Nelson continued to read the journals *Casabella* and *Quadrante,* which kept him apprised of the latest issues and alert to the debate that was beginning to tip in favor of more conservative tendencies, he was not partial to the rationalists. As a matter of fact, he left them out of his picture altogether. By 1934, and certainly by the time he actually published his articles in 1935 and 1936, Nelson's omission of Giuseppe Pagano (who was then editor of *Casabella*), Giuseppe Terragni, Pietro Lingeri, and Adalberto Libera shows that Nelson had formed an independent view of what mattered. Instead of partisanship, he betrayed an affinity for Gio Ponti's interior design and his book *La casa all'italiana* (1933).[56] Nelson's talents as an artist probably made him appreciate the share that artistic practice still claimed in Italian architecture. He admired Gio Ponti's ability to decorate stylish porcelain vases with one hand and design a thirteen-story high-rise in Milan with the other. He even fell for Ponti's exhibition at the Milan Triennale, where he showed a bedroom for a "very hypothetical Italian gentleman."[57] One of Ponti's most accomplished buildings, the Mathematics Faculty at the Città universitaria, which lay at Nelson's doorstep, rightly garnered special praise.

Italian periodicals continued to publish the work of German architects after it had become anathema in their own country. *Casabella* carried an article by the highly respected art historian Lionello Venturi, "Sette note per i Luckhardt," perhaps prompting Nelson to add the Luckhardt brothers to his list of architects to visit in Berlin, aside from Mies van der Rohe and Walter Gropius.[58] Nelson sounds scathing when he describes the circumstances in which he found the Luckhardt brothers living in Berlin after Hitler's *Machtergreifung,* when verdicts of "unpatriotic" and "un-German" rained down on anyone previously associated with public housing or an interest in modern art and architecture. Decried as "Bolshevik" and "decadent," the Luckhardts were put out of work overnight. Now, Nelson reports, "they have no work. What is more, they can't do any work: it is forbidden by law." The consequences of this

Erich Mendelsohn's Ufa-Palast, Berlin, and Frederick Kiesler's Film Guild Cinema, New York (Sheldon Cheney, New World Architecture, 1930, p. 360).

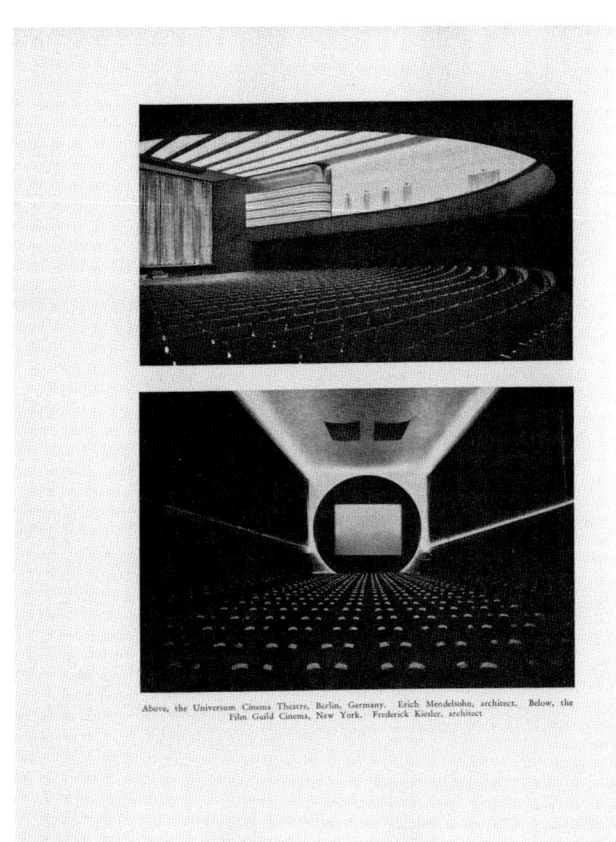

new policy were apparent everywhere: "So Mendelsohn is in England, the Luckhardts have an empty office, and Mies van der Rohe and Gropius must look elsewhere for recognition. It is apparently the taint of internationalism that is taboo."[59] Some readers of *Pencil Points* seemed to agree. The March 1935 issue, which carried Nelson's report on the dilemma of the Luckhardts in Berlin, also shed light on American attitudes toward such tendencies. The columnist Harold Van Buren Magonigle (1867–1935) inveighed against "modernistic" and "modern" architecture, taking Richard Neutra and Rudolf Schindler to task in a tone that drips with vitriol, because they are "foreign" in more ways than one but active in the United States. Magonigle's stentorian dismissal could be matched word for word by Nazi journalists when he claims that he has "yet to see one 'modern' house (or 'modernistic' according to the 'master' you follow) that is truly functional, really logical, structurally and aesthetically."[60]

All of this made even less sense because many architects, artists, and writers had begun to think of their work as European rather than strictly national (and some, like Mendelsohn and Le Corbusier, even thought in intercontinental terms), and held architecture to cultural and industrial standards that necessarily transcended political boundaries. Especially with regard to industrial progress, interest was bound to follow the latest developments rather than cling to parochial models. These developments might be American mass production and organizational theory or the elegant

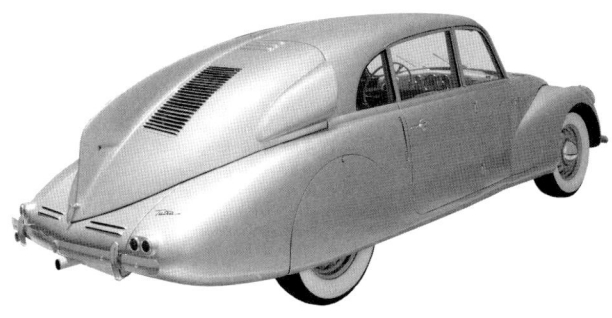

new cars designed in Czechoslovakia for which Wassily Luckhardt expressed a preference. For an American in Italy and Germany–rather than in Paris, where only the claxons of cruising cabs made it into Gershwin's music–the cacophony of political upheaval and routine violence could not be overlooked.

WHO'S WHO, AND FOR WHOM?

For a man in his mid-twenties, Nelson cast a precociously knowing eye on a culture that was certainly new to him. His intuition was keen, even in matters where he had little experience, such as the professional life of architects in Europe. He even tempered his praise when he had reason to approve, as in the case of public competitions, a subject of vivid debate in the pages of *Pencil Points*–the advantages seemed obvious to Luckhardt because competitions allowed young talents to emerge quickly and independently.[61] However, Nelson cautioned against an overly enthusiastic appreciation, insofar as "one might be tempted to inquire in this more deeply," only to resign oneself that "it would be fruitless."[62] He went even further, because he recognized that an all-powerful figure in the profession, such as a Marcello Piacentini, is revered only because he knows how to deal with authorities and cleverly turn legal and social safeguards to personal advantage. In a word, corruption is the correlative of success. Piacentini's accomplishments inspired respect, nonetheless, but Nelson saw through the rhetoric and the sham when he concluded his thumbnail sketch of a man who appeared to him to be a veritable "bundle of contradictions" with these words: "A wily politician and utterly unscrupulous, he is at the same time a man of wide learning, passionately interested in his work and all that has any bearing upon it."[63]

What intrigues us is how Nelson arrived at his choice of subjects and what kind of larger picture of European culture he created for them. One unavoidably thinks of the first exhibition dedicated entirely to modern architecture ever held in the United States, the Museum of Modern Art's International Style show of 1932, as an obvious point of departure. We can be sure Nelson knew it well, for he refers to it matter-of-factly in his very first article, observing that "the international style had no attraction" for Piacentini.[64] Nelson did not navigate in Europe with anything like the International Style in hand, for his interests were both more individual and more expansive, albeit less sure. He certainly came to know the chief European publications and made ample use of them. Several of them have remained landmarks: Walter Gropius' *Internationale Architektur*[65] and Walter Curt Behrendt's *Der Sieg des neuen Baustils*[66] were written simultaneously. Their titles furnished the terms that were combined in the naming of the New York exhibition. To Gropius and Behrendt must be added the first European "survey" of contemporary architecture, published in the prestigious Propylaeen series by Gustav Adolf Platz, and two "picture books," one by the English photographer F. R. Yerbury, the

opposite:
Tatra 87, designed by Hans Ledwinka and manufactured by Tatra Werke, Nesseldorf, Czechoslovakia (1937). Restored by Ecorra.

right:
Raymond McGrath, Twentieth Century Houses (1934, pp. 56–57).

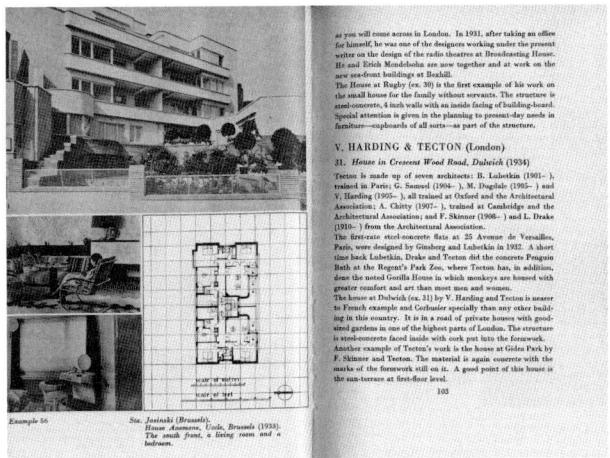

other by the Italian architect Alberto Sartoris.[67] As if to make comparisons between American and European perceptions of the "new" explicit, an English (hence, "extra-Continental") perspective opened up just as Nelson was leaving Europe: Raymond McGrath's curious but fascinating compilation *Twentieth Century Houses*.[68] It left a lasting mark on Nelson's thinking and later approach to design. Perhaps the only real sleeper among books of its kind, it gave every promise of success, for McGrath deliberately wrote it in "basic English," using no more than 850 words, and yet managed to give a lively personal view of the evolution of houses as a staple of architecture since the late nineteenth century based on 128 examples from around the world.

European architects who might have appeared eccentric or impure to the advocates of the International Style—figures such as Helweg-Moeller, Gio Ponti, and Raymond McGrath—do not fit into anyone's scheme and were considered only peripherally, if at all, in other accounts of new architecture. In virtually every book published on both sides of the Atlantic, only one country aside from Germany could claim a pioneering role: the Netherlands, heavily favored by Hitchcock and declared by Yerbury as early as 1928 to be "the only country of which it can be said that it has a very pronounced modern national architecture."[69] Nelson included no Dutchman among his subjects, and he never discussed social housing and community planning, except with Le Corbusier and Walter Gropius, who must have brought

it up. Even then, Nelson quickly turns to prefabrication and the educational programs at the Bauhaus rather than dwell on housing. Education and collaboration rank high on his list of burning issues. He is enthusiastic over a group of seven young architects, Tecton, who have established an office of their own in London in order to take on major planning projects with little or no prospect of realizing them. The Tecton group is relentless in its attention to detail, which in the absence of actual construction takes the place of practical work. "Any detail left to the contractors," Nelson is told, "will certainly be done wrong. Better to spend a month drawing than spoil the building forever."[70] Tecton's assiduous attention to the details shortly brought results. First they housed zoo animals, then they addressed the expectations of the highest primates with a high-rise in Highgate. For Nelson, "the Penguin Pool—it deserves capitals: there is only one in the world like it—[was] a piece of pure constructivism."[71] In this case, as in others, Nelson put a premium on personal qualities, enamored as he was of a "unique" building or a remarkably individualistic way of working. Ever fascinated with personal solutions rather than accepting standard "types" and submitting to inflexible programs, Nelson proves to be an "American" in Europe rather than the returning son of eastern European (or Russian) immigrants to the United States.[72]

Nelson's years in Europe coincided with the time when the aspiration to an "international" architecture ran counter to the demands for "national" identity.

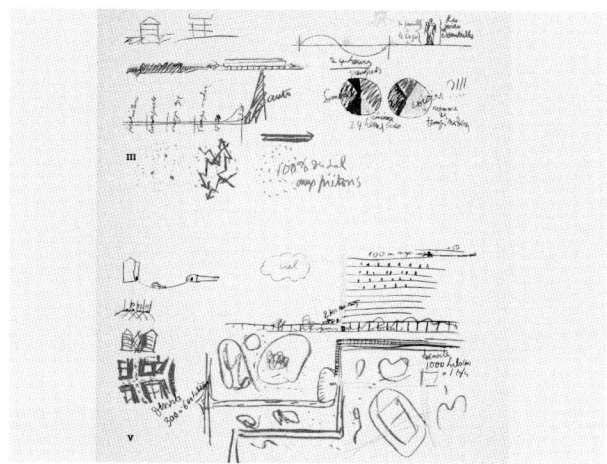

Drawing by Le Corbusier for his lecture in Rome, after Quadrante *13 (May 1934).*

The debate tore the parties far apart. While the cries for autarchia, the exclusive reliance upon national resources and manufacture, became as strident in Italy as the idolatry of race grew in Nazi Germany, a remarkable number of Italian intellectuals continued to advocate a broader vision of Europe. One of them, Armando Ghelardini, edited the journal *Occidente,* which began appearing in Rome at the time of Nelson's arrival in the capital.[73] *Occidente* aspired to a notion of world literature, echoing the periodical press of Europe and America, and including writing on film and anthologies of current poetry.[74] Issue 9 even introduced readers to the editorial offices in Rome, elegantly appointed quarters with an array of the latest tubular furniture and lamps à la Bauhaus. But architecture as an international field soon found itself stalemated by politics: the League of Nations withered, and totalitarian notions of the state not only gained intimidating power but also exercised it for territorial expansion and the establishment of regimes at home. Whereas Nelson was a largely apolitical observer, "national" terms of reference came naturally to Hitchcock, who characterized the initially laggard role of Italy by the standards of other nations: "Such excellent buildings as Piacentini's Cinema Corso and Banca d'Italia, both in Rome, might easily be respectively Austrian and Swedish."[75] Piacentini, to be sure, expressed only scorn for glass façades, huge windows, and other architectural features common to "northern Europe." Yet his invectives, and those of many others, were only ripples on the surface of an increasingly stormy sea that was to suck entire nations into the abyss of war and wholesale subjugation. The architectural debate had definitely turned away from *couleur locale,* from the finer shadings within a common ideal, clamoring instead for an indigenous, "original," and intrinsically superior character. Its advocates everywhere raised their voices to a chauvinist pitch. *Pencil Points* carried an editorial by Ralph Walker in summer 1936, when Italy had just liquidated Ethiopia as an independent nation, in which he notes that "we are too apt to forget in our proud moments of being pure rationalists, of being hard-boiled realists, that we are ruled sentimentally by the symbol. The European world is relearning it–the Fasces, the Swastikas, the Sickle and Hammer, are as potent as the cross and the crescent ever were, and in their rule architecture is just as much affected."[76] At the Paris World Exhibition the following year, even the fairground turned into an arena of mutually threatening self-affirmations: the oddly brittle but rational colonnades of the new Trocadero lent its frame to the "sentimentally" posturing pavilions of Germany and the Soviet Union. A pantomime of power acted out in the confines of a chauvinistic "theme park" *avant la lettre.*

The only thing new among the architects of the new was politics. Nelson had to travel to England to meet Gropius, now impatiently testing the ground in the "only country left in Europe where architecture has no political significance." Gropius, ever the *Geschäftsmann,* was still hedging his bets at the time: "He is not

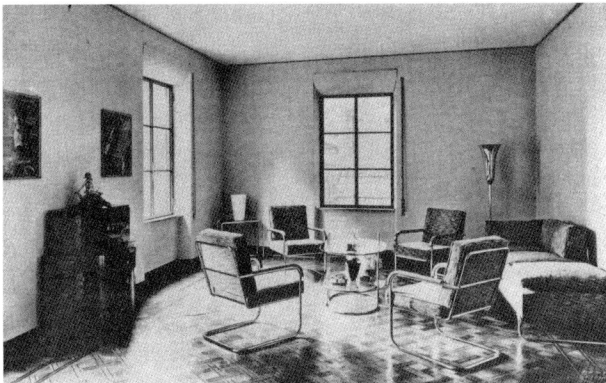

"*La Nuova Sede di Edizioni, d'Italia,*" Occidente *9 (1934).*

against the present regime [in Germany] and his departure was considered as temporary."⁷⁷ Nelson is not fooled. He recognizes that "when Germany repudiates modern architecture as Bolshevistic, Russia, because it is bourgeois, and Italy embraces it because it is Fascist, there is little difficulty in drawing a conclusion."⁷⁸

FINER POINTS

Because we lack archival sources, we cannot say exactly when Nelson composed his essays, how much of his "word portraits" may have been drafted while he was still in Europe, where he certainly must have collected illustrations, and how much he added after returning home. When his requests for pictures were not filled, as was the case with Le Corbusier, he had to fake the evidence.⁷⁹ Naturally he would draw on publications, as when he imitated Le Corbusier's sketch of the Campo Santo at Pisa, which was published in the first volume of the *Oeuvre complète,* in order to juxtapose it with the Palace of the Soviets, which had been included only in the second. Le Corbusier concluded the second volume of his *Oeuvre complète* with a report on his visit to Italy, adding a highly promotional flourish and including illustrations that had appeared in *Quadrante*.⁸⁰ Nelson sneakily mimicked Le Corbusier's impromptu sketches, but he may also have felt a tinge of revenge doing so, because the photographs he already paid for never arrived from Paris. Corbu condescended to playing confrère with an American greenhorn on a hot afternoon in May, but didn't care to follow through with the pictures. His Roman lecture, given on the invitation of the editors of *Quadrante,* was not only a spectacle to behold, but it also was fully transcribed in the May issue of the journal.⁸¹ Even his drawings were reproduced there in full color, printed on tipped-in pages.⁸² The journal indulged the curiosity of its readers with a somewhat bizarre "interpretation" of the architect's psychosomatic disposition, as if the peripatetic monster had to be assessed in all its phenomenal manifestations.⁸³

When Nelson reached the halfway point in his series of articles with a particularly persuasive piece on Mies van der Rohe, his opponents at *Pencil Points* were hitting back in a ping-pong of polemical repartee: H. Van Buren Magonigle fired one of his last shots, lobbing a tirade against modern architecture into Nelson's advancing camp, before withdrawing into Paul P. Cret's bulwark against all things evil.⁸⁴ But the secret working of irony had not yet run its course, for Nelson's article on Mies, which prominently displays a photograph of the New York City apartment he designed for Philip Johnson, is followed by copious documentation of the "radio shrine" of the Little Flower (Royal Oak, Michigan).⁸⁵ This was, of course, the project commissioned by the Reverend Charles E. Coughlin, the very man with whom Johnson sought to align his own short-lived political campaign after resigning from the Museum of Modern Art.⁸⁶

PENCIL POINTS

MARCH 1936

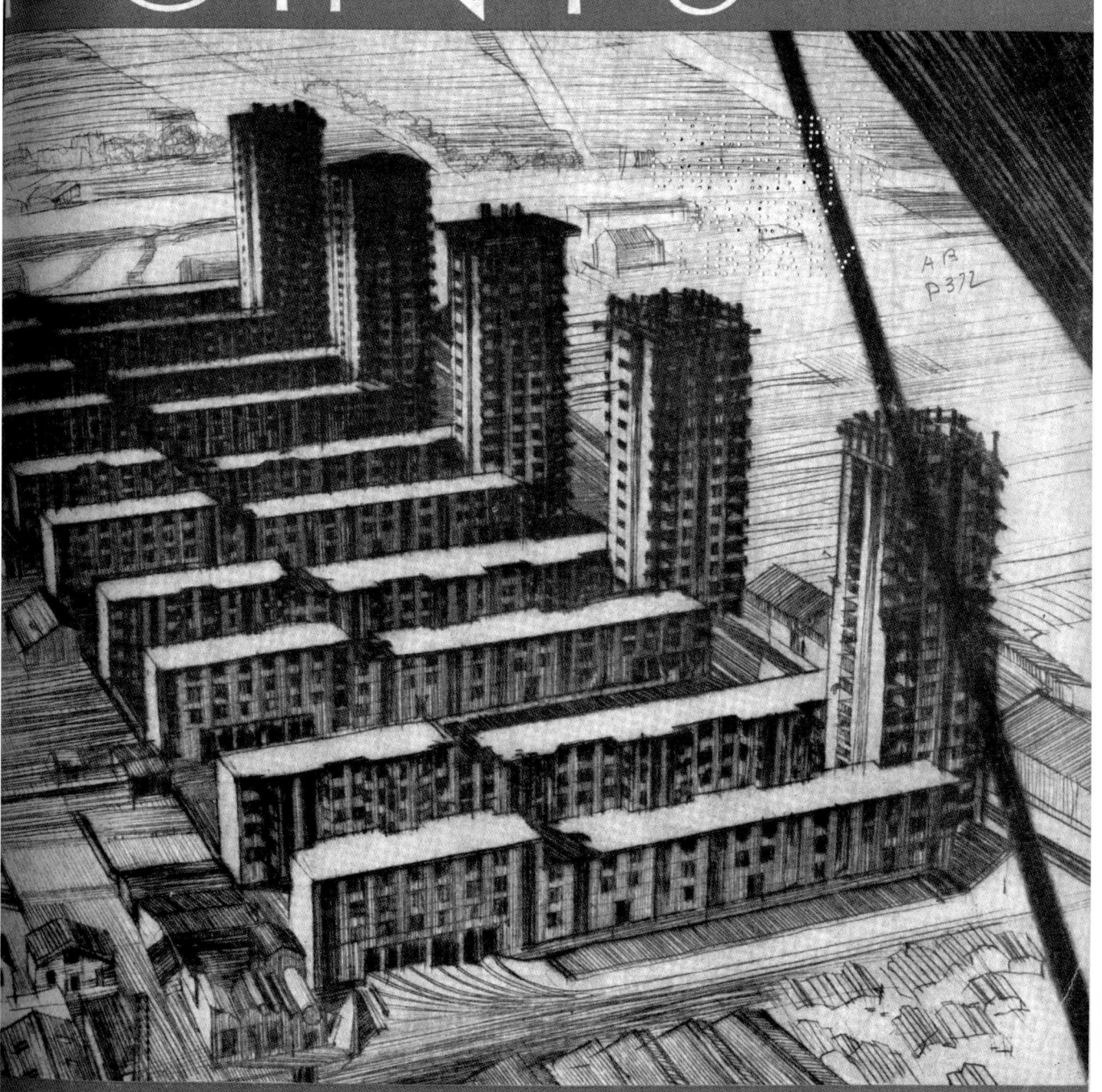

Newly designed Pencil Points
(March 1936).

Cover of Das Werk
(October 1930).

THE VIEW FROM NEW YORK

Nelson's articles for *Pencil Points* began appearing with the first issue of 1935, accompanied by the following editorial caveat: "We are definitely not interested in publishing examples of contemporary European architecture for the purpose of encouraging the sort of stupid copying of mannerisms that is unfortunately sometimes done." Nelson eloquently introduced readers, hitherto fed "Something for Everyone in the Architectural Profession," to astonishing buildings and fascinating personalities from across the Atlantic.[87] His articles not only stirred curiosity and controversy but left the journal thoroughly altered. In April of the following year, *Pencil Points* conducted spring cleaning and shed its bland covers, which had carried chiefly etchings, in favor of beautiful monochromes with just a touch of contrasting color.[88] In this regard, too, the models were European and specifically architectural: The Swiss monthly *Das Werk* avoided images on its cover, giving full play to its new typography of bold capitals sans serif. In Italy, *Quadrante* had adopted a similar cover at its inception in 1933, using a sturdy, monochrome board that was the aesthetic equivalent of linoleum. Building materials of a pastelike substance, such as rubberized or linoleum flooring and terrazzo, were just coming into their own for residential use, along with visually intriguing displays of aluminum, copper, and etched and tinted glass.

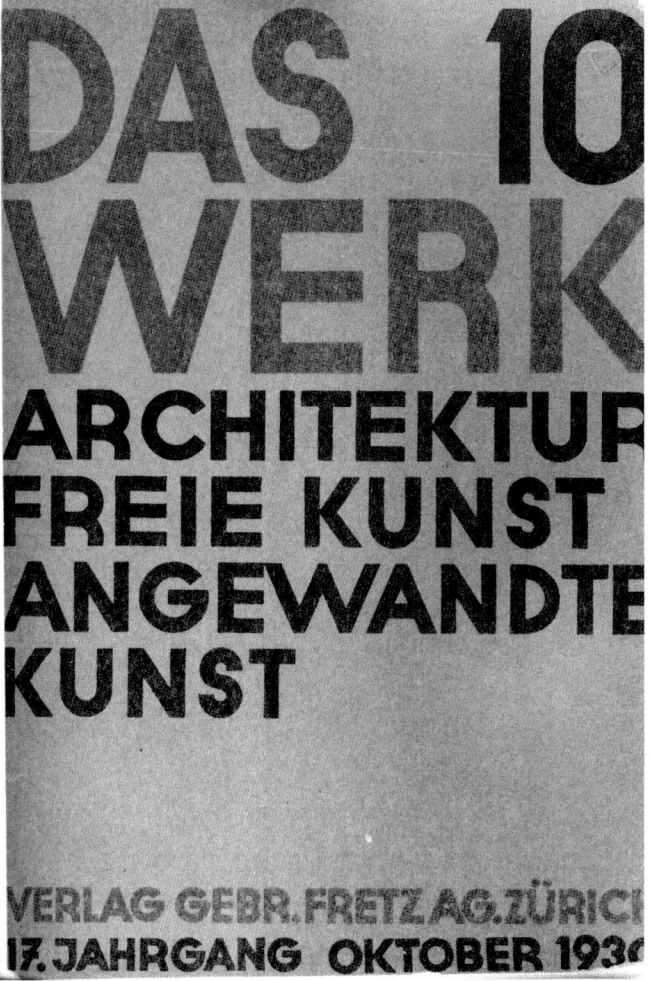

QUADRANTE 1

RIVISTA MENSILE
MAGGIO ANNO XI

MASSIMO BONTEMPELLI
P. M. BARDI: DIRETTORI

opposite:
Cover of Quadrante *1 (1932).*

below:
Alcoa advertisement in
Pencil Points *(April 1936).*

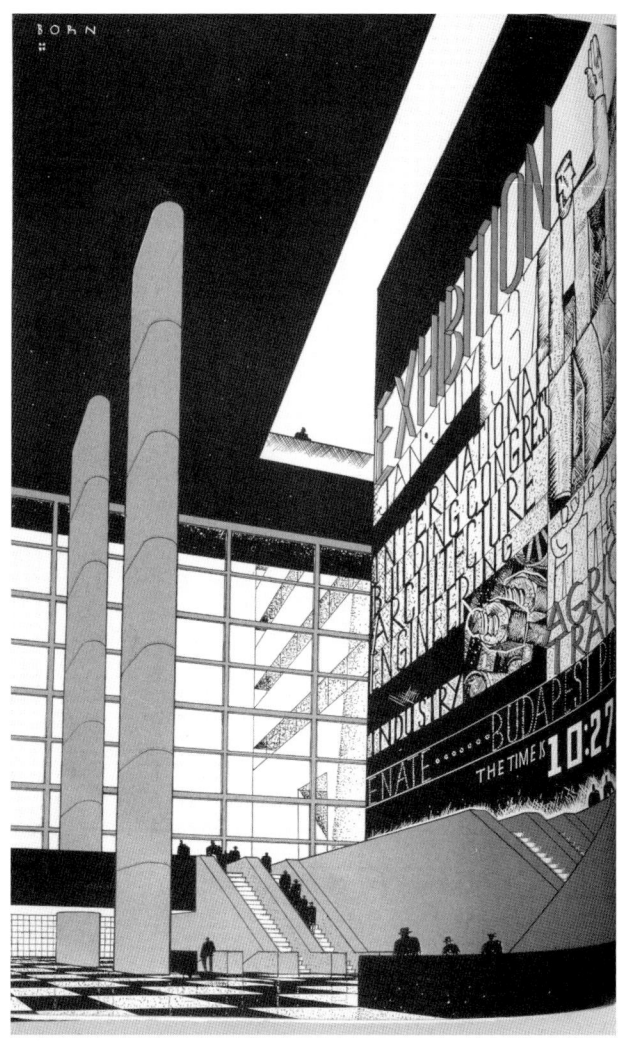

The new typography on the cover of *Pencil Points* – including the addition of the word DESIGN in the left margin – was striking, but not simply conformist with regard to models set by the International Style. Nor was the next step, taken in May 1936 when the title page was redesigned, in any way faddish.[89] As a matter of fact, the rival *Architectural Forum* followed the lead and switched to monochrome covers that changed every month. In its new garb, *Pencil Points* kept up its competition with the *Architectural Record,* where, under the editorship of A. Lawrence Kocher, "so much contemporary foreign building had been brought to American attention."[90]

More than adding appeal to the package, Nelson's articles introduced a fresh approach to layout: the photographs grew larger, even into full-page illustrations without borders, and gradually a touch of Bauhaus montage made itself felt when editors began to run two images across the same page or cropped the traditional margins. This kind of layout distinguished Nelson's articles, and only his, from the conventions that held sway at *Pencil Points.* Even if Nelson may not have caught a spirited letter published in *Quadrante* 8 (1933) under the heading "La tipografia è la cristallizzazione del pensiero" (Typography is the crystallization of thought), he acted in the spirit of graphic invention that made such headway during his stay in Europe. He shared the conviction expressed in the letter to *Quadrante:* "Thought and spiritual life are the fleeting abstractions of every moment, but the imprint [of letters] reveals them, like photography illuminates certain mobile manifestations that escape the eye."[91] This aesthetic extended well beyond the printed page. When Nelson began designing furniture, he treated his cabinets in similar fashion, dividing their front into balanced fields of unequal surfaces. By means of thin cuts he set off doors, loudspeakers, and drawers, adding the slimmest handles as if they were mere captions. Any surface area thus demarcated within the cabinet's front would slide, turn, or fold flush into place.

After 1936, *Pencil Points* featured more contemporary work, less for its radical nature than for its usefulness in clearing the way for a better appreciation of architecture tout court. The September 1936 issue carried a lengthy, richly illustrated article on Eliel Saarinen by the managing editor Kenneth Reid. By this time, Nelson was already working at the *Architectural Forum,* where he became an associate editor. He was able to recruit almost anyone he wished to publish, even so obstreperous a fellow as Frank Lloyd Wright, who in 1938 celebrated his near-miraculous return to leadership with a single issue of the magazine, in which the typography, layout, and photography were entirely of his design. Nelson's departure left *Pencil Points* searching for a direction of its own. The potion of fresh thinking that he had administered worked its magic. *Pencil Points* evolved in due course into the successor journal *Progressive Architecture.* But that is another story.

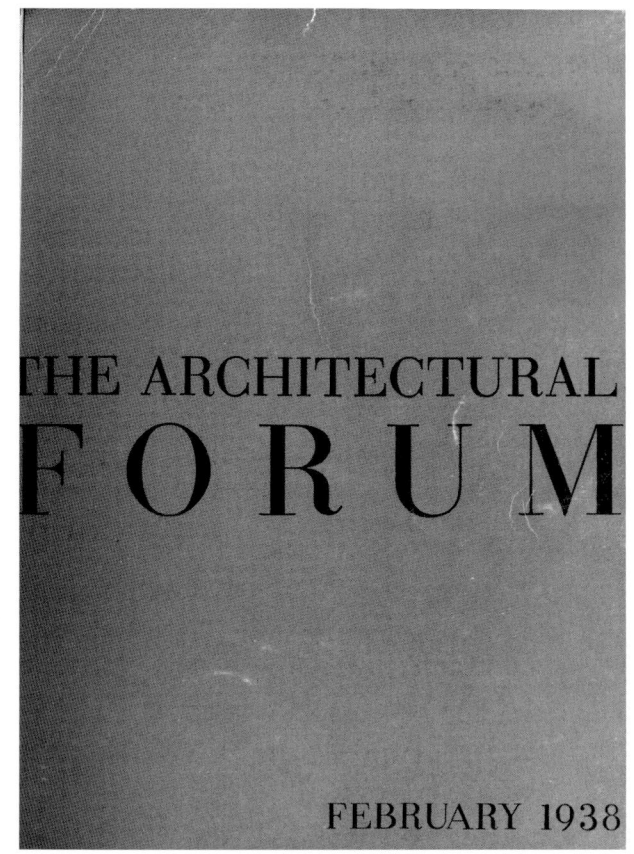

opposite:
Cover of the Architectural Forum *(February 1938).*

below:
George Nelson, modular radio and phonograph cabinet (1947).

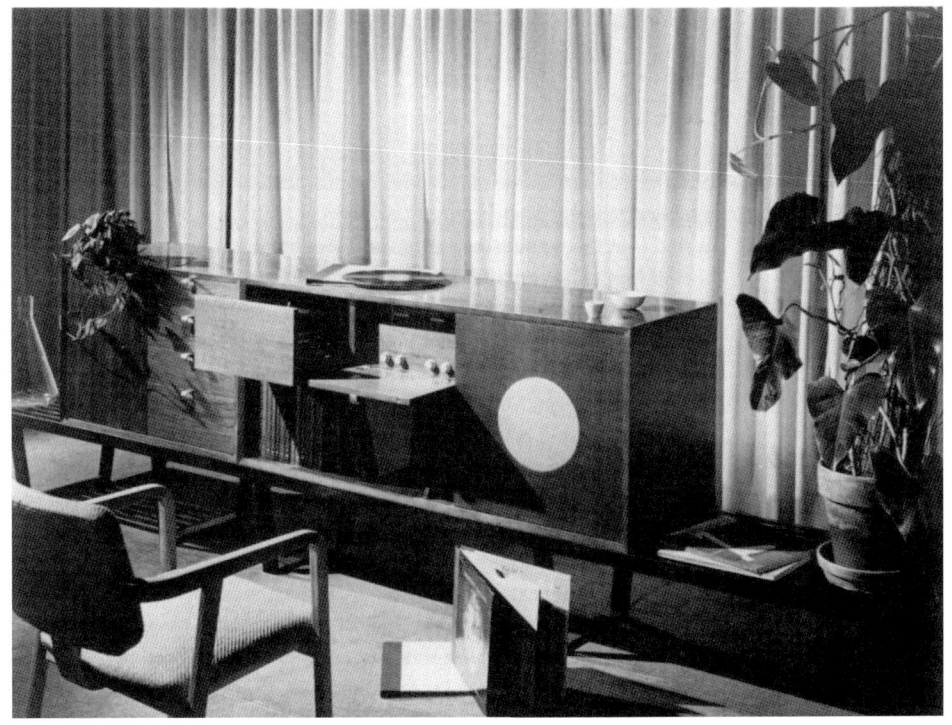

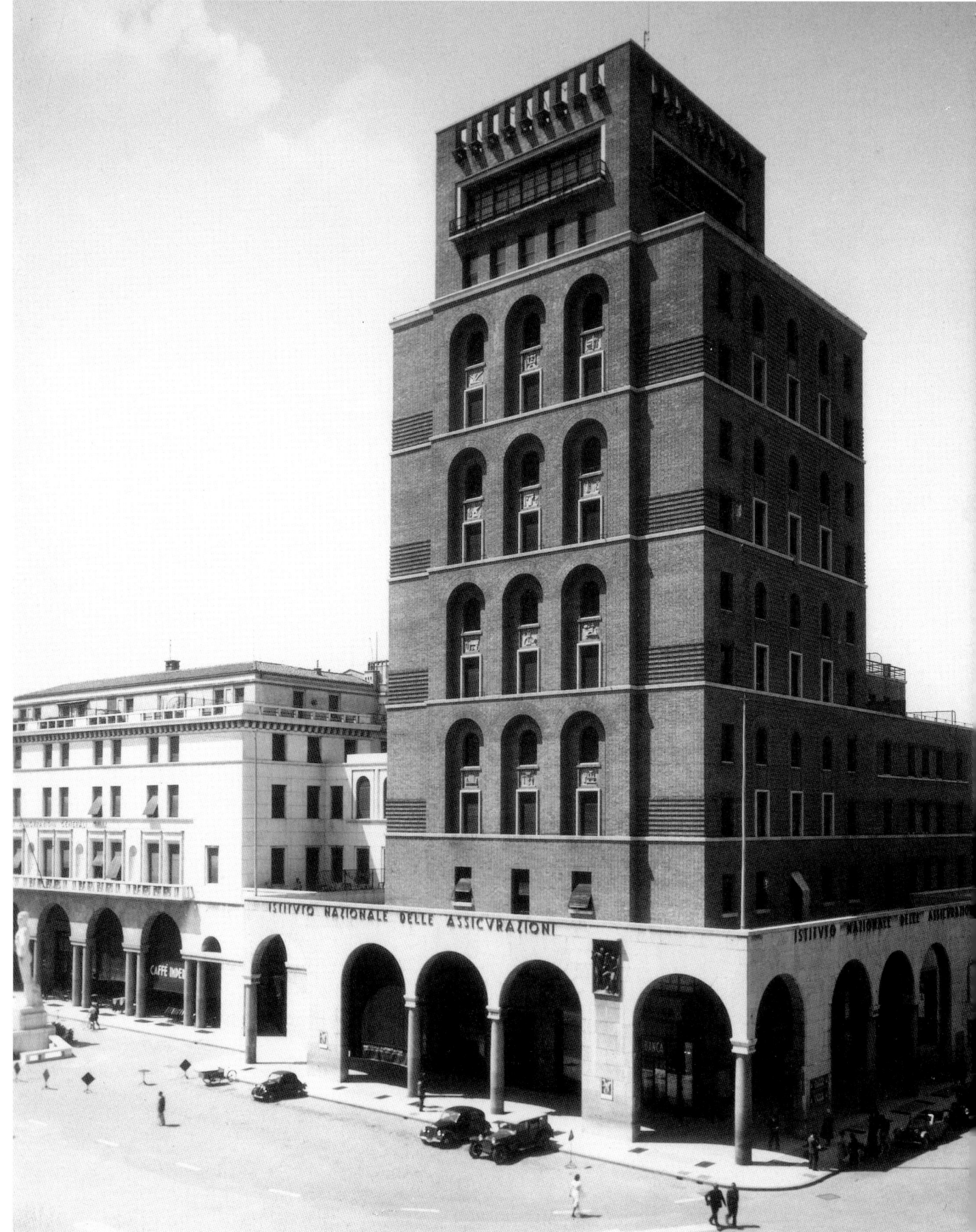

MARCELLO PIACENTINI
ITALY

FROM
PENCIL POINTS
JANUARY 1935

Editor's Note: *We are definitely not interested in publishing examples of contemporary European architecture for the purpose of encouraging the sort of stupid copying of mannerisms that is unfortunately sometimes done. We do feel, however, that something can be learned from what is going on in Europe today provided we look at the buildings with full knowledge of the men and philosophies responsible for them. With this thought in mind, we commissioned George Nelson, Fellow of the American Academy in Rome, to interview a number of most important Continental architects and write for us a series of twelve articles to run during 1935.*

Irreverent legend has it—and there would seem to be some foundation for the tale—that sometime in the early '20s Piacentini was in a select group which became familiar with the taste of castor oil, that persuasive lubricant so generously administered to the wavering ones by the enthusiastic Fascisti. Today, under the same regime, it is His Excellency Marcello Piacentini, official architect to the government, Secretary of the Royal Academy, President of the Nation Committee on City Planning, director of the magazine *Architettura*, official organ of the Fascist Syndicate of Architects. All of which goes to indicate that we are here dealing with no ordinary man. And if it is true that at the beginning he and the new order viewed each other with mutual suspicion, it is equally to be remarked that had the present government, with its huge building program, never come into existence, Piacentini would not have reached his present unique position of power and eminence. Success he would have had under any conditions: it is in the man to be a leader; but the opportunities would have been lacking. The sluggish country of pre-Fascist days had its grandiose schemes, to be sure; the trouble was that it never did anything about them.

Piacentini came to his profession naturally: he was born into it. His father was an important architect in his time and the son was given the best education the country afforded. In 1901 he took his final diploma, after having demonstrated unusual ability as a student, and two years later, at the age of twenty-five, he won first prize in a large competition for a new civic center for the town of Bergamo. This was indeed no little plan for a boy just out of school, and in one stroke his reputation was made. It is characteristic of the way things were done that the project was not completed until the present government took it in hand, a quarter of a century later. His record of successful competitions is phenomenal. In 1908, his design for a vehicular tunnel under the Quirinal hill in Rome took first place; it is still one of the most successful constructions of its kind. In 1910, he was back in Bergamo, having won another competition, this time for a new university. The same year he did the Italian Pavilion at the World's Fair in Brussels, receiving the Grand Prix for it. On the strength of this he was put in charge of all the buildings for the exposition in Rome, which took place the following year, this time not only winning another Grand Prix, but a gold medal as well. Shortly afterwards his plan for joining the palaces on the Capitoline hill was accepted, and with the architect Brasini he worked out an arrangement whereby the curiously elongated Piazza Navona might better be adapted to modern traffic needs. At the Panama Pacific Exposition of 1915, the Italian Pavilion won the only Grand Prix given to any of the seventy-eight competing nations, and he took advantage of the opportunity to go to America. By the time he was thirty he had become a recognized leader in his profession.

Piacentini's career illustrates clearly some of the advantages of giving out important work on a competition basis. It allows a young man of ability to come quickly to the fore. The better men set a pace which raises the standards of the entire competing group, which in the case of Italy is very large. Best of all, it makes for progress in design: men who would play safe on a commission that had been handed to them, often experiment on competition drawings. In the case of a dishonest or mistaken judgment, superior solutions still have a chance to win recognition, the best case of this, of course, being Saarinen's *Chicago Tribune* [building] design. In Italy the numerous competitions which are held have become a kind of proving ground where all of the most radical ideas of the younger group are passed upon. And while there have been cases of the most flagrant abuses of the system, its educational effect, to judge from publications in the numerous interesting reviews, has been very great indeed.

Private commissions began to come Piacentini's way after the first winning competitions, and he soon demonstrated his outstanding abilities in the difficult business of job getting. His skills at negotiating and [his] powerful connections often made him the logical choice for architect when his undoubted talents as a designer would have been of no avail. One family in Rome that had chosen to build its town house on a site complicated by all sorts of restrictions due to the proximity of several national monuments, was practically forced to engage him because no other architect in the city could have designed the house it wanted and then forced it through the Building Department. And he had the most uncanny flair for getting a maximum of publicity out of ordinarily commonplace jobs. One example will serve to illustrate. He was commissioned to do a moving picture theatre in 1915. He analyzed the problem of how to treat the façade in a manner years ahead of the time, and designed it as a simple screen with accents of flat decoration, rather than the pompous arches and colonnades that the Romans had come to expect on the fronts of their theatres—as well as on everything else, for that matter. It created a furor. Everyone who could talk or use his hands joined the controversy, and the howls raised by the arch-loving populace were so great that he finally had to do the façade over at his own expense. The battle went on for months in the cafés and newspapers, and while he did lose a good bit of money on the job, infinitely more important was the fact that when the excitement had died down there was hardly a man, woman, or child in all of central Italy who did not know that there was an architect named Piacentini in Rome. The proprietor of the theatre was highly gratified by the uproar: not only did he get a new façade for nothing, but the daily free advertising kept his house jammed for months. There was an amusing sequel to this tempest in a teapot. An American movie magnate, who happened to be in Rome at the time, called on him and offered him vast sums if he would design him theatres that would produce similar outbursts in America. Piacentini, familiar with the happy unconsciousness of the American citizenry where matters aesthetic were concerned, regretfully declined.

As he began to settle down to a prosperous career devoted to designing villas and an occasional theatre or bank, the war broke out, ending his architectural activities for several years. In the troubled days that followed the war he worked intermittently, doing a large building for the Bank of Italy, more villas, [and] a new bridge over the Tiber, and made many town planning studies. Then came the March on Rome and Fascism, the slight misunderstanding already referred to–a matter that was speedily cleared up–and Piacentini entered upon the greatest phase of his career, under a government whose program included plans for a virtual rebuilding of the country in the shortest possible space of time.

Today his offices are housed in the modern building he designed, almost directly across the river from Castel Sant'Angelo. The busy clatter of typewriters, the air of energy and efficiency that pervade the place make it seem almost American by contrast with the studios of his more leisurely contemporaries. He receives visitors in a large room, impressively bare save for a huge desk and a few modern chairs. Not particularly striking physically, except for a pair of remarkably keen, noncommittal eyes, he somehow makes felt his extraordinary personal charm from the first instant. Behind the charm lies a cold detachment and an inflexibility which are not so pleasant, perhaps, but much more revealing.

He talks well, and courteously opened the conversation by speaking of his trip to America and the impression it had made on him. Like most Europeans he had an almost wondering admiration for the rich, unfamiliar beauty of the large cities, but never for a moment did he confuse this sentiment with approval of the system of unregulated building that made such sights possible. In Rome there were laws to take care of that sort of thing, he added, and a very good thing it was, since the streets were already crowded to capacity. On the subject of modern architecture he was outspoken. The international style had no attractions for him: his sympathies were all with the efforts to produce a distinctly national modern architecture, and for the attempts of some of the younger men to introduce the glass façade and other features of the architecture of northern Europe, he had nothing but scorn.

"It is all very well to do these things in Russia," he snapped. "Here in Italy we have another problem. With a blinding sun for eight months of the year it is difficult enough to keep out the intense heat without removing what protection we have and then substituting glass for

The "Tower of the Revolution" indicates the Italian feeling that the last word on towers has not yet been said. A blending of old and new.

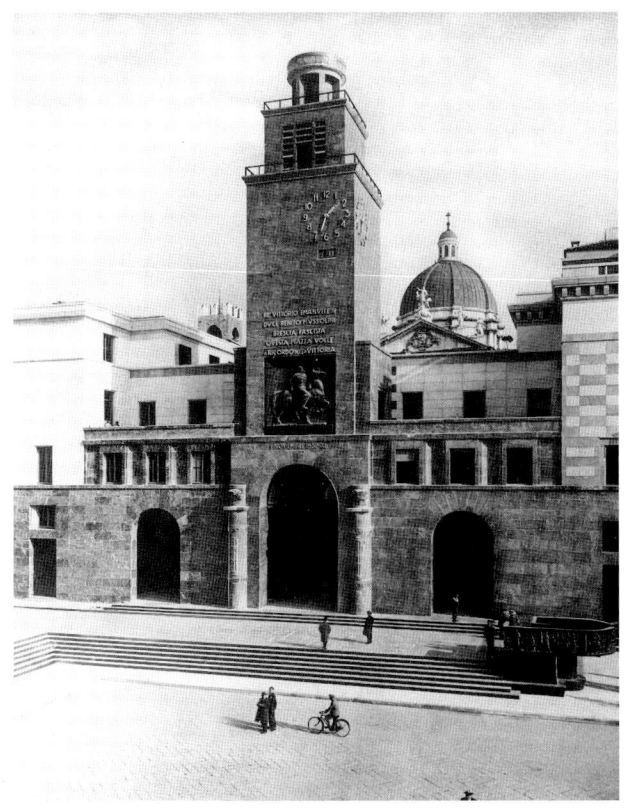

it. Look as this studio"–indicating a small row of horizontal windows–"just because I increased only slightly the usual glass area, even now in early spring this room becomes uncomfortably warm in the afternoon. This preoccupation with the least adaptable features of German architecture is clearly a case of slipshod thinking, of infatuation with forms while they pretend to talk about functions."

There was nothing out of the ordinary in all this talk: there rarely is in the reasoned conclusions of the practiced builder who has found that theories are no good unless they can be successfully built. "Why this mad rush to create a new architecture in a day?" asked Piacentini. "Rome has seen many styles come and go; they all developed slowly. So today. What I build now is better, more truly modern than what I built last year. One must progress step by step–*passo a passo*–testing as one goes."

For all his expressed conservatism, his work tells quite a different story. How may of our architects, in a position similar to his, would abandon their bastard Gothic, emasculated Colonial, or the other shaking props which they substitute for lack of convictions, and make as radical a departure from established forms as in the Church of Christ the King, which was completed last year in Rome? Another example was the Via dell'Impero, and streets subsequently built in the heart of Rome. There had been plans made for years to remove the picturesque slums that fringed the Forum and put in streets to relieve the frightful congestion in the heart of Rome.

MARCELLO PIACENTINI

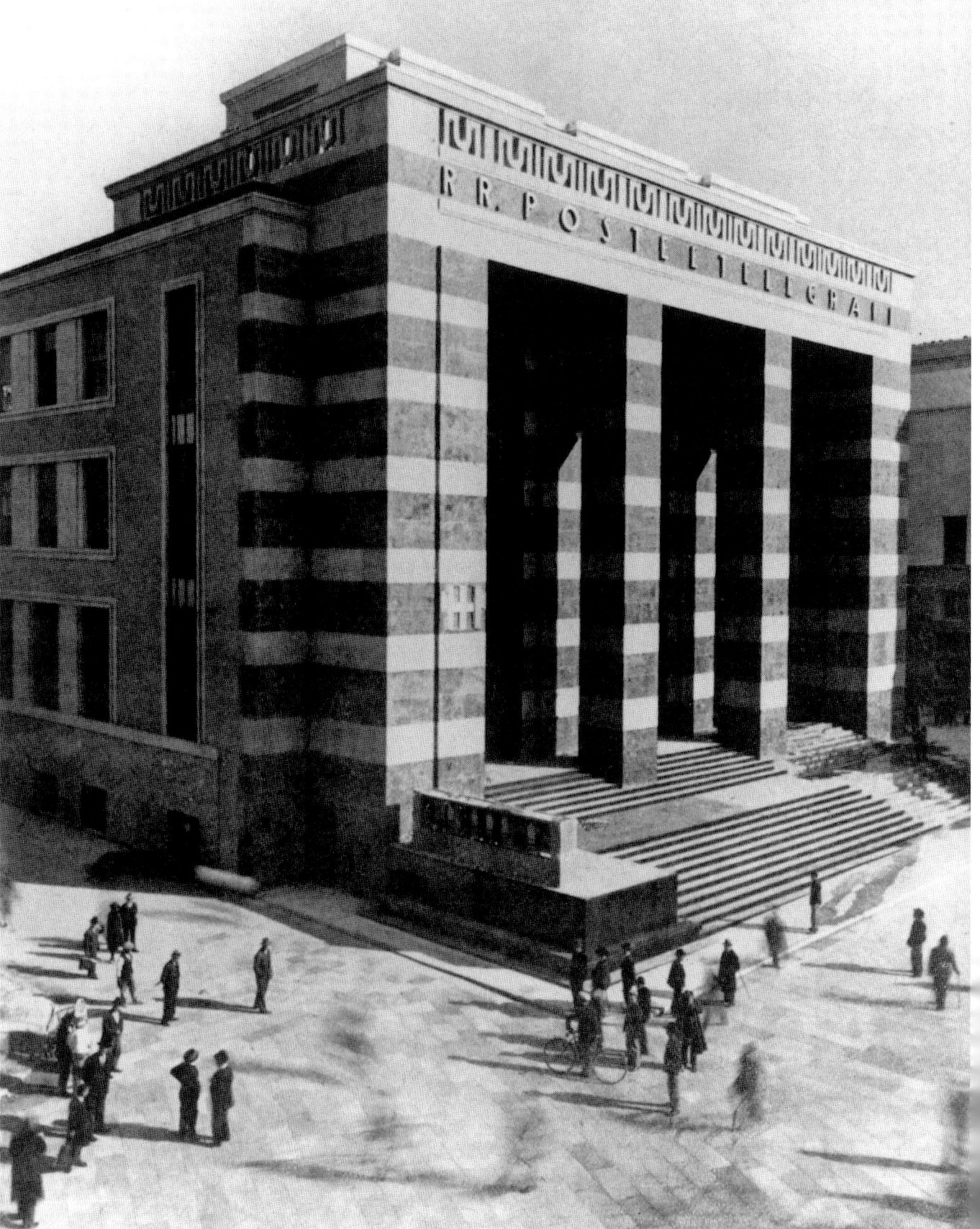

Italy finds in the Post Office at Brescia that a government building can be modern and still dignified, as well as possessed of a national flavor.

Nothing, as usual, was done about it until Mussolini came into power. It would have been very easy to side with those sentimental souls who preferred to leave the malodorous tenements as a background for the ruins and to bewail the vandalism that would remove this scenery. Instead, as head of the commission, he worked wholeheartedly for the scheme until the government was interested, and then it was done. The spectacle of fast cars going down the street, past the ruins, only increases, if anything, the sense of their magnificence and power.

A few years ago one of the greatest of all the competitions was held. The town of Brescia, a thriving commercial city midway between Milan and Venice, needed a large new center for its growing needs. There were two existing piazzas, both inadequate, and between them lay a choked area of tangled slums. All of Italy's architects submitted plans, with the exception of Piacentini and others who were on the jury. The drawings were judged inadequate, six of the best were purchased, and one year after the judgment it was announced that the City of Brescia had awarded the commission for the design of a new civic center to Marcello Piacentini. One might be tempted to inquire into this more deeply, but it would be fruitless; besides, as a cynical acquaintance remarked, no other architect in the country could have pushed the project through to completion. There were municipal funds, and there was money from the Government, but the success of the venture depended on the big companies which might be induced to buy or rent space in the buildings that were to surround the piazza. It was one of the biggest jobs Piacentini ever undertook; he succeeded finally, and in 1932, a scant three years after the demolition of existing buildings had begun, the Piazza della Vittoria was inaugurated with much pomp and ceremony by Mussolini, who afterwards privately expressed his gratification to the architect, as well he might. It was a splendid piece of work. In one stroke a blighted area was removed from the center of the city, its inhabitants were transferred to more sanitary quarters, a new open space, well placed in relation to existing traffic arteries, was created, automatically becoming the logical business section of the city. There are ten large buildings around the piazza, a post office, an insurance company, a bank, and so on. While easily accessible, the piazza accommodates no through traffic, and has consequently become the favorite gathering place of the people. One can criticize, of course. It is all a bit garish in its sleek coating of varicolored marbles. There is a curious vacillation between Lombard, Venetian, and nontraditional modern influences, and the very virtuosity of the architect makes for restlessness. Amid all the marble rises a thirteen-story skyscraper of brick, with apartments on the upper floors and a restaurant at the top. The post office, done in horizontal stripes of black and gray marble, is a simple and monumental edifice, not to be passed over lightly when one considers what we have been getting in the way of post offices for many long years. Piacentini was practically a dictator on the work, and his powers extended to the point where

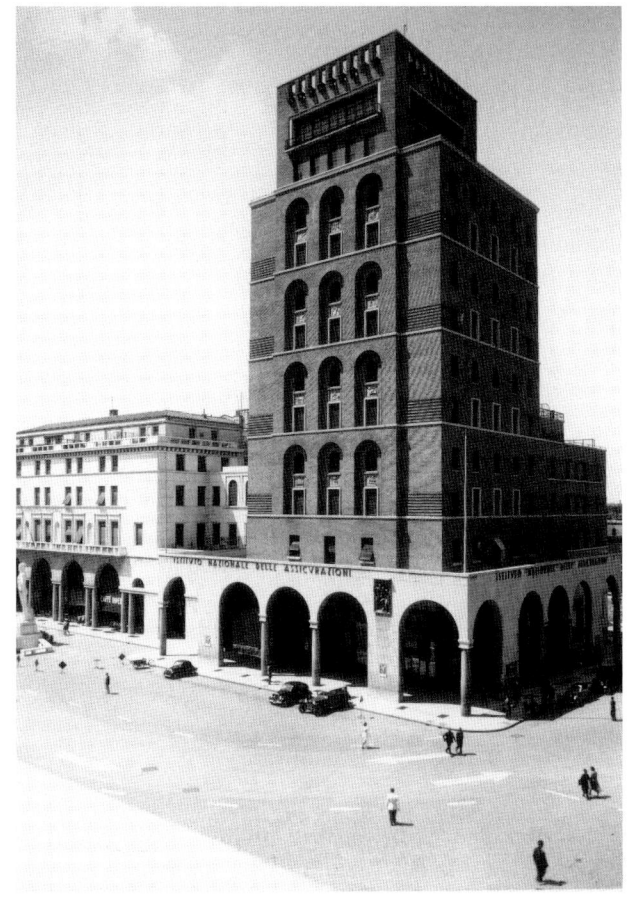

The "New York Skyscraper" of the National Insurance Company in Brescia, designed by Marcello Piacentini, architect. For once in history a building of this type comes by its Lombard brickwork honestly.

he could say what kind of a shop was to go in any given space. It is to be noticed how he spotted cafés and restaurants on the corners so that the limits of the piazza would be marked at night. No opportunity of this magnitude ever came the way of the great builders of the Renaissance. Borromini and Bernini cut each other's throats for chances much smaller than this, and the best that any of them could do was to make complete plans that they hoped would be followed, and, during their own lifetimes, change the plans of their predecessors.

Last spring Piacentini was reported to have the equivalent of about twenty-six million dollars' worth of work in his office. Large as this figure looks to any American architect in these days, when considered in relation to the wealth of Italy, by no means a rich country, it becomes staggering. Small wonder, then, that he is feared and flattered, attacked behind his back. Last winter opposition came to a head, and he was bitterly denounced—not by name—in Parliament. Why, came the question, should so much of the government work be concentrated in one or two offices when so many of the able younger men could get nothing? The picture is not quite as black as it was painted. Few countries in the world have entrusted so many commissions of importance to men barely in their thirties. Sabaudia, the new town in the drained Pontine Marshes, was designed lock, stock, and barrel by Cancelotti and his group, all young. The new railroad station of Florence, popularly known as *"la bara di vetro"*—the glass coffin—is being done by young men. So is the Naples post office and

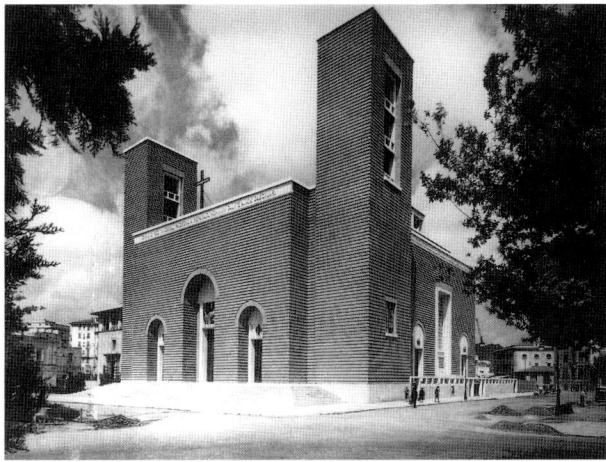

The Church of Christ the King in Rome, at left and below, a radical departure from established forms.

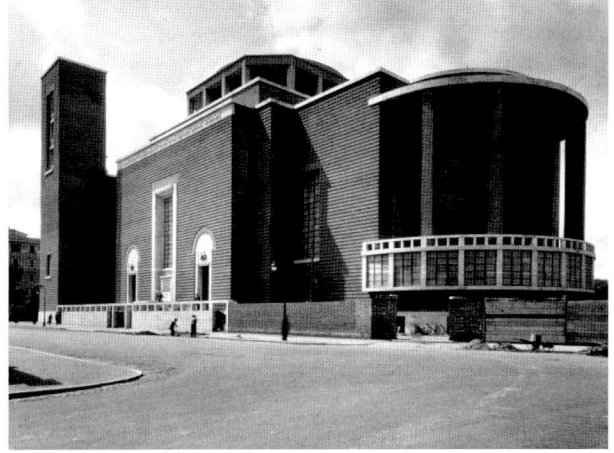

innumerable similar buildings being done all over the country. But someone has to be attacked, and Piacentini is the biggest target.

Personally, the man is a bundle of contradictions. In his character are to be found all the inconsistencies that have made the Italian temperament a mystery to the people of the north since they first became aware of it. A wily politician and utterly unscrupulous, he is at the same time a man of wide learning, passionately interested in his work and all that has any bearing upon it. A wealthy and conservative businessman, he has written books on modern architecture, has held the chair of Town Planning in the Royal School of Architecture since its foundation, and is an authority on the subject. Indisputably an extremely able architect, he nevertheless made the serious error of signing his name to another man's design for a new street in Rome. The mistake lay in his getting sued and losing the case. A firm believer in a modern architecture of a distinctly Italian cast, his Church of Christ the King has no prototype south of the Alps, plenty north of them. He is to be distinguished from his Renaissance forbears only in his dress, and of the determination and energy of the regime that is making over his country, he might be a symbol. Today he is at the peak of his career. Bound up intimately with a government beset by financial difficulties within and political worries without, it seems that he would of necessity rise or fall with the group now in power. But it is not safe to predict. He is a shrewd man.

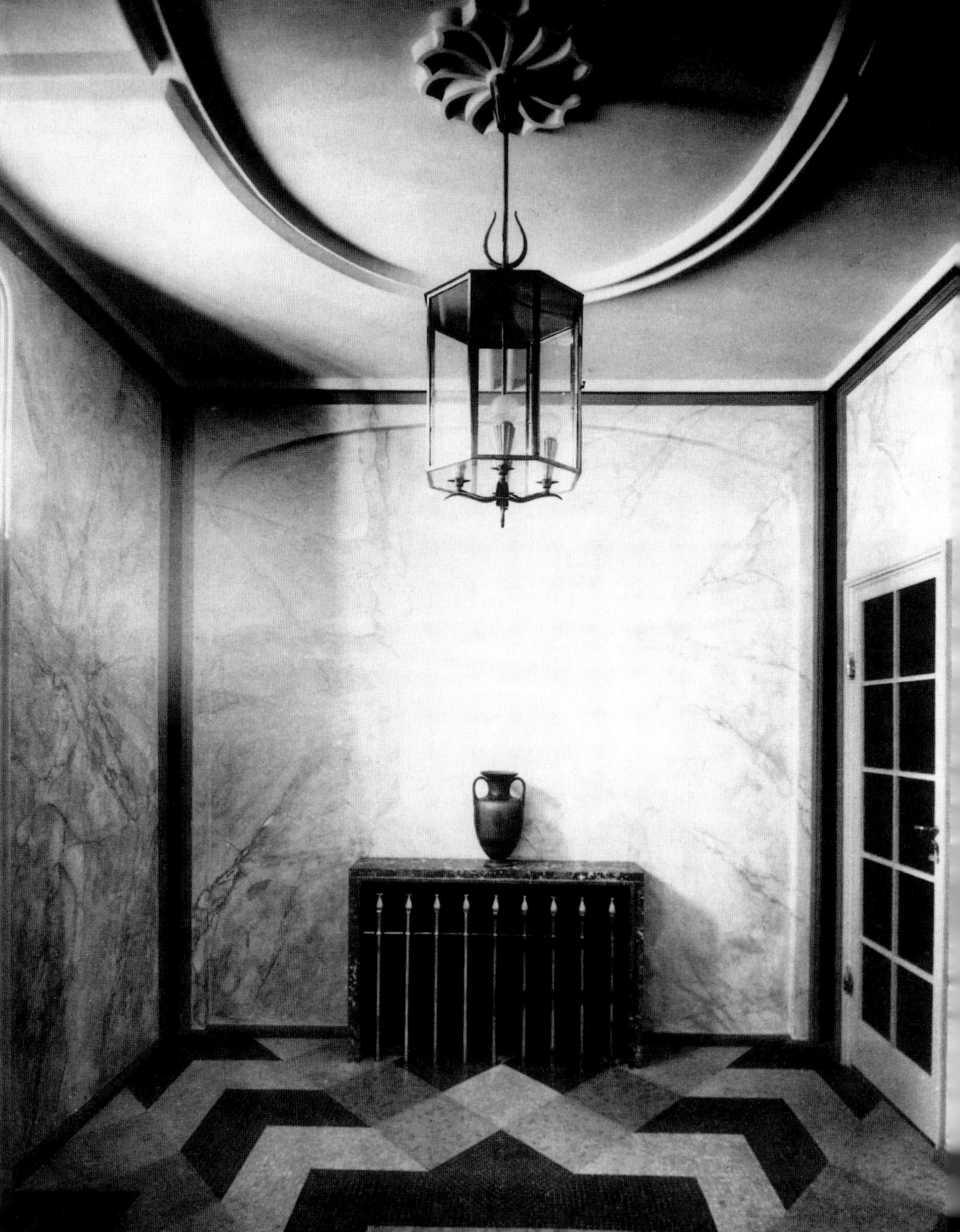

BENT HELWEG-MOELLER DENMARK

FROM
PENCIL POINTS
FEBRUARY 1935

Georg Brochner, in his entertaining volume on Denmark, remarks that the Danes are not a demonstrative race—a comment as Danish in its understatement as anything one could imagine. It would be much nearer the truth to say that the inhabitants of this pleasant little country carried reticence to the point of being a vice. Not that it isn't a most agreeable change from almost any of Denmark's neighbors to the south, noisily suffering from paranoia, inferiority complexes, and other European ailments. Quite the contrary. But it is probably due largely to this reason that so little attention has been paid to the modern architecture of Denmark in spite of the considerable and growing interest in things Scandinavian. Sweden, to be sure, would in any event come in for more notice if only for the greater amount of work of high quality done there—it is a vastly richer and larger country, and its highly organized industrial enterprises are of a nature that permits building on an extensive, not to say monumental, scale. In Denmark the case is quite different; it is small, agricultural, with a large part of its population and wealth concentrated in the busy and charming city of Copenhagen. Yet it is safe to say that there is no country in the world where such a relatively large quantity of work of the highest quality is being done at the present time. But, unless one happened to go there and see, one would never know anything about it. The Danes would never say anything. Certainly for one just a bit weary of the high-pressure whimsy and romanticism of Ostberg and some of his contemporaries, and the quite German (of pre-Nazi vintage, of course) appearance of the most recent work, the modern Danish architecture has a strong and pleasing individuality that is refreshing in the extreme.

Far and away the best of its producers is Helweg-Moeller. He is entirely a native product, which may partly account for some of this strong individuality. His architectural training he received in the Royal Academy of his own country, and as soon as possible he got himself a job and started to work. One gathers that he was a bit impatient with academic methods. Curiously, the job he got was not at all the sort of thing he had prepared himself for, and just how he got into it he didn't say: he became a designer in the Royal Copenhagen porcelain factory. To one who is at all familiar with the history of this extraordinary institution there is nothing surprising in this. One of its leading designers was an architect, and collected under its many roofs one finds today the most fantastic diversity of types, from the savagely religious Jais Neilsson to the realistically sensual Malinowsky. Helweg-Moeller stayed four years and then decided that it was not enough. "Small things," he said. "If you can do large things you can do small ones, but the reverse is not true." So he left, and started his search for large things.

For a number of years he did the usual small jobs that fall to the lot of the young architect, did them with a finish and originality of treatment that attracted and satisfied an ever-increasing clientele. There was no ballyhoo about it. He did his work and that was all there was

Helweg-Moeller's prize-winning Danish Pavilion for the Paris Exposition, 1925.

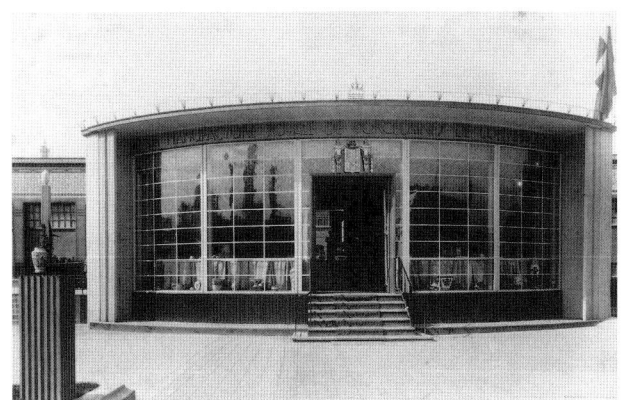

to it. Recognition came in 1924, when he was selected to do the Danish Pavilion for the Paris Exposition. He made his designs and went down and showed them to whatever committee was in charge of buildings. The committee, it seems, was greatly disturbed by what it saw, and became voluble. It protested. Surely Helweg-Moeller had made some mistake—the building was of wood. One couldn't do a wooden pavilion for the great Paris Exposition. But one could indeed, said Helweg-Moeller—he was doing one. He didn't go into further details about later struggles with the committee. His wooden pavilion received a first prize for the exterior, a second prize for the interiors.

It was in the following year that he received his largest commission up to that time. Heering's Gaard, situated on one of the old canals of Copenhagen, was having growing pains. In spite of Danish reticence, too many people, apparently, had been hearing about the soothing qualities of Peter Heering's cherry brandy, and the firm needed more space to satisfy their demands. One of the heads of the company was a friend of Helweg-Moeller's, fortunately for both of them, and together they worked out the plans of the greatly increased buildings down to the last detail. Nothing was omitted; the furniture, lighting fixtures, the smallest accessories were all designed specially for the places they were to occupy. Old Mr. Heering had seen the pavilion in Paris; he had liked the pattern on the exterior, so it was repeated in plaster on the ceiling of the main office, stenciled on the walls of a private passage. In

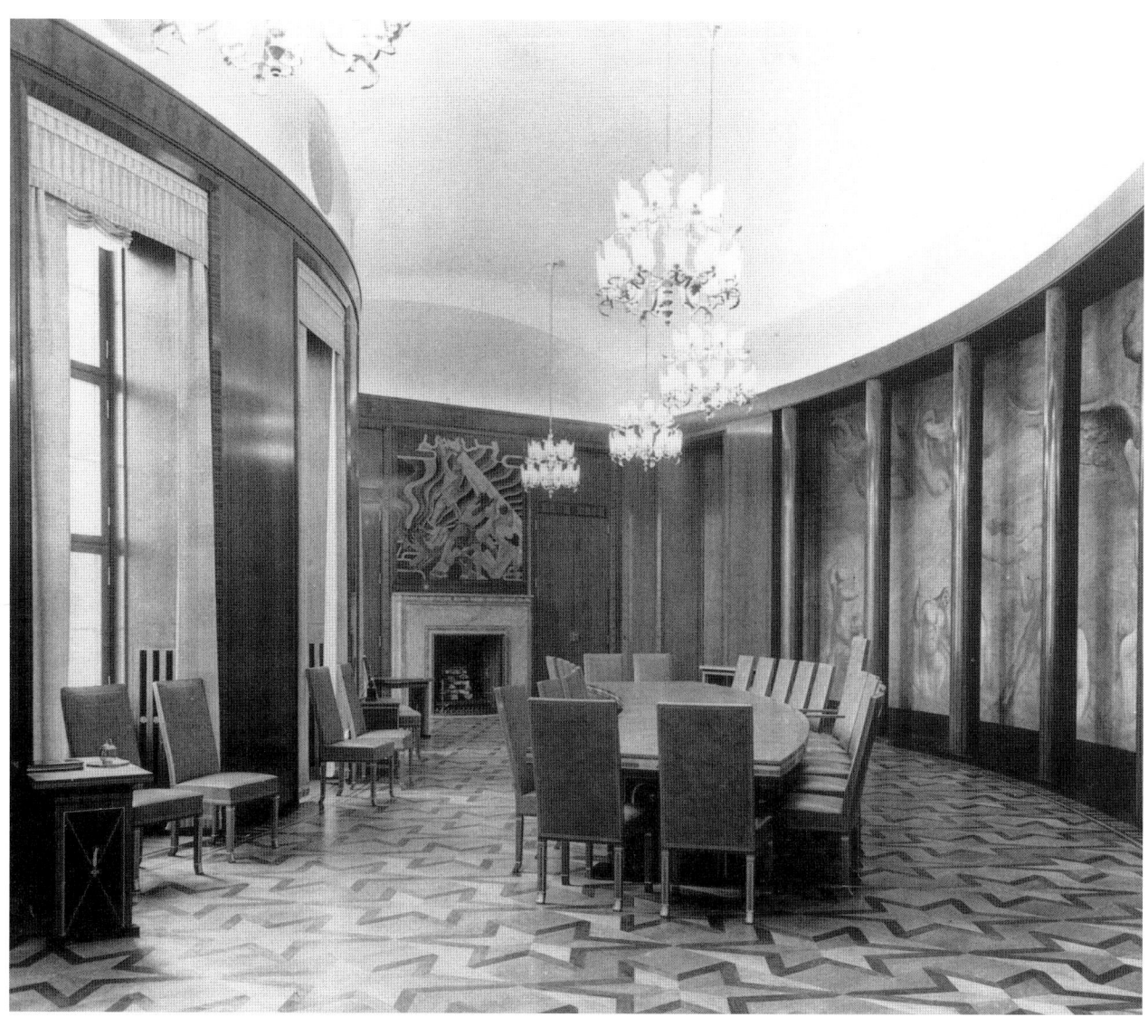

below, opposite:
Interior views of
Heering's Gaard.

PORTRAITS

an exhibition of their wares they had once used a large map of the world, showing all the distribution centers for their product. Helweg-Moeller had it cut up and used it to cover the walls of the office which kept in touch with these agents. It was highly successful. The exterior he did in yellow painted brick to keep it in harmony with the eighteenth-century building across the court in which the first Peter Heering had laid down his oak casks.

After this, more and bigger commissions came. The various economic crises which had paralyzed building in so many countries left Denmark almost untouched. His work from this time was almost entirely commercial and residential. Copenhagen was very well equipped with monuments, palaces, churches, and a huge Town Hall, and had no need of more. But there was a crying need for places in which to live and work in the busy and growing city, and Helweg-Moeller was called on to do his share of it and more. Perhaps the most interesting thing about all this commercial work that he did was that not a single thing came out of his office that did not have a remarkably strong personal character. It is not easy to take work of the most nondescript sort, build it for a minimum, and still make it look like something quite out of the usual run. And he got this quality not by little gadgets hopefully tacked on "to lend interest to the design," but by his conception of the fundamental character of the building, which was invariably original, and very sound.

Let us look at some examples of this. A while ago he

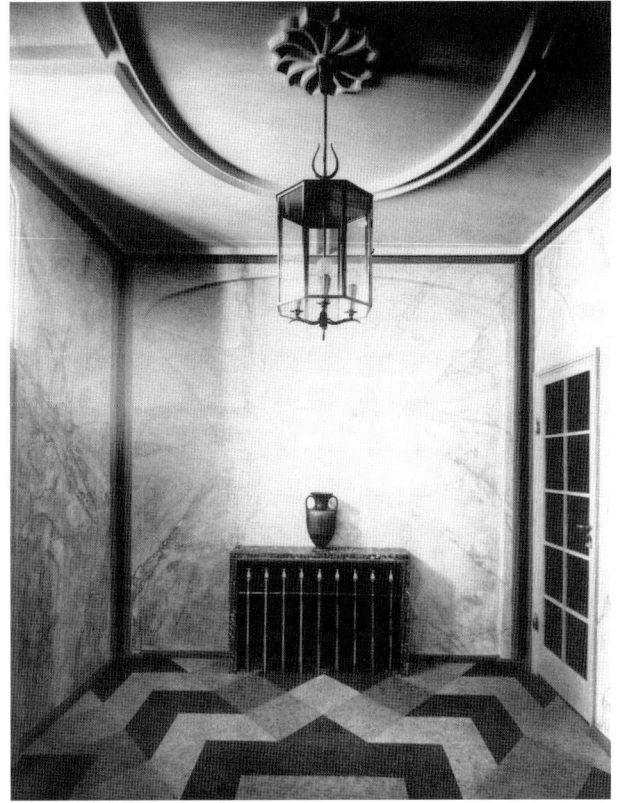

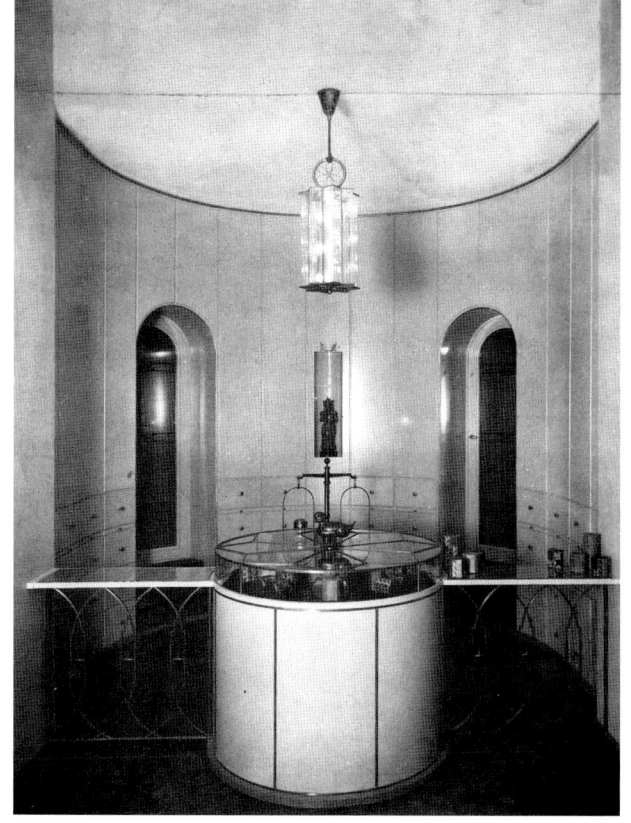

Helweg-Moeller's fondness for simple surfaces is noticeable in this Copenhagen shop where fine teas are sold.

was commissioned to do a large temporary building for a department store. A one-story affair, built of wood and plaster, it was to cover a plot of ground in the center of Copenhagen to give the store the extra selling space it needed, and to serve as a "taxpayer." Going on the basis that a store should function as an advertisement as well as a place of doing business, he designed the whole thing, inside and out, from this point of view. Metal fire screens were required over the shops by the building department, and he turned an originally disfiguring element into a motive of considerable interest. Particularly at night, when large block letters above the show windows cast their shadows on the corrugated screen above, is the design effective. The strong horizontals of the windows and screens above were stopped on the corner, which formed one end of an open square, by a two-story motive of glass which was excellent display space by day or by night, and in the cheapest possible way succeeded in giving a quite luxurious and spacious appearance to a building that was really neither one nor the other. The large moon sign is interestingly composed in itself, in relation to the building and to the square on which it faces. Inside, with the utmost ingenuity, he designed decorations of materials like iron wire, and odd bits of woven materials which were used to advertise the various branches of the firm over Denmark, and to illustrate the organization's growth. Outside, in the center of the square, he built a little circular affair with display windows. Here the best materials were used, and it is worked out with the greatest of simplicity and refinement. The whole is surmounted by a column made of green glass tubes, and crowned by a little gold figure. For the figure he had a competition, and the best sculptors in Denmark turned out for it. The effect of the whole is precisely the same as that of a decorative feature, such as a fountain, in spite of its distinctly utilitarian purpose.

Perhaps his four years of work with "small things" was not wasted. It was this training, perhaps, which made him so conscious of every detail, once the scheme was settled. He will design anything. A few years back he did a tea shop, and when he got through with the store he designed the packages in which the tea was sold. There are few men today who can design a lighting fixture, keeping it simple and practical, and get something so far removed from the banal. The fixtures in the Heering Liquor Pavilion in Tivoli Gardens are among the best examples of this. Helweg-Moeller says that this little building, which has been up for over ten years, is still being mistaken by visiting architects for one of the most recent designs. It is typical of the things he has done that none of them look out-of-date: they have an elegance and a refinement that has nothing to do with passing fads.

The man's very appearance is reassuring. In his early forties, apparently, in very good condition physically, with the lightest of blond hair, a very ruddy complexion, and kindly eyes of the palest, coldest blue imaginable, he is the best type of the true northerner. Thoughtfulness, decision, energy, and moderation are expressed in every word and action. One can at once see how such a personality would be entrusted with work by people who valued reliability, strength, and fine workmanship, and the shortest of walks through the city will show how well this confidence has been justified. As to the future, one can only make speculations.

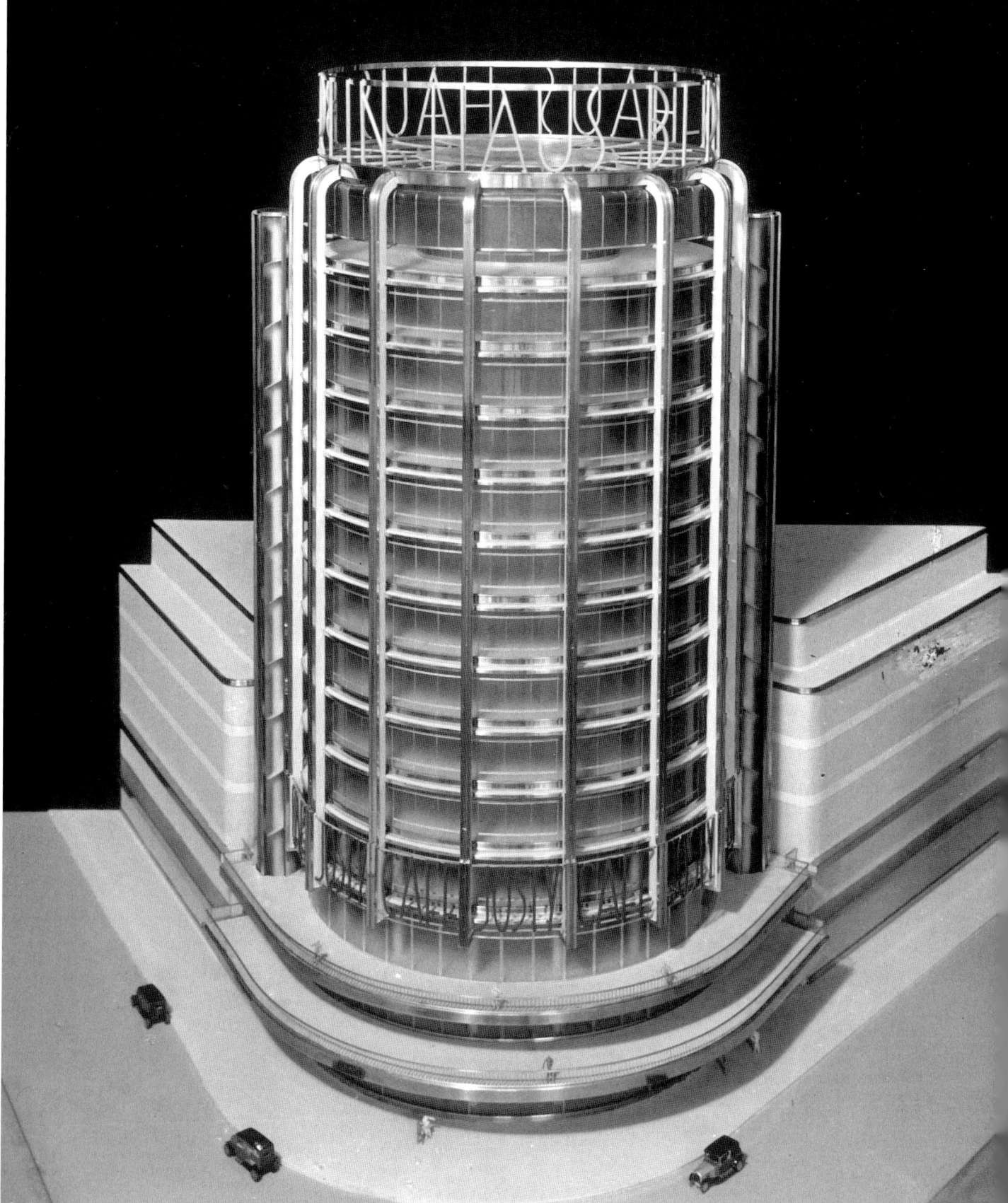

LUCKHARDT BROTHERS
GERMANY

FROM
PENCIL POINTS
MARCH 1935

Editor's Note: *This is the third of a series begun in January with the object of acquainting our readers with the men and philosophies responsible for the trends of architecture in Europe today. The examples of their work used as illustrations are definitely not presented for the purpose of encouraging the sort of stupid copying of mannerisms that is unfortunately sometimes done by men without understanding.*

To speak at all of the work of the brothers Luckhardt one must use the past or the future tense. They, along with Le Corbusier, Oud, Gropius, and a few others, may be considered as the pioneers in a new way of building. They built the first modern house in Germany. They anticipated the house built of prefabricated standardized units which is today the subject of so much experimenting in America. They were among the first to study the city plan in intelligent relationship with the serious problems presented by fast-moving traffic, and they began the revival of the use of models for the study of buildings. Now the office is empty. They have no work. What is more, they can't do any work: it is forbidden by law.

This doesn't mean that Hans and Vassili Luckhardt have been singled out for attention by an outraged government. Take any of the names which put Germany in the front rank as a contributor of highly important developments in architecture after the war, and you will find most of their owners in the same position. Their offense was to design buildings that took advantage of the great technical advances made since the beginning of the century, and reflected a new way of living. Just what manner of reasoning led to the conclusion that the sort of thing these men were doing was un-German would be interesting but unprofitable to inquire. Let us be generous and assume that it was the outcome of a semi-divine revelation, probably of the Aimee Semple McPherson variety. In any event, when the Nazi moguls came out of their huddle there was a whole new credo ready for the great German people. That the flat roof was not German was one of the fruits of their lucubrations. In some benighted countries the inhabitants decide whether a roof should be pitched or not by means of certain practical considerations, and perhaps taste; here the criterion is political: you can tell how good a German your neighbor is by the pitch of the roof he builds. Horizontal windows prolonged beyond a certain point are unpatriotic. Finding the "certain point" is to be compared only with the equally difficult task of the movie censor who must be prepared to say after how many seconds a kiss becomes immoral. It is all very uplifting, and from time to time out pops another astounding truth for the edification of the eager citizenry. One of the most advanced ideas as yet put forth by the brown-shirted Solons is that what the good untainted and undiluted Nordic needs is his own little home. The long conferences, the scratching of closely cropped heads that preceded the birth of this astounding notion are not even hinted at by the patriotic thinkers, but the great housing exhibition in Munich last summer gave all of the results. It seems that the ideal habitation for

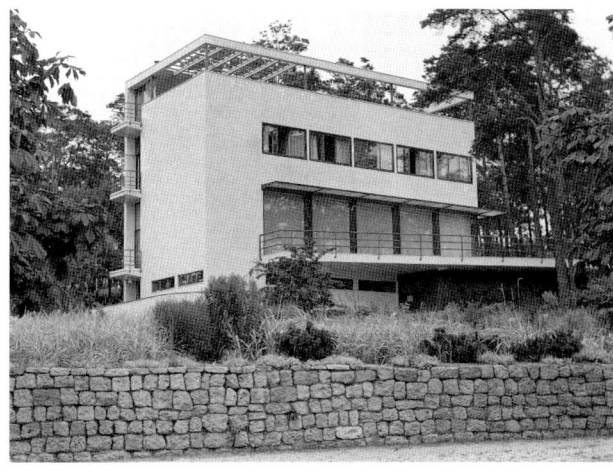

Two houses in Berlin designed by the Luckhardts with Alfons Anker.

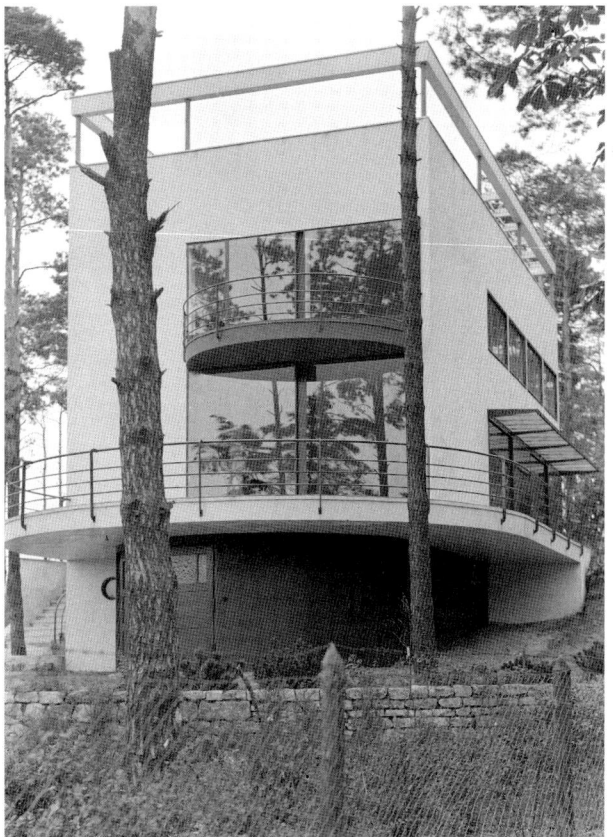

the average citizen, the great national dream dwelling, is a ducky little white cube, with four or more rooms in which to hang pictures of Hitler, *and* a pitched roof. The show was beautifully presented, and we soon found ourselves wishing that we had a little white cube to live in, surrounded by lots of other little white cubes. There was something degrading, we began to think, about living in a great apartment house with many other people one never sees, and central heating and incinerators and built-in kitchens. Most other races, lower down in the scale of human values, to be sure, still have the option of deciding for themselves whether they will inhabit single or multiple dwellings—it is only the Germans who are fortunate enough to be told what they want.

On this grand march towards a government stamped and approved ideal, a purging process has been under way for some time. Certain elements that have shown a dangerous interest in artistic and social endeavor on the wrong side of unjustly reduced frontiers had to be removed from the social fabric, or at least rendered incapable of doing more harm. So Mendelsohn is in England, the Luckhardts have an empty office, and Mies van der Rohe and Gropius must look elsewhere for recognition. It is apparently the taint of internationalism that is taboo. There has been one rather amusing exception: the tubular furniture which has been developed to such a high degree of beauty and comfort by Mies van der Rohe and other designers, and has since spread all over the world, was on the list of verboten articles drawn up by the new potentates. In the first philanthropic flush of saving the German race from the base contamination of the foreign devils a great many such articles were forbidden. Just what it was about tubular furniture that aroused such odium was not announced; it was just un-German. Something must have been wrong somewhere, because no sooner had this conclusion been arrived at than a few embarrassing facts were brought to the notice of the fiery reformers. The tubular furniture industry, it would appear, was a large and lucrative one. The gentlemen who owned this industry were very rich and influential. Moreover, they had one and all been born with silver swastikas in their mouths. With a truly Nazi broadmindedness and spirit of fair play the edict was instantly reversed. Tubular furniture was as German as the Iron Maiden of Nuremberg, as Aryan as frankfurters and sauerkraut. Let all good Teutons rally around and buy lots of tubular furniture!

But the Luckhardts are more…than…mere victims of a national catastrophe, and Vassili, with whom I spoke for a considerable time, had little to say about his misfortunes, much about the tremendous change in architecture during the past decade. The subject of politics was avoided, and the above account of the situation in Germany was obtained not from this man who might reasonably be expected to resent his career being destroyed but from sources more authoritative and much less biased.

It was shortly after the war that the brothers Luckhardt, together with Max and Bruno Taut and Walter Gropius, began the studies that later brought them into worldwide prominence. Undreamed-of technical developments had made available new tools which demanded new means of expression. An acute housing shortage had to be met—and at minimum cost. It was out of the work on these two major problems that most of the elements of the international style have come. Gropius went on with his studies at the Bauhaus at Dessau where his students learned about architecture as an art of building instead of a collection of rules which involved the wholesale cribbing of façades out of whatever books happened to be popular at the time. The Tauts put up the colossal settlements in Berlin's outlying suburbs, and the Luckhardts built a studio in Dahlem, a charming suburb where they built a number of modern houses which served as a sort of experimental proving ground for their systems of construction.

Luckhardt is a most amiable gentleman who appears to be perfectly content to talk indefinitely about his beloved modern architecture, and in the tour of inspection around his offices he pointed out many models, . . . all marvels of delicacy and precision. The use of models for the study of projected buildings had by 1920 become a lost art. The brilliant draftsmanship that appeared with the Beaux Arts, the prodigious facility of its leaders, soon became an end in itself, and it was forgotten that architecture had nothing to do with lines on pieces of paper. Small wonder, then, that the use of models had been abandoned. The Luckhardts and their group discovered, after throwing the styles overboard, that nothing remained but a set of blocks devoid of all

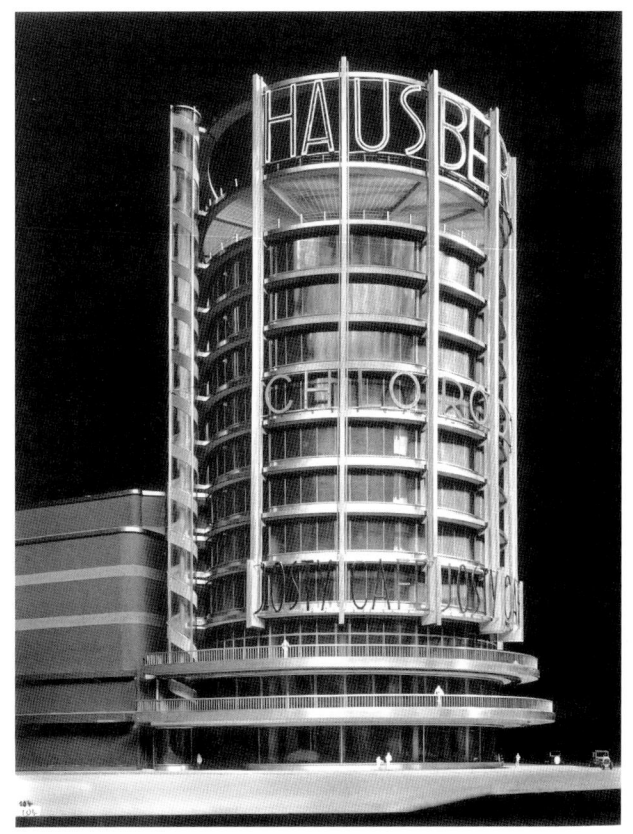

Designs by the Luckhardts for an open square in Berlin. The central building was worked out with models, the final one being executed in white metals and glass with accuracy in every detail.

ornamentation. There was nothing left to indicate on paper, and they were forced into the study of volumes in three dimensions. In their final state everything was shown in these models, even wall and floor sections. At the present time there are increasing numbers of men who are returning to this truly architectural way of studying buildings.

Long before most architects were even conscious of the word, the Luckhardts were studying methods of prefabrication. Intensely aware of the rapidly increasing industrialization of all countries, they saw that sooner or later the machine was going to replace the hand laborer in building, and instead of wasting time bewailing the fact, they studied to find the best way of utilizing the new techniques. In Dahlem one can find some of the results: light, fireproof buildings of steel, terra cotta blocks, and cement—planned for the utmost in convenience, compactness, and economy.

Their findings bear a remarkable resemblance to some of the experiments made in America nearly a decade later. Some of the requirements they set up were as follows: (1) The walls, inside and out, must be clean, as smooth as practicable, with a minimum of jags and breaks. (2) The exterior should be impervious to weather, always remaining the same in color and appearance. (3) The interiors must be hygienic, easy to keep clean. Unnecessary recesses and projections in walls should be avoided. (4) Speed and efficiency of construction must be made possible by the design, and economy is of prime importance. (5) All of the latest improvements

below, opposite:
Plaster model of a large garage in Charlottenburg shows a strong Mendelsohn influence. The ramps were studied with exterior supports but were finally cantilevered for structural and aesthetic reasons.

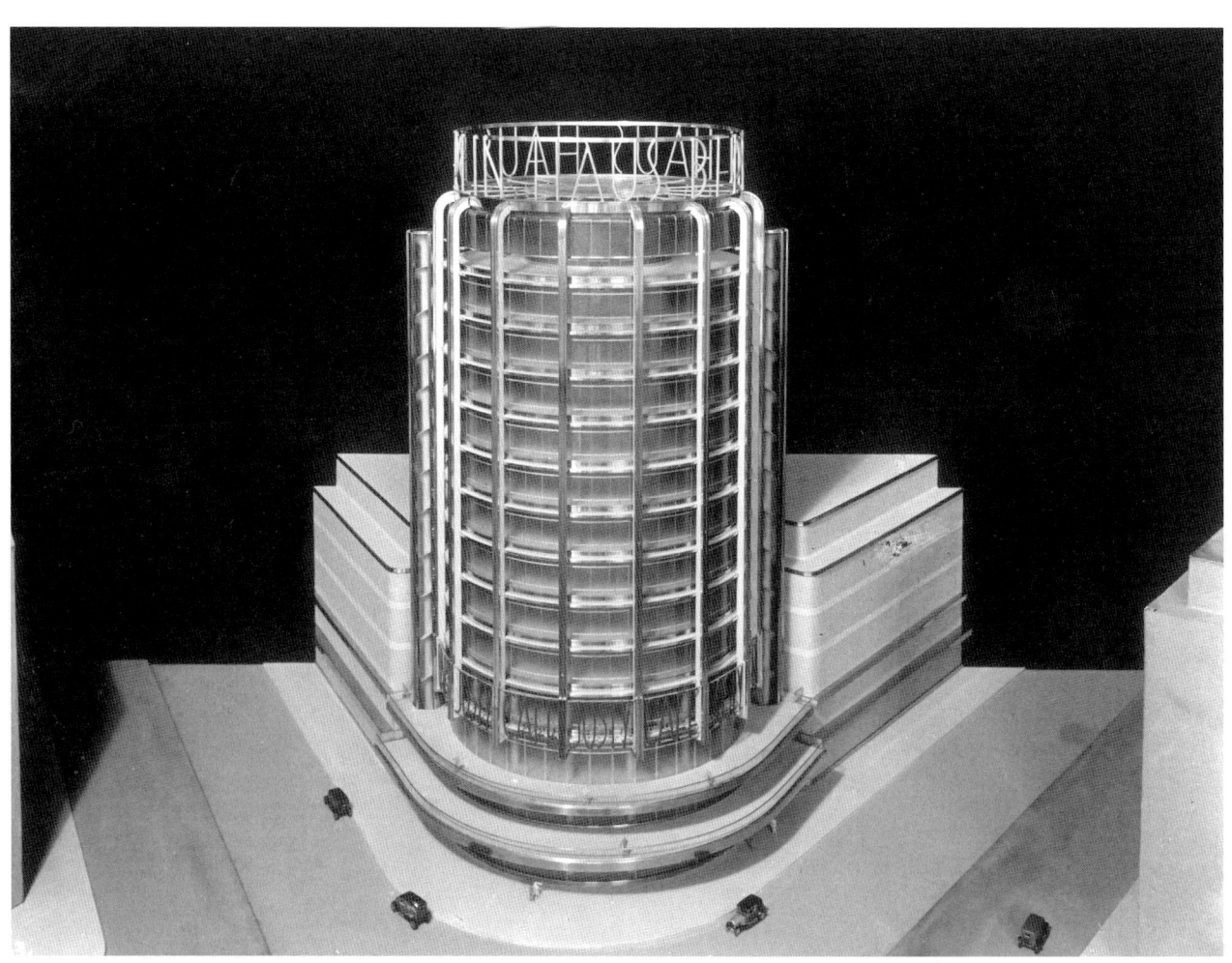

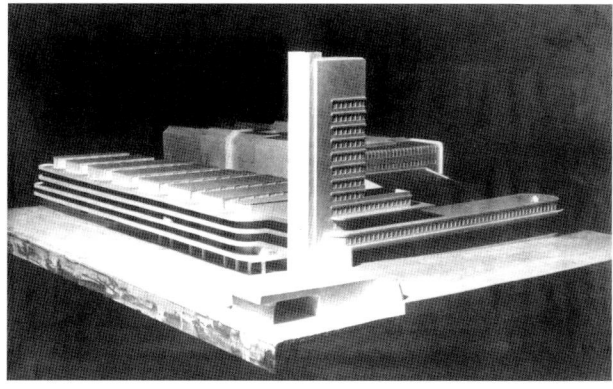 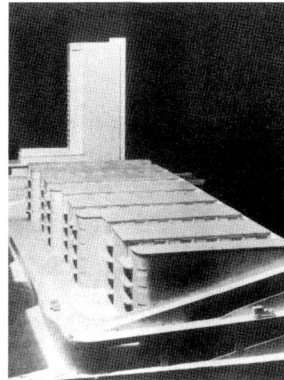

are to be taken advantage of, as much of the equipment being built in during construction as possible. These and similar requirements are now being so generally adopted that one remembers with surprise that a short while ago they were thought almost revolutionary.

Recently considerable interest was aroused by the Lescaze Town House, whose façade of glass brick and stucco stands out in sensational contrast beside its rather dowdy brownstone neighbors. Without wishing to belittle Mr. Lescaze's most ingenious and tasteful solution of the problem of a town house with a narrow frontage, it is worth noting that the Luckhardts had long since realized the potentialities of glass brick and were among the first to use it. Although changes in design come about very rapidly these days, one has yet to find any marked improvement over the room illustrated which was built in 1931.

While Le Corbusier was mulling over his grandiose visions of a new Paris—a scheme which involved the destruction of a huge section of the city, Vassili and Hans Luckhardt were making excursions into the field of city planning in a much more practical fashion. A competition for a new design for the Alexanderplatz in Berlin was announced, and they entered it. From the beginning, traffic was a controlling factor in their design. They realized that in a great open space, regardless of its shape, traffic naturally tended to go in circular lanes, and they based their scheme on this observation. Above the street great curved façades were created, their long lines of horizontal windows recalling the form of the building on each floor. The traffic was studied with great care, and every known device which might facilitate the movement of automobiles and street cars, and separate them from the pedestrians, was employed. The great daring of the scheme, its simplicity, reasonableness, and lovely flow of line, captivated the jury, and it was awarded the first prize. The winning design was published widely, everywhere arousing great admiration, but in the end it was just another competition winner that was never built. Just what happened is not quite clear, but in any event, when work was finally begun on the new buildings for the Alexanderplatz, Peter Behrens was the architect, not the Luckhardts. Behrens made some clever sketches which were never followed, and today the Alexanderplatz is one of the biggest, dullest, most completely commonplace squares to be found in all of Europe. They had one other opportunity to work on a grand scale in Berlin. Their project had for its main feature a skyscraper of metal and glass, circular in plan, placed on the long axis of a great open rectangle, and flanked by Erich Mendelsohn's Columbus Haus on one side, and a replica of it on the other. This was also never executed and Berlin lost its second chance to show how effectively modern architecture fulfills the requirements of present-day life.

During the conversation, Luckhardt wandered frequently from the subject of architecture to discuss developments in design in other fields. Automobiles and furniture seemed to interest him more than anything else, and he took much time to rail against the fake

below, opposite:
The Luckhardts' winning design for the Alexanderplatz in Berlin. The complete harmony of the design, which solves a difficult traffic problem, makes it a distinguished example of modern city planning.

streamlining of cars in order to make them sell rather than run more efficiently, and the Czechoslovakian car with the engine in the rear was the only one which had his complete approval. He was entitled to speak with authority on modern furniture, having been one of the first to use bent steel tubes for that purpose, and it was extremely interesting to inspect some half finished chairs in the office. It is difficult to see how simplification could be pushed any further—a bent tube, a sheet of metal welded to it, some upholstery, and some just had the tubes and leather straps.

Still talking, we left the studio and went down the street towards the subway station. There were many people in brown shirts, dripping with swastikas, symbols of the new Germany that has ruined the men who brought her worldwide respect. And of these wasted talents, the brothers Luckhardt are, in my humble opinion, by no means the least.

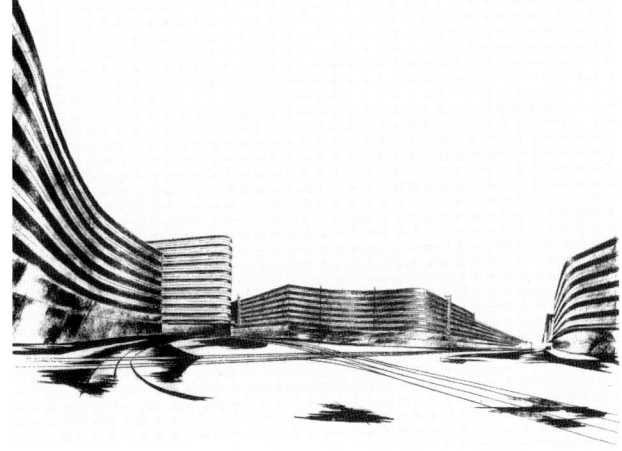

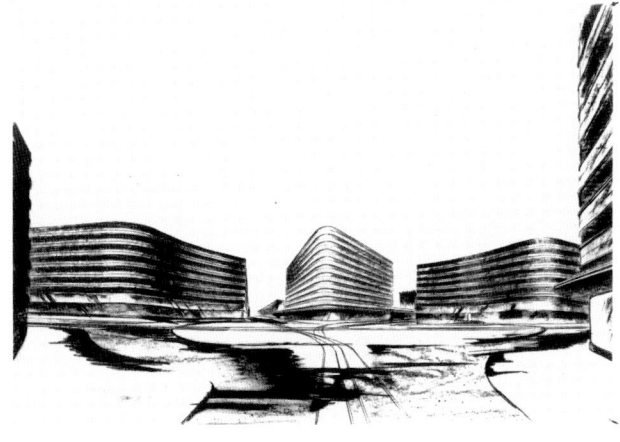

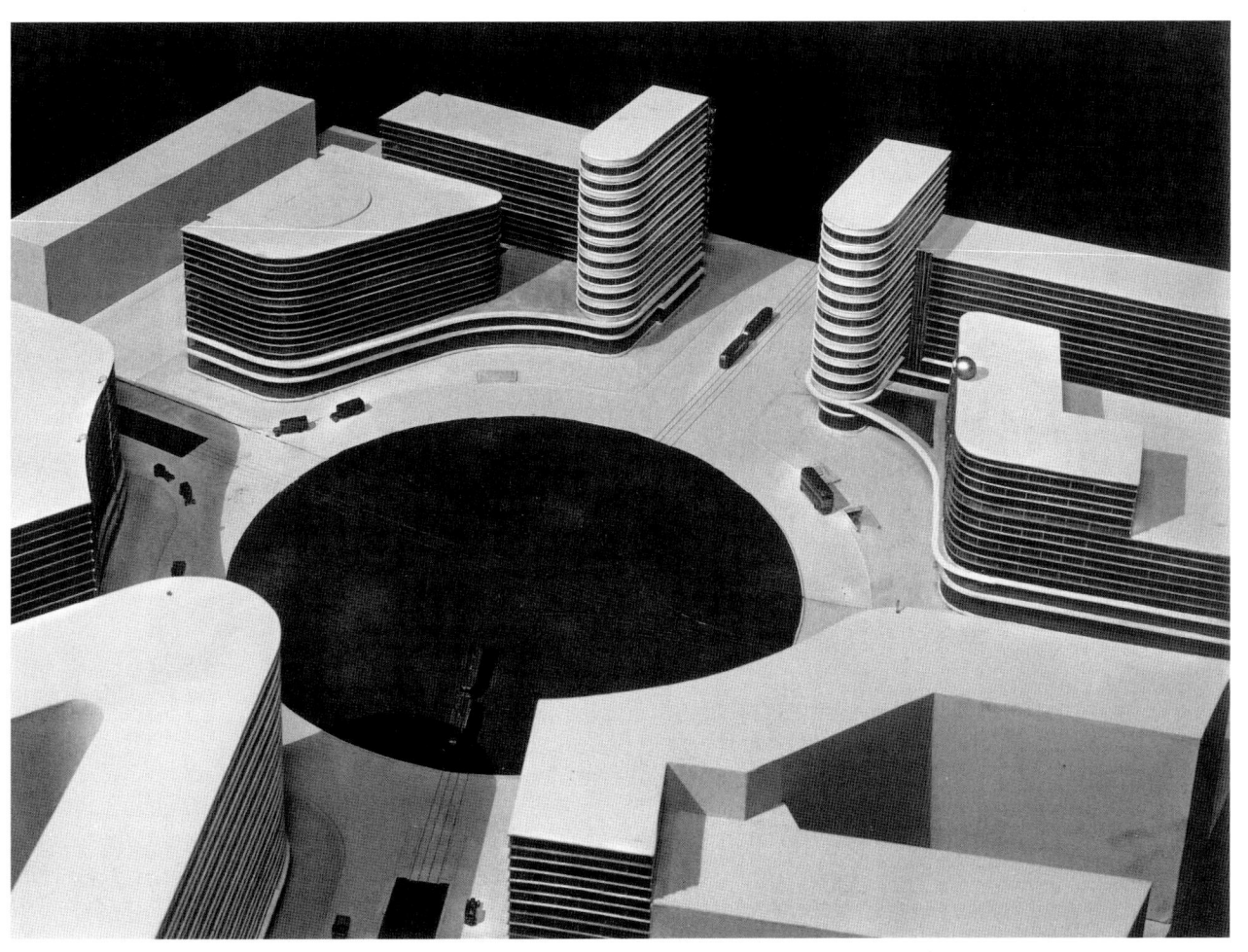

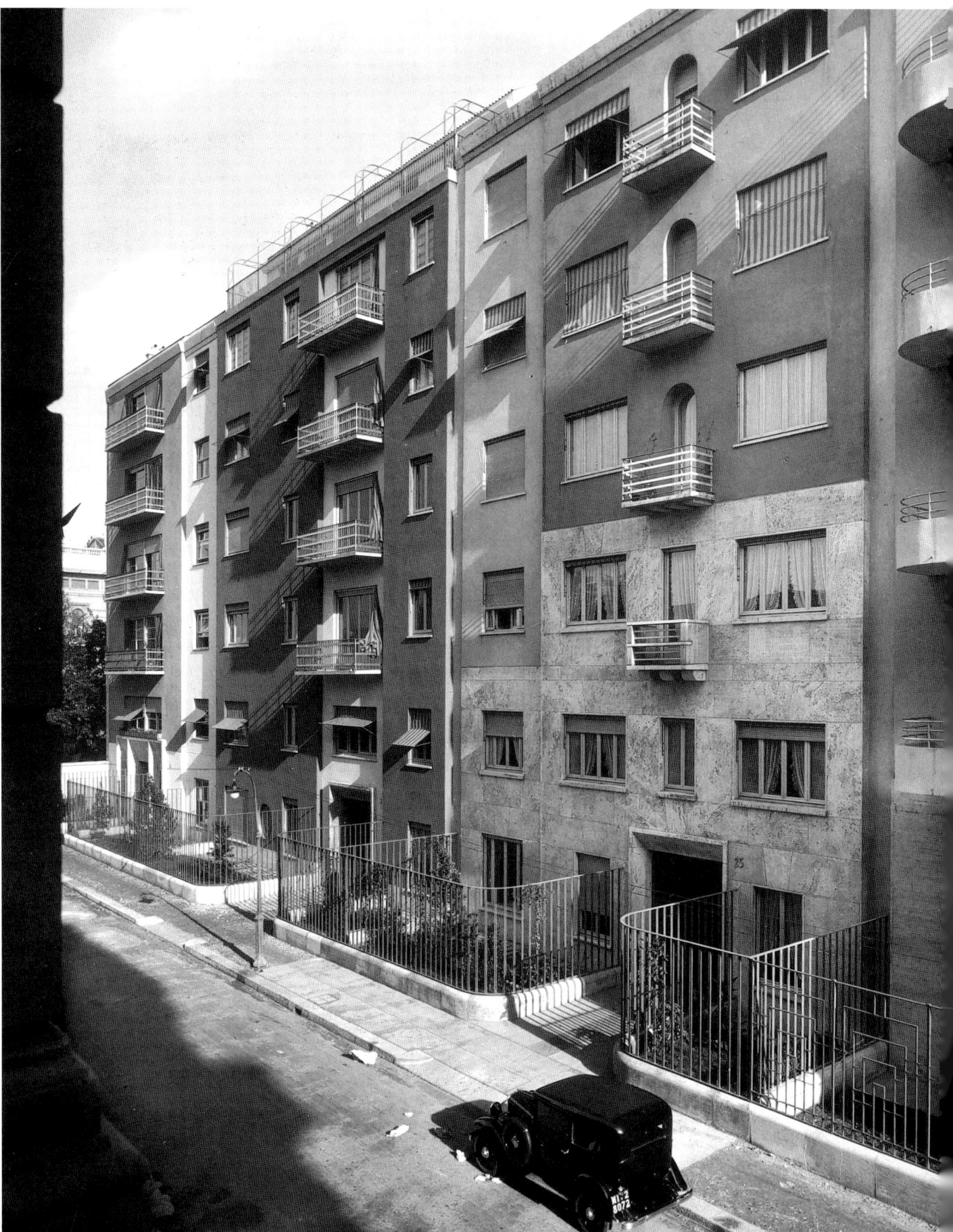

GIO PONTI
ITALY

FROM
PENCIL POINTS
MAY 1935

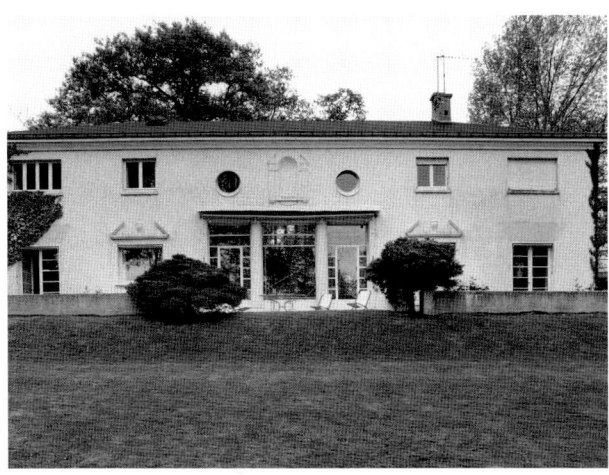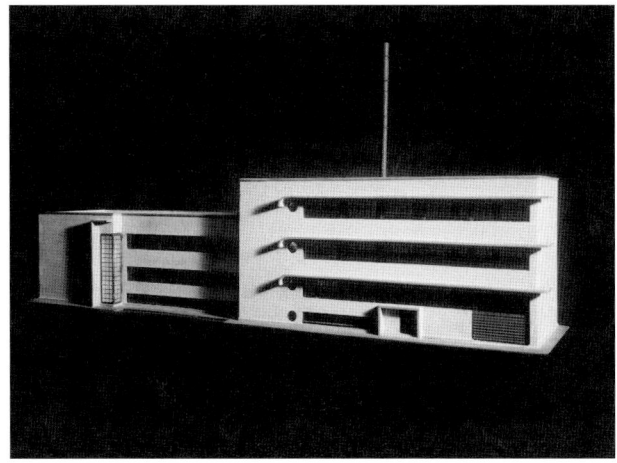

Editor's Note: *This article continues a series begun in January with the object of discussing the men and philosophies behind the contemporary European architecture, examples of which are so often published in American periodicals, usually without explanatory text. We believe that it is important to understand why architecture in Europe is taking the forms that it is, for with understanding the American practitioner can profit from the good and reject the bad, avoiding the unintelligent copying of mannerisms that is unfortunately sometimes done for the sake of being "smart."*

For centuries Italy in her inexhaustible vitality has been producing men like him. Sculptors who were architects. Painters who turned from the production of incomparable masterpieces to decorate ballrooms, devise plays and pageants, and puzzle over the problems of medieval plumbing. One of the greatest engineers of his time did a series of superlative paintings and saw nothing odd in it, nor were his contemporaries in the least surprised that he could design a palace in Rome which was even then recognized as one of the peaks of a great style. The causes of this amazing versatility are far to seek, and moreover have no place here, but whatever the reason, there remains the fact that the history of art in Italy presents the astonishing spectacle of a series of men who knew no boundaries between the arts. And today, with the depressing picture of a world made up of increasing numbers of specialists, busy subdividing minute tasks, we have the cheering example of Gio Ponti, who found early in life that no one profession was sufficient to use up his energy or exhaust his interests, and added others with the nonchalance of a small boy increasing his collection of marbles. It would be hardly accurate, perhaps, to describe him as a modern version of one of the giants of the Renaissance, sculpting new Medici tombs for munitions manufacturers, or painting Sistine Chapel ceilings for moving picture palaces. Ponti's gay talents are to be found in other, more typically twentieth-century fields.

He began by wanting to be a painter. His parents, who were prosperous people, were surprised but not pleased by these tendencies in their only child, who otherwise seemed normal and healthy enough, and they voiced their displeasure in a fashion which left no room for misunderstanding in the mind of the would-be artist. So he went to a school where painting was omitted from the curriculum, and he had a very dull time of it indeed, until rescued by a very exciting war into which Italy entered in 1915. He went into it in his usual impetuous fashion, coming out untouched several years later. Family influence was still uppermost, however, so he put away his uniform and the medal he had acquired, went back to school, got his diploma, and, shortly afterwards, a wife.

Marriage is a very serious business in Italy, but it is only rarely that it marks as complete a turning point in a man's life as it did in Gio Ponti's. His father-in-law was a member of the firm of Richard Ginori, the most important ceramics works in Italy, and before anyone quite knew what was happening the factory was turn-

opposite:
Ponti's first and latest excursions into architecture. His enthusiasm for the International Style is tempered by an appreciation of its limitations, and he reserves it for such things as the chocolate factory shown here (near left). The villa in Paris (far left) looks like a villa yet it is modern enough to be distinctive.

right:
A number of examples showing Ponti's varied and sensitive approach to the design of modern ceramics.

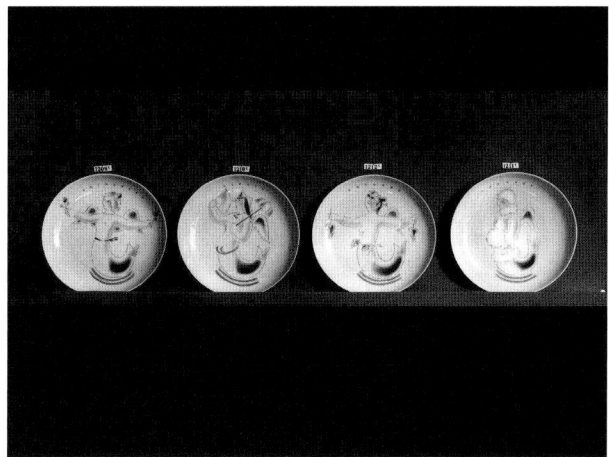

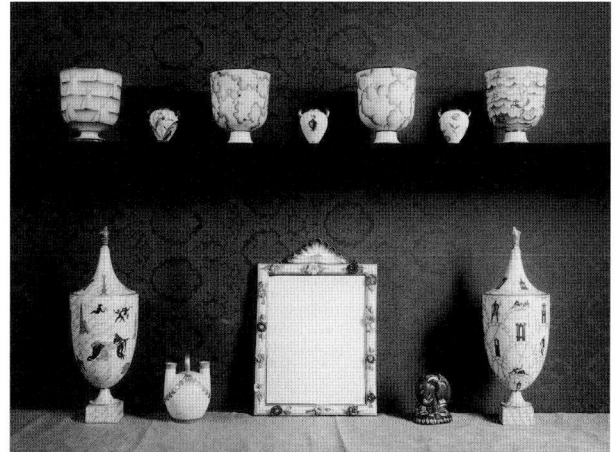

ing out pieces designed by Ponti which for lightness of treatment, grace, and vigor were without precedent. Under his direction a vast quantity of ceramics in the modern manner were produced, distinguished at the same time by an unusual individuality and by an evident appreciation of what had been done in the past. They were not serious in theme. Pottery, according to Ponti, should be amusing, giving the gay note of color in the home that was formerly supplied by the rubber plant. Classical forms and subjects were used, but not with that reverent spirit which inspired so many of our railroads to use Roman baths for stations. Ponti handled a pipe or a bag of golf clubs with the same understanding of their decorative qualities as when he used more classical forms. A fair test of the quality of his work is that most of the pieces made for the Paris Exposition in 1925 still look well, something which cannot be said for many of the exhibits.

Success in his early thirties did not content Ponti. He had never forgotten his thwarted ambition to become a painter. Also, he was discovering unsuspected talents as an organizer and executive. Impressed by a growing conviction that Italy needed to realize the importance of artistic creation of a sort that had some meaning in a rapidly changing age, he started the triennial exhibitions of industrial arts at Monza. They rapidly increased in size and importance, and eventually a school was founded, based on the same idea. He worked on other committees, usually as a director, and under cover of all this activity he painted and worked on his game of golf.

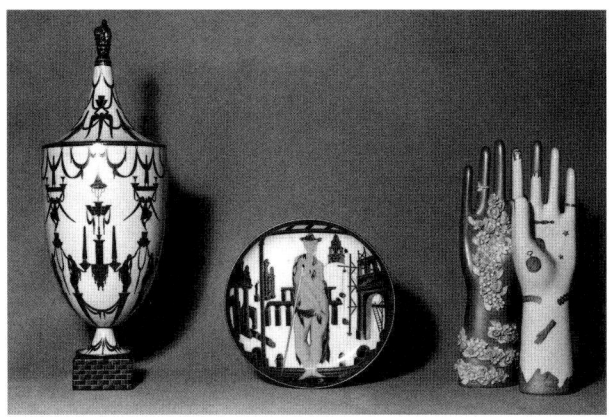 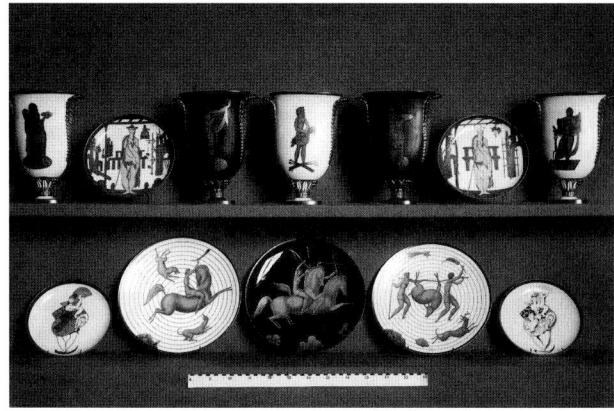

His greatest problem, apparently, was what to do with his spare time, so he became an architect.

It didn't happen all at once. He was well known in Milan, and architects called on him to collaborate when they had need of a decorator. There was considerable work being done by architects on new shops, apartments, and cafés. New materials were found capable of producing smart and amusing effects cheaply, and businessmen soon discovered that engaging one of the numerous young architects about town helped their sales. It was also learned that when Ponti was mixed up in these jobs the result was in better taste, and was more successful advertising, than when others were called in. Ponti, completely unimpressed by the maze of technicalities surrounding the profession of architecture, turned from decoration and collaboration with architects to designing buildings himself. Some of his first commissions were villas, nothing remarkable, but good to look at and to live in. He occasionally tried to be serious, but even a mausoleum could not suppress the natural grace and lightness of his work. When confronted with the sober problem of doing a large apartment house, he managed to break up the façade into a number of variously colored sections. It was highly successful; the bright colors were selected and combined with skill, and the division of the long façade brought it into better scale with the other houses along the street. He seems to like doing apartment houses. He made a sketch while he was talking, showing what he would do if he had one to build on the piazza of the Cathedral, or some such place where the view was of interest. Each apartment was arranged so that its view was different from its neighbors', and he even went so far as to say that the windows in each apartment should be different, so that they would frame the vista in different ways. He loathes uniformity. In practice, of course, he has necessarily modified his theories considerably, but his latest job, a "skyscraper" apartment of about thirteen stories, has a remarkably interesting form due to the varying arrangement of the apartments and terraces on the upper floors. People like the idea, it would seem. The building was not completed last summer, but all the apartments had been taken.

As he became more and more absorbed by architecture, he lost interest in ceramics. Like his contemporary in Denmark, Helweg-Moeller, he found that large things held a fascination which quite overshadowed anything ceramics had to offer. He abandoned an active part in the Ginori factories, and to fill the gap he took on a great many odd jobs. He designed a new banner for the Ospedale Maggiore–the main hospital of Milan. A deluxe edition of a cookbook was published, and he worked on some of the illustrations. It is typical of Ponti that even this cookbook should be unlike any other ever done: in addition to being a valuable contribution to a great art, it is most amusingly written and ingeniously presented. He sent dozens of drawings to the Biennial Exposition in Venice, most of which found their way into one collection or another; he painted portraits and did a large painting on glass for Milan's newest and smart-

opposite:
More ceramics designed by Ponti, ranging from decorative treatment of useful objects to sheer fantasy.

below:
Sketches for the two sides of a banner for the Ospedale Maggiore in Milan. Ponti made this design problem the excuse for two brilliantly executed drawings in full color.

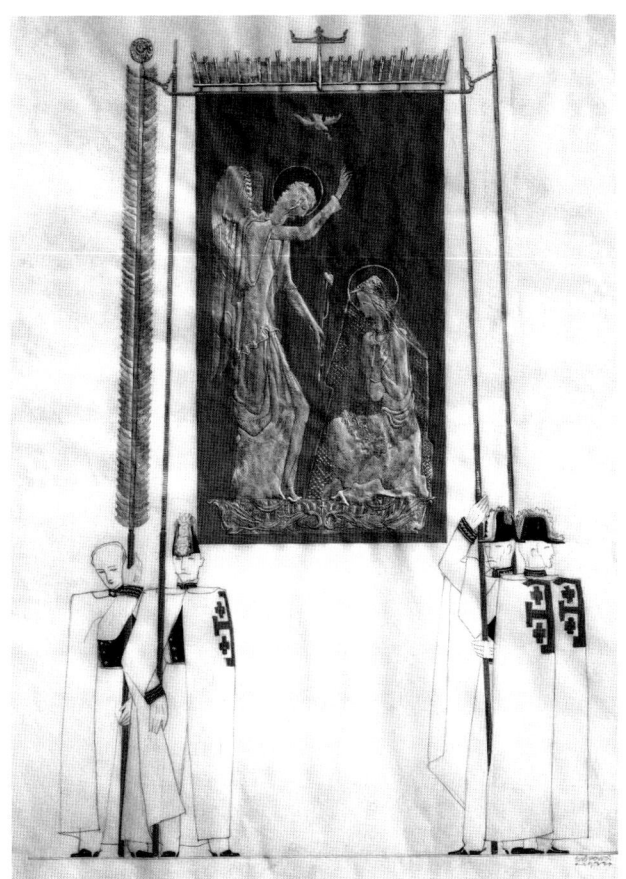
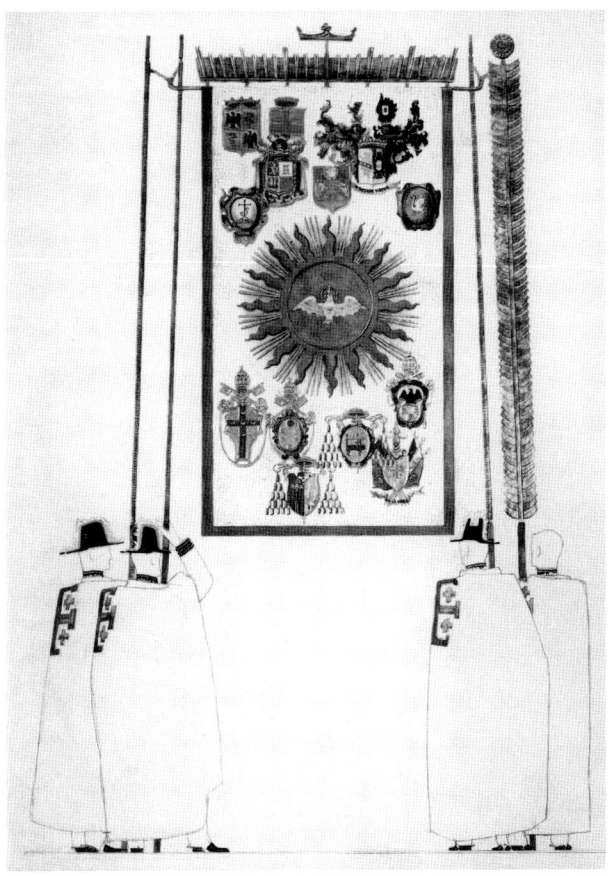

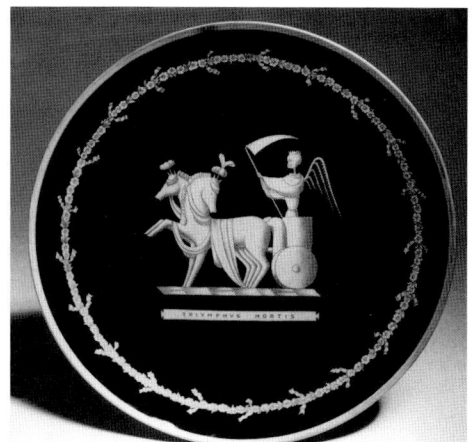

left:
"The Triumph of Death," executed in blue and gold.

below:
Two illustrations from "La Cucina Elegante," a privately printed and most irreverently written treatise on the art of cooking. The recipes therein are of surprising excellence.

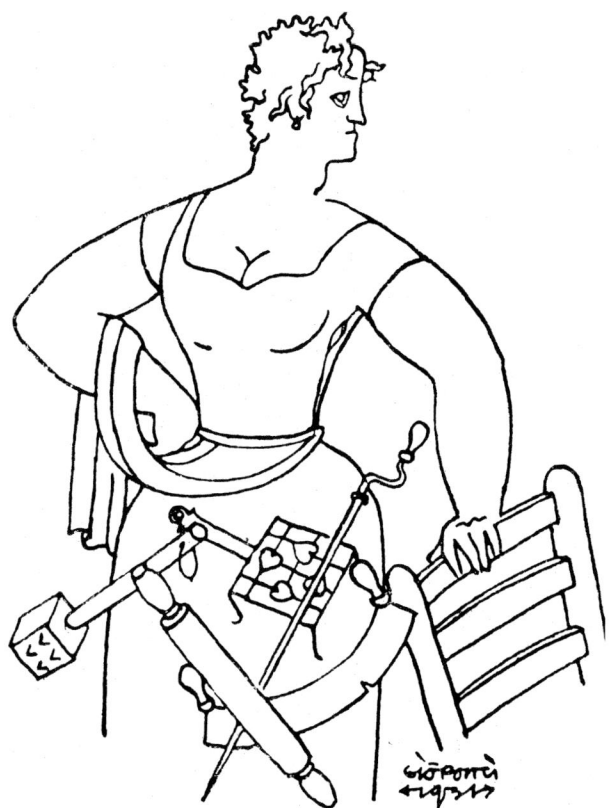

Leonarda o la cuoca collerica

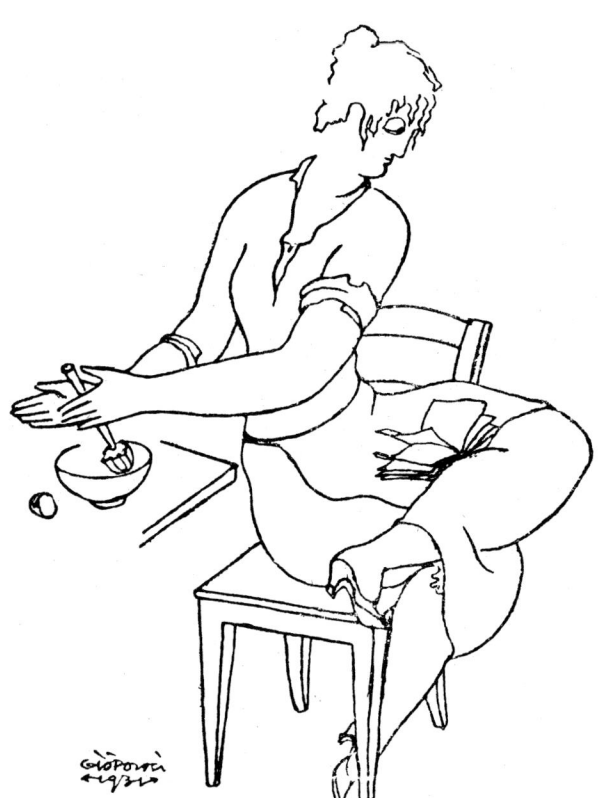

Remigia o la cuoca letterata

PORTRAITS

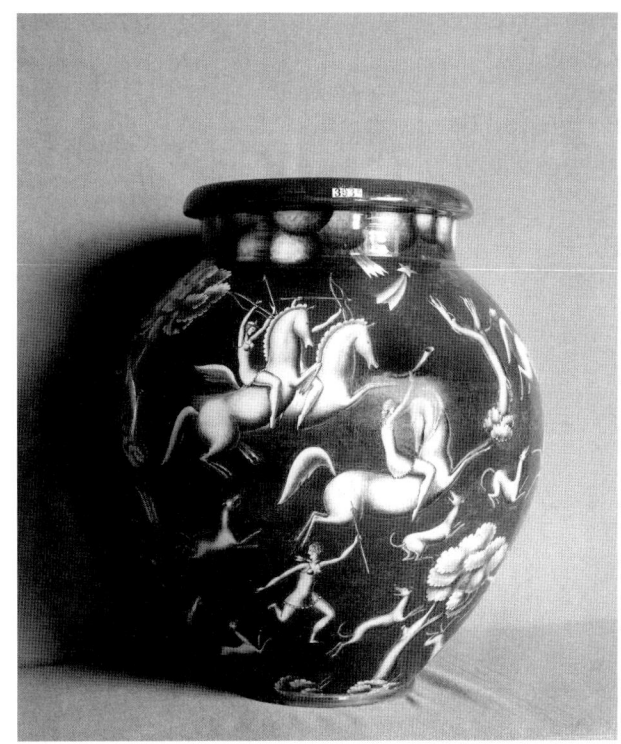

"The Chase," a large vase in majolica depicting in a modern manner the classic hunting scene, all lively and colorful.

est café. Even these activities were not enough for him, and he became an editor and publisher. *Domus,* his first magazine, was devoted to the arts and crafts that have a place in the home. Material from the world over was collected, making it a valuable periodical for reference. This was followed by a second publication, *Casabella,* a more purely architectural magazine, in many ways the most interesting in Italy. He also published books of the most diverse sorts, from technical publications to the famous cookbook, and many of them are notable for the freshness of their design. He wrote articles for the *Corriere della Sera,* a widely read Milanese newspaper, and he wrote a book, *Case all'Italiana,* houses in the Italian manner. Recognition of this extraordinarily varied and successful activity came this year from the Royal Academy. He was awarded the Premio Mussolini, a prize of 50,000 lire, given to the man who had done the most for the advancement of art in Italy. There was no discussion about the selection of Ponti as the winner.

There is no longer any doubt as to his main interest: painting has definitely taken second place. The problem is to know what he is going to do next. His work as an architect has shown really remarkable progress, and the same qualities which made his ceramics outstanding are now coming out in his buildings. Perhaps the most interesting from the point of view of "parti" is his School of Mathematics, which will form part of the new University City in Rome. It is fairly involved in plan, something the Italians seem to have difficulty in escaping, but his solution of the problem of arranging

Milan's version of the Eiffel Tower. Ponti points with pride to its construction of tubular steel, its twelve-table restaurant at the top, and to its elevator, the fastest in Europe.

opposite:
Ponti's winning design for the School of Mathematics in Rome. The design shows varied influences, but the effect of the whole is definitely Italian.

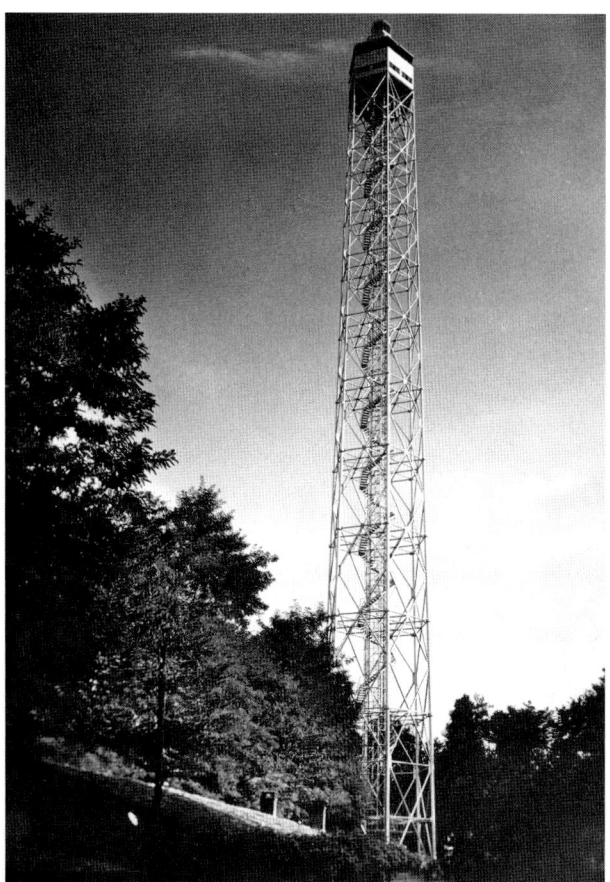

a number of large lecture rooms is most ingenious. He arranged them vertically rather than horizontally, the sloping floor of one hall becoming the sloping ceiling of the one below, and so on. The group functions as a unit, has separate entrances and circulation. In the rest of the semicircle he has placed the large drafting rooms, and in the main portions with the main entrance are arranged the offices, professors' studies, conference rooms, and a library. One may take issue with the façades, perhaps, but it is a question whether they are any worse than what greets us on more than one American college campus, suggesting nothing so much as a cross between a setting for *Hamlet* and a country club for decayed or decadent millionaires. Ponti's design, whatever its defects, looks very much like what it is—a building to work in.

Ponti, certainly, has no doubts about the course he has chosen to follow. His ideas on architecture are definite and can be had for the asking. There is nothing extravagant about them. He is completely in favor of taking advantage of all technical means at his disposal, and of treating the resulting forms in a manner consistent with their construction and function. The use of "standards" to facilitate building and to reduce costs is to be encouraged. But there must never be a "standardized conception." Here is where the break with the German school comes. The "siedlung" idea is anathema. Series of standardized dwellings, whether in one-family houses or large buildings, may be only used when the life is similarly standardized: barracks, convents, prisons,

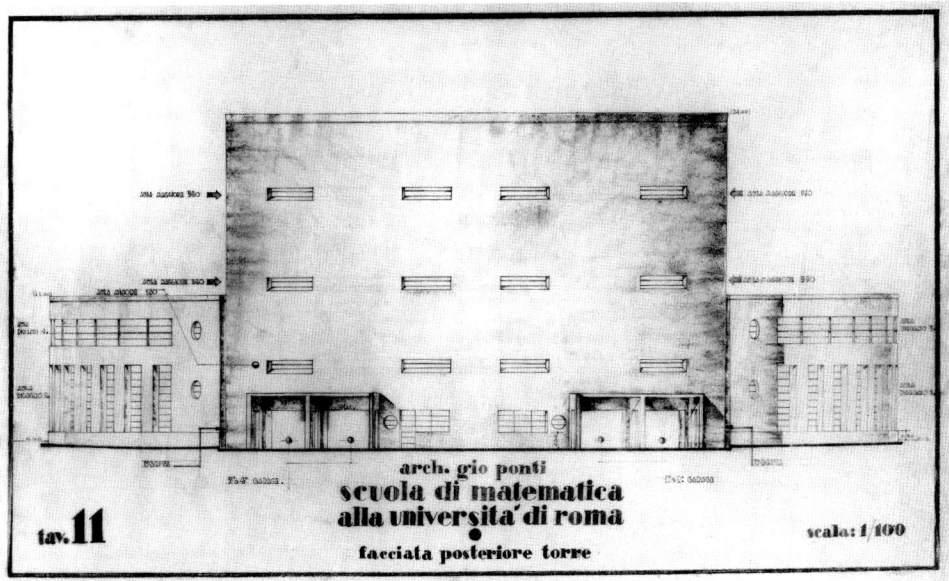

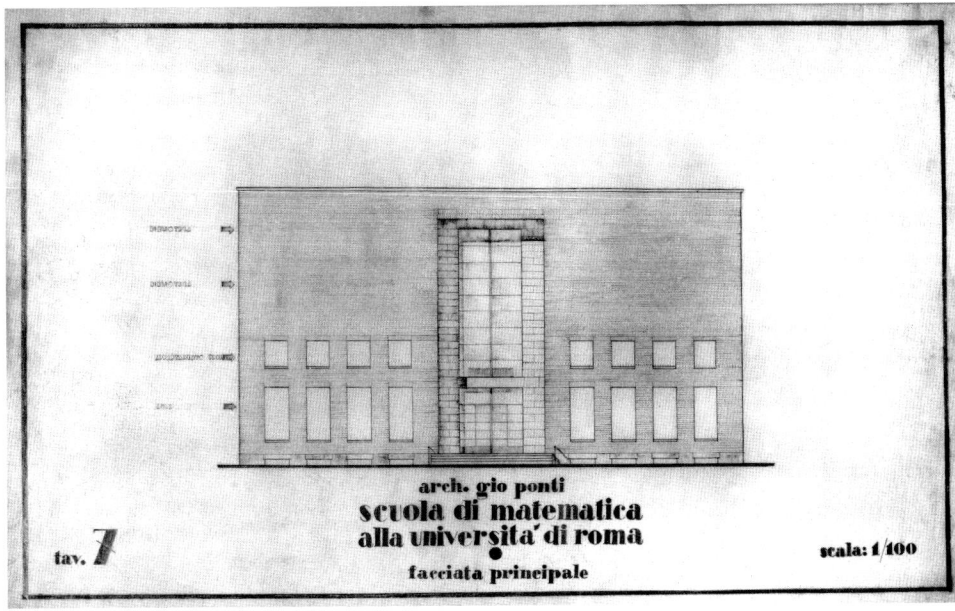

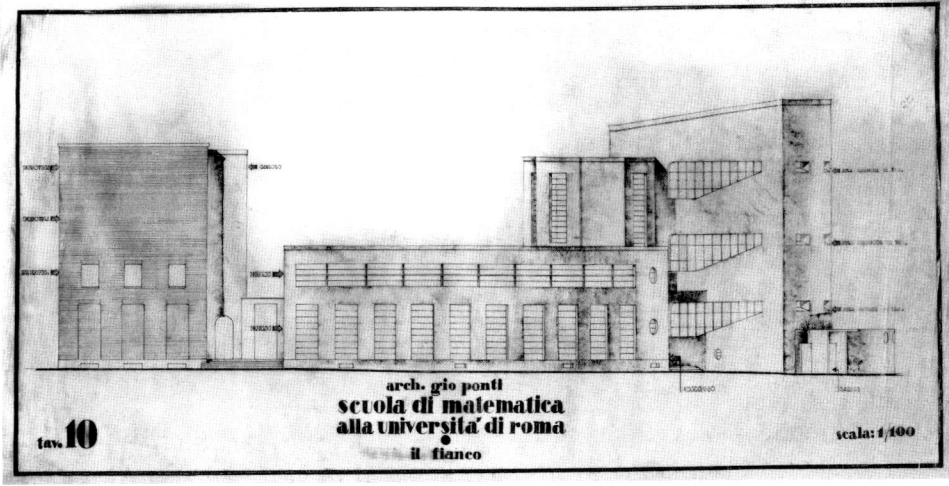

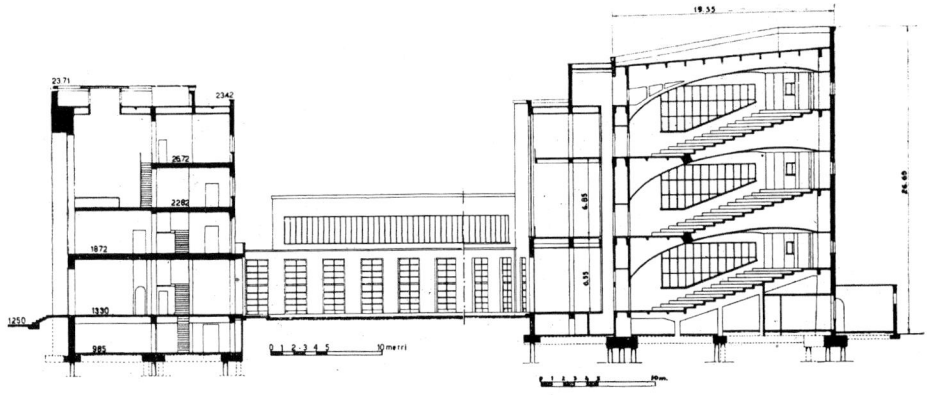

Section and plan drawings of the School of Mathematics, a part of the University of Rome. The section is most unusual.

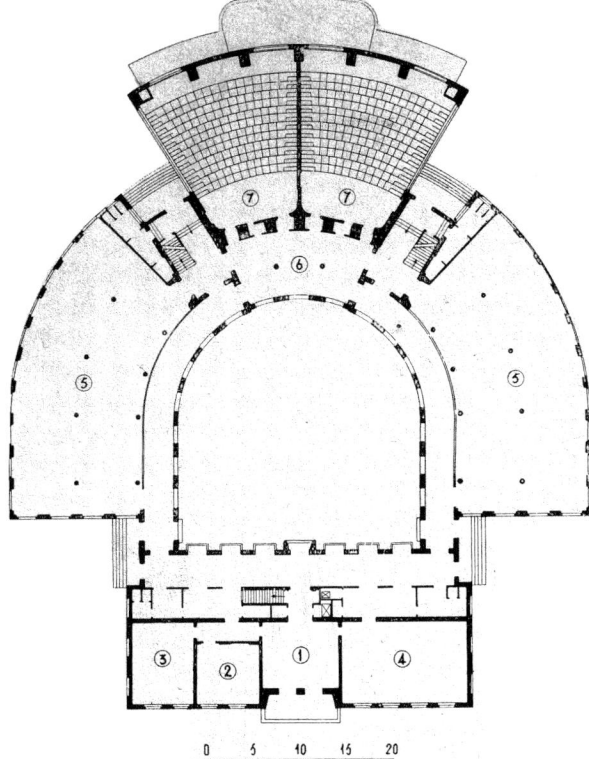

dormitories—but never for families. This idea is by no means exclusively Ponti's; it is only another expression of the intense individuality of the Italian, and he carries it out in his architecture.

A forecast of the future activities of such a person is a rather risky business at best. He is only forty-three, looks much younger, and is apparently thriving on the hectic existence he leads. He seems to think of himself as primarily an architect, for the time being, at any rate, and the commissions he has will keep him one for quite a while. There are indications of a growing restlessness, however. He talked a good bit about town planning with a look in his eye that might lead one to suspect that he was beginning to find designing buildings one at a time rather dull. Recently he has entered some of the larger competitions, and according to word I received as I left Milan, he had just won the competition for the new buildings in the University of Padua. Certainly, if his ambitions lie in this direction, he could not be more fortunately situated. Almost every town in his country has plans made or projected which involve clearing of slum areas, creation of suitable traffic arteries, and bringing up to their full effectiveness the monuments of the past. Two new cities have arisen in what used to be the Pontine Marshes, and there may be more. Ponti, with his rich and varied experience, his sure feeling for form and color, and, above all, his highly personal way of solving any given problem, should be able to make interesting and valuable contributions in a field richer in promise than good examples. Follow-

Apartment houses designed by Ponti are invariably rented before completion. The gaily colored façade of the buildings on the Via dei Togni is accompanied by a plan more modern than those to be found in Milanese apartment houses, but still far short of American ideals of arrangement.

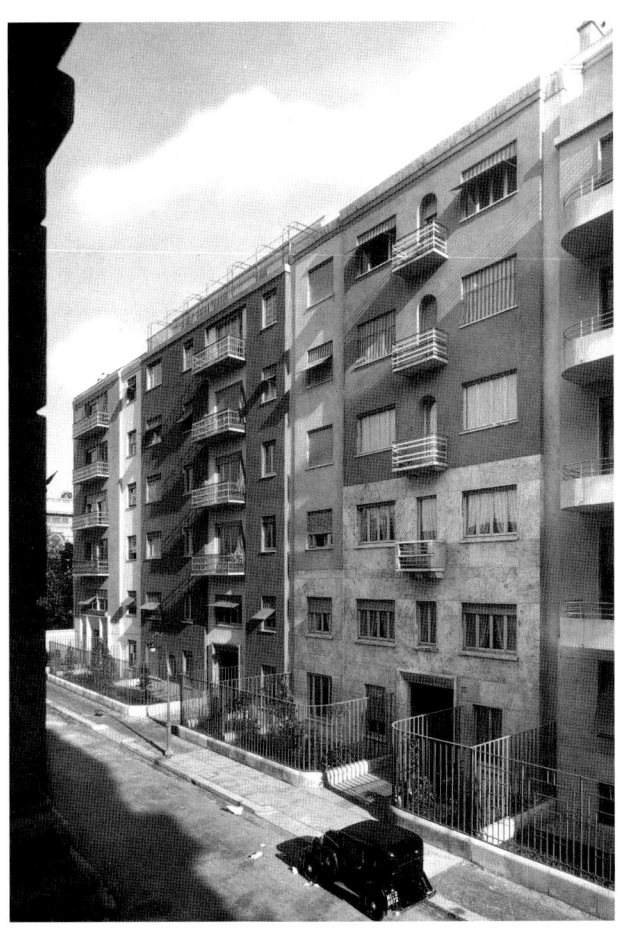

ing neither the rigidly formalized plan of an outmoded Beaux-Arts on the one hand, nor the restless horizontals and delicately balanced asymmetry of a Luckhardt or Mendelsohn on the other, there is little doubt that he would have something fresh to offer, vigorous in conception, typical and worthy of the magnificent spirit of his profession in contemporary Italy.

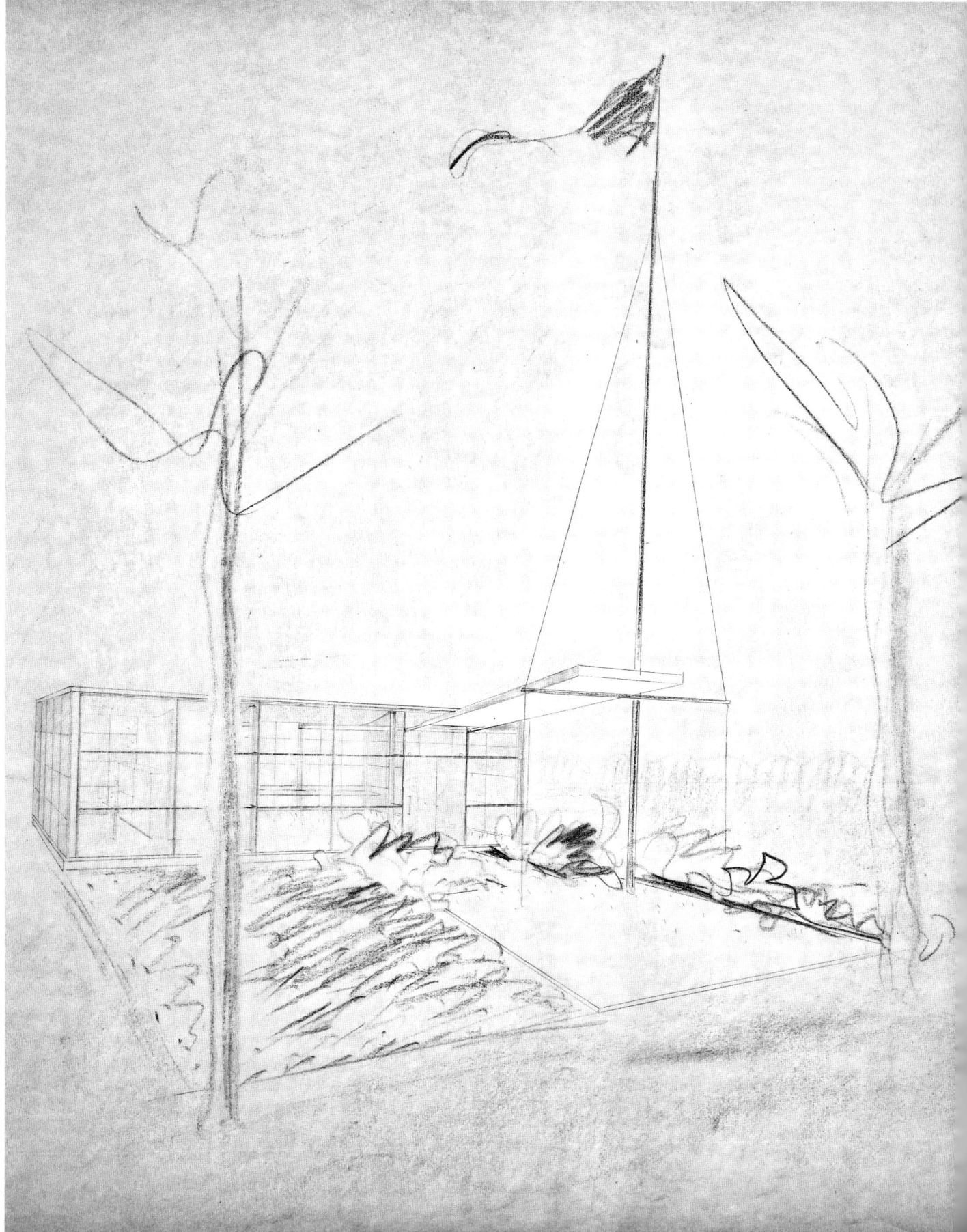

LE CORBUSIER
FRANCE

FROM
PENCIL POINTS
JULY 1935

Pavilion at the 1925 Paris Exposition.

To anyone who has followed the development of architecture in the past two decades the name is hardly unfamiliar. To the layman who has dabbled in such matters, he is the man who builds houses that look like packing boxes, who asserts that a man's house in not his castle–it is a "machine for living in." He has been more widely copied, more bitterly attacked, than any living member of his craft. At the Paris 1925 Exposition his pavilion was herded into a corner, hidden from view by a larger one. His designs for remodeling a section of the city were barred from the Salon d'Automne with the comment that they were an insult to the city. He has "poisoned the minds" of the youth of France (of Italy, too, adds an architect in Rome), and his very name is anathema to the Academicians. Today there is scarcely a country in the world that cannot point to at least one construction based on his work, and there recently appeared an article on architectural education whose sole comment on France was that the ateliers of the brothers Perret and of Le Corbusier were worth all the schools in the country put together. A slight difference of opinion here!

It was more to get some idea concerning the man himself, to see where he stood in this turmoil of conflicting opinion, than to broadcast to a waiting world his already well-advertised theories that I took advantage of his unexpected arrival in Rome to interview him. He commented, "Alors, vous faîtes ce sacré métier d'architecte?" It was hot, he added, did I not think beer was in order? We went around the corner and found some beer in a quiet café. The café itself is worthy of notice. Old, even for a city like Rome, it has had generation after generation of artists, poets, tourists, diplomats, all meeting for the once with a common aim. Byron had frequented the place, so had Keats and Shelley, probably. Now you can see the pensionaries of the various Academies, long-haired folk from the artist-infested Via Marguta nearby, elegant gentlemen with ladies who are possibly a shade too elegant, and on a good evening it has a vivacity which recalls Paris, but not for long. The weight of the centuries is too much. This day there was no one, and the rooms were dark and cool after the blazing sun and heat out of the doors. The contrast between this dank place and the theories of the man with me was striking, and I said as much. The best thing about Rome, he answered, was the sky. It was incredible. Rome was best in the early morning. It was impossible after that; the noise, the congestion–frightful. The climate was bad, it gave him a headache. The hotel rooms were ghastly; dark except where light shot through the windows as if out of the mouth of a cannon. How could one live in such conditions? No, Paris was no better.

He is a plain-looking man, this Le Corbusier. No striking irregularity of feature, nothing unduly prominent except possibly a high forehead. He wore large tortoiseshell glasses whose blank stare disguised any facial expression; one could see only an immobile face, tremendous areas of glass, and thin hair. That such ideas as the organization of traffic in Algiers on fast motor highways three hundred feet in the air, and the demolition of the center of Paris, could have originated behind this noncommittal façade seems a bit incredible until one hears him talk. Then anything is credible. He speaks invariably in a quiet, matter-of-fact way, whether talking to one person or addressing a hall, moving from conclusion to conclusion with a direct and relentless logic that nothing can budge. His more fantastic schemes are all traceable to this method, which, taken to its conclusion, often neglects the demands of existing conditions, becoming in consequence a kind of "reductio ad absurdum." But this is his method, and he stays with it. He is absolutely incapable of compromise solutions. He possesses a devastating sincerity so complete that to me it is a miracle that he has ever been able to get anything built. There is the example of his museum design. A Russian had been sent by his government to study all the museums of Europe; in time he got around to Le Corbusier, who is well known in Russia, and spoke with him about it. "But you are going at it all wrong," protested the architect with impatience. "You are studying what has been done, and what has been done is bad. These museums are expensive, they are tiring to go through, they are badly lighted and ventilated, they cannot be enlarged without the greatest difficulty, and often it is impossible. Look, I will design you a museum as it should be. It will start with a few rooms, perhaps, and as need arises it can be extended indefinitely. It will be cheap to build and cheap to run. It will always be well lighted, there will be no glare on the pictures, and day or night the light will come from the same source. It will have no façade." He sketched on a piece of paper as he talked.

"What would you do if someone came to you and said, 'We want to build a museum. It must be an ideally working mechanism in which to show our collections. But it must also be a beautiful monument which improves the appearance of our city.' What would you do then?" I asked.

"I would say, 'Monsieur, vous êtes un imbecile.'"

He spoke at some length about his work in Paris. There is a group associated by common interests: a sociologist, a heating and ventilating engineer, designers, and others. They work on problems which reach all through the social fabric; he expresses their findings in his architecture. "We are of necessity revolutionary," he explained. "Not that we have given ourselves any particular name, but to realize with any degree of completeness the implications of the modern social and technical structure means that one will inevitably fall into this category. People say to wait, that changes will come automatically, naturally. They are going at it backwards. A given situation must be studied, a program must be formulated, then we can go ahead." He was insistent on this point. His writings are full of it. We talked about Italian architecture for a while, but he would say little beyond remarking that the young group in Milan seemed to be on their way to something or other. He was a guest in their country, and besides knew that what he said would be held against him, so to speak. But on the subject of new towns built in what used to be the Pontine Marshes, now a great tract of planted fields, he waxed more eloquent. City planning is a topic very dear to him. "Look at this town plan," he said, pulling out his pencil again. "The young men who did it are sensitive artists. Here we find they have put their little poem of a town hall, here a bank, a church, a post office. Fine. And then see how they have scattered these little cottages all over the landscape. Why cottages? *The man who lives in a single house is a slave.* He has an infinity of little things to worry about that are a constant drain on his energies. Let these people be put in one great communal dwelling, perhaps two or three. Then these little things could be taken care of by people whose entire job it was. The inhabitants could enjoy advantages utterly unattainable under present conditions. Here is how I should do this town," and he drew his town center, then a large mass representing his apartment house, and that was all.

"These peasants wouldn't like it," I commented. "They don't give a damn about these comforts of yours. A house, once it is theirs, is something solid to own, to fall back on. See how they put their money into gold jewelry, pawn it when they have to, redeem it when they can. It is a different economy." He shrugged.

He will talk about air conditioning for hours. He and his group have studied it at length. The idea is at the base of his design. Air conditioning is not a gadget you buy and install, it is a method of reaching a new way of living, and has to be designed for. The first conclusion in designing for it is that windows must be hermetically sealed. He did an apartment house in Paris for sixteen families, designed for air conditioning, and considers it a substantial backing-up of his theories. He told several stories about it. Women, particularly, made a fuss about the sealed windows.

"Monsieur l'architecte, I will not live in such an apartment. I cannot open the windows!"

"Why, Madame, do you wish to open the windows?"

"To be able to breathe God's good fresh air, of course! Why else?"

"But this is not God's good fresh air, Madame, this is the air of Paris. It is filthy, full of coal, of bacteria, of poisonous fumes, of all manner of things that will do you harm. It is, in addition, either too warm or too cold, too dry or too humid. It is bad, this air of Paris. If you don't believe me, go for a walk on any warm day and look at your handkerchief when you return home."

It is a passion with him. One must get good air. He will, at the beginning of a lecture, illustrate a fundamental problem of city planning by drawing a pair of lungs, and the sun. Not light and air. Light and good air. Only a machine will provide it in the cities; it doesn't come in the windows. A machine will give the right proportion of moisture, the right temperature, absolute purity. Working conditions improved, living conditions improved, increased efficiency as a means of doing work more quickly so that there will be more time to enjoy life in his ideal cities. His sealed apartment house is full, he said, and the lives of the tenants have been

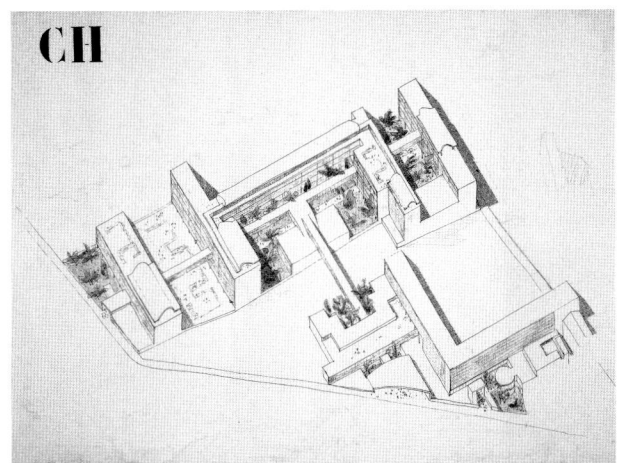

The Armée du Salut, one side of which is all glass.

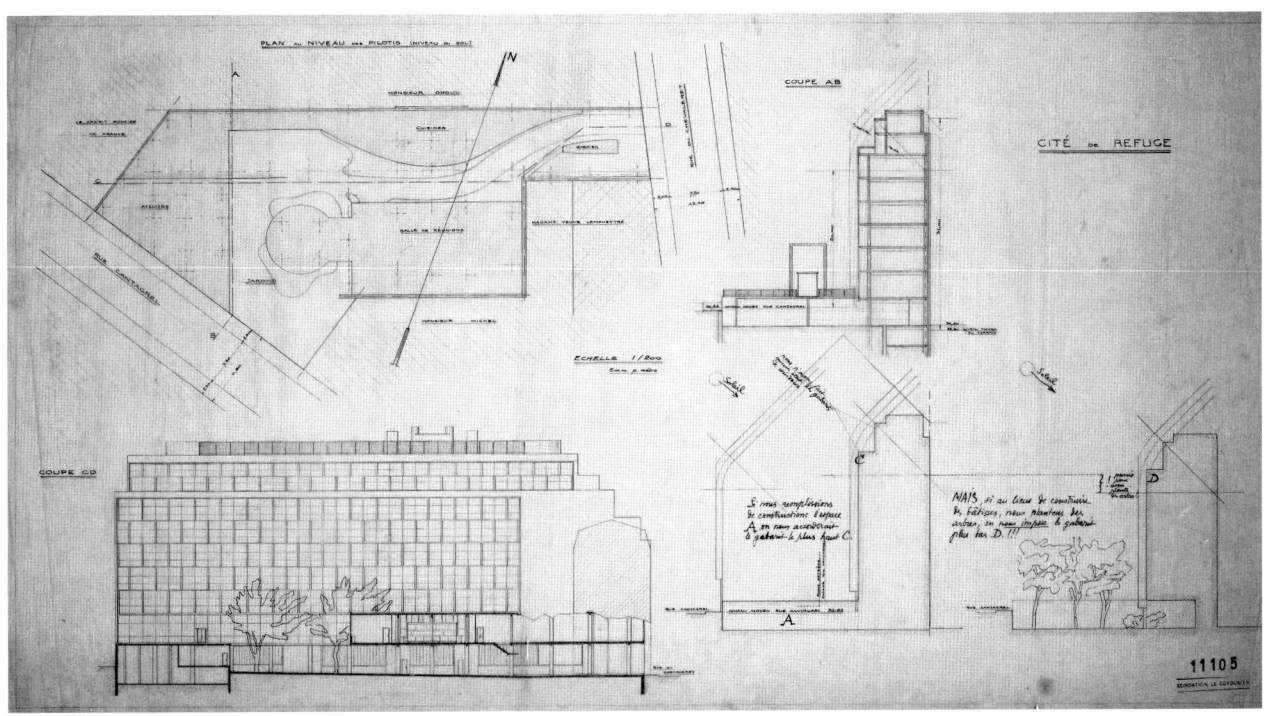

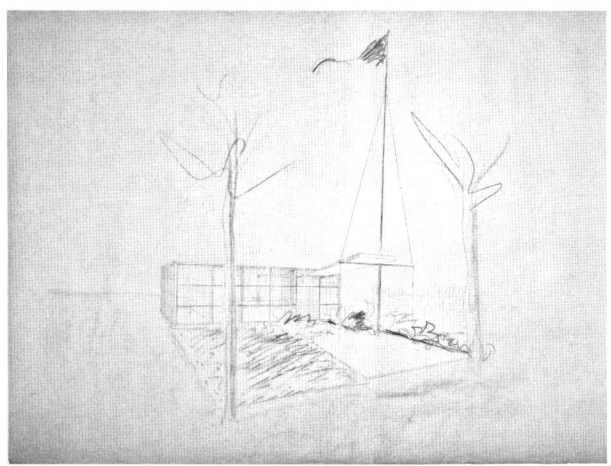

Flying Pavilion, constructed mostly of metal and glass.

transformed, literally transformed.... As he spoke his own face underwent a sort of transformation. Architecture, to this man, is not a series of monuments to the architect. It is a means of attaining a way of living.

I quoted what one of the biggest Italian architects had said to me about his great expanses of glass: "Impossible in a country where the sun is blinding for eight months of the year." He started impatiently. "I know them, these people! They say a thing cannot be done before they have tried, before they think. They are afraid. They think their positions are secure if only they can keep things from changing. In Russia I had a large building to do. I designed it with a glass façade, double walls of glass through which warm air circulated. The engineers said, 'Impossible! Here in Russia we have a cold which is indescribable. With this temperature on the outside and warm air on the inside the glass will crack.' 'The glass will not crack,' I replied. 'Very well,' they answered, 'suppose it will not crack. Look at this butcher's shop. Of what use is his plate glass window? It is covered with frost. Your great glass façade will be covered with frost. Also, to maintain a comfortable temperature inside will require an enormous quantity of your heated air moving at a tremendous velocity. The expense will be prohibitive.'

"I went back and made experiments. We built a double wall of glass to a room. Inside we ran through warm air. Outside we maintained a temperature well below freezing, and waited for the glass to crack. Nothing happened. We raised the temperature inside, lowered it outside, still nothing happened. To maintain a comfortable temperature within the room a small quantity of warm air moving slowly was all that was necessary. Frost? How could there be frost? The amount of moisture in the air can be controlled, and if there is no moisture, there is no frost."

The conversation veered back to Paris. "When we had the inauguration of the Armée du Salut, people came and looked at the building. One side, you know, is all glass. 'Poor devils,' they said, 'how will they stand the cold in this place?' The poor devils stood it very well indeed, and people then said, 'Wait until summer. They will roast behind that show window.' Summer came and went, and still the poor devils did very well. One must not speak without thinking, without finding things out. People are very stupid, particularly the ones who should know better. Academicians, of course, one expects . . . but aviators! I did a pavilion on a flying field. It was a simple little thing, made of metal and glass, mostly. Do you know, it caused a furor. Where were the walls, the windows? The directors were incensed, insisted it would have to be done over. There was a prospect of annoyance, but the papers got hold of the story, ridiculed the objectors, and fearful of undesirable publicity they stopped their action. Think of it, aviators! They daily trust their lives to beautifully designed creations of metals and fabrics, they work in lovely concrete or metal hangars. And they want a pavilion with Renaissance windows!"

He talked about Algiers. A coal merchant had come to

Design for open terraces and sun protection in a project to house two thousand families in Algiers.

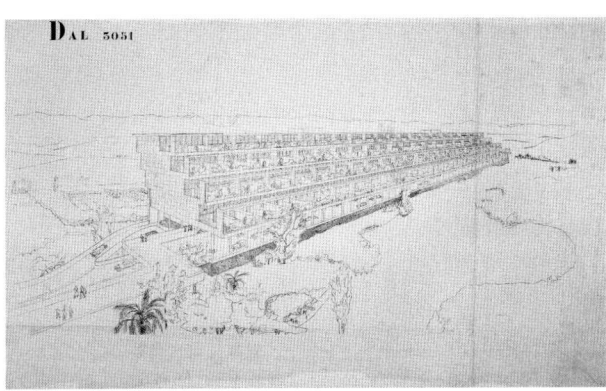

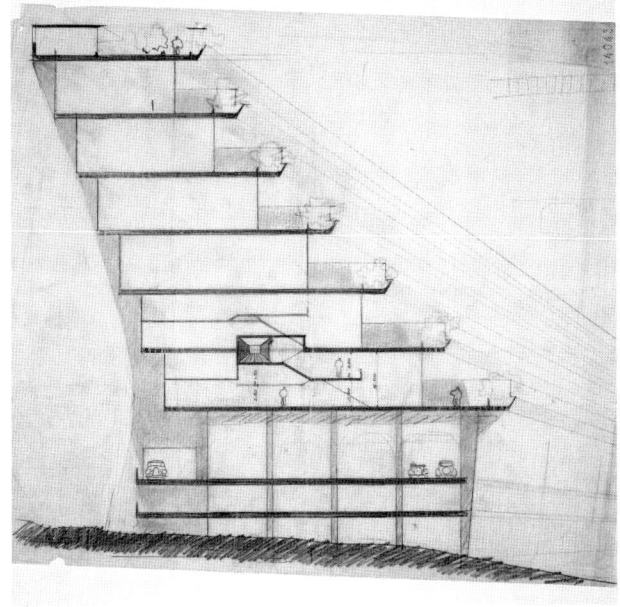

him one day with a map of some property he had, and a project to cover this land with low-cost housing for two thousand families. He had a sketch showing the houses laid out in rows. "This is how we will do it," he said.

"No. This is not how we will do it," replied the architect. "You are covering a fine piece of land with many miserable dwellings. Look about you. On one side you have a magnificent view of the mountains, on the other, the wide expanse of the Mediterranean. You cannot put them in rabbit hutches. You must put them in great buildings from which they can enjoy the view. If you group them together the buildings will cover but a small percentage of the ground area; the rest will be available for gardens, for recreation. But down in Algiers there is a sun which is terrific, so, on the south side of each building we will have glass, for the view, but each floor will project out above the one below and form a screen from the sun during the hottest hours. The other side will be a series of open terraces." The coal merchant looked at the sketches, listened, was convinced.

Indubitably these constructions have a strange appearance. To the unaccustomed eye they are absolutely incomprehensible. For one taught, as most of us have been, that any example of architecture consists of a base, shaft, and crowning motive, these huge boxes perched precariously on concrete pillars are foolhardy efforts made in defiance of the law of gravity. To him, however, they evidently have no such odd appearance. It is not that he sees in them a kind of abstract charm, much as a mathematician may be said to find a sort of

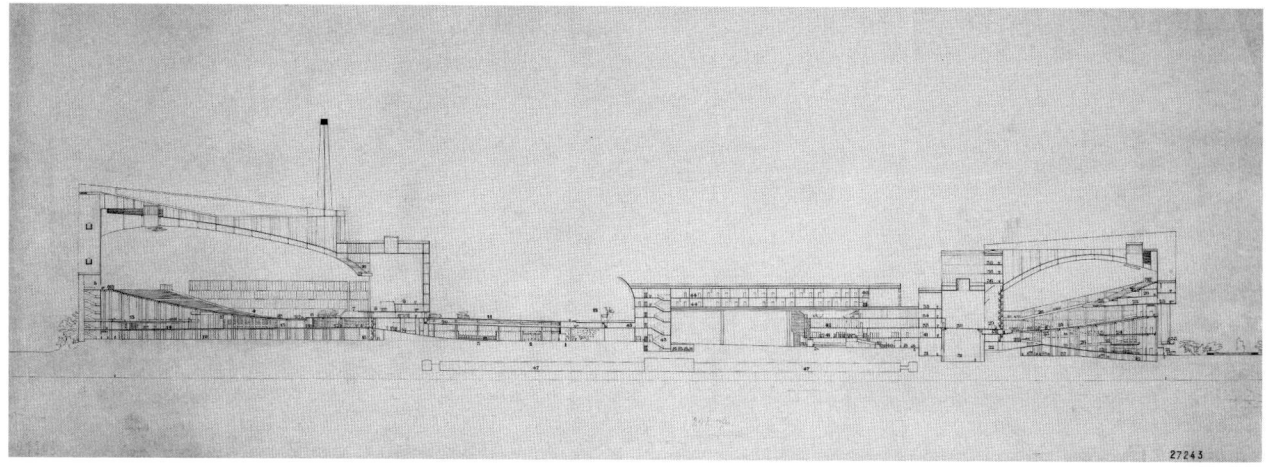

austere beauty in his graphs and equations. He sees no difference between these airy three-dimensional projections of his thoughts and the great monuments of antiquity, as far as essentials of composition are concerned. This is no guess of mine, put down here as a feeble attempt to justify anything he may have done. He told me so, in as many words.

We were looking at a perspective of his design for the Palace of the Soviets in Moscow. He pulled out a notebook from his pocket, turned to two sketches in it. One was of the drawing at which we were looking; the other was a rapid sketch of the group of the Baptistery and Cathedral at Pisa, apparently made from a train window. "Look at these two compositions," he said. "Each has a consistent design, a repetition of certain elements at a certain scale. Each has a unity of color, of material, of texture. One has studied volumes, consistency of surface treatment, and of structure, quite as much as the other. There is no difference."

"You are called by some a cold logician," I said, "either incapable of producing effects which appeal to the emotions, or uninterested in them. Why, then, did you curve the façade of the Maison Suisse?"

"It is very simple," was the calm rejoinder. "The plot had an odd form which demanded some such solution. The entrance had to be where it is. Walls met at an oblique angle, and blending them into one curve simplified the form and improved the appearance. It is very interesting," he added suddenly, "to notice how the slight curve in the wall gives a suggestion of tremendous extent to a small building; it seems to pick up by its concave surface the whole surrounding landscape, and so to establish a relationship that carries its effect far beyond the actual bounds of the structure itself."

Of interest to those who consider him responsible for most of the inanities of the so-called "international style" are his comments on cities. "The problems of architecture are international. They are fundamental in that they relate to man and his needs, and today the mechanics of solving these needs are pretty much the same everywhere. Style? Style comes of itself. You can't prevent a city from assuming a characteristic physiognomy, and consequently it is useless to worry about finding one for it. This physiognomy is influenced by topography, climate, and a multitude of other conditions, but these too are fundamental, *not* national." A case in point is a design for some houses in Algiers. Once again the blinding sun was the problem. He solved it by putting a *"brise-soleil"* in front of the building. It is a device which "breaks" the rays of the sun, a kind of grid which looks like the top of a General Electric refrigerator rolled out flat. The result looks anything but "international." "We got it from a trick the natives use," he explained.

To those who try to pin the man down to one category, he is impossibly exasperating. Tags don't cling to him. He has been identified with a certain type of house, with all-glass façades, with a doctrine of hopeless uniformity, with a dogma that everything, no matter what, must be built at a minimum cost, and

Section and elevation of the Palace of the Soviets in Moscow.

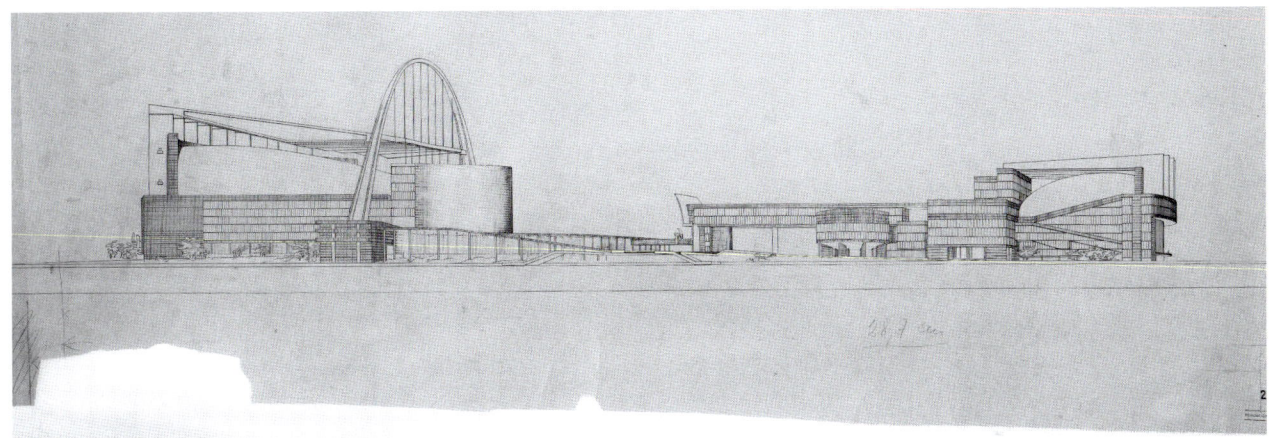

*Interior perspective view
of the Palace of the Soviets.*

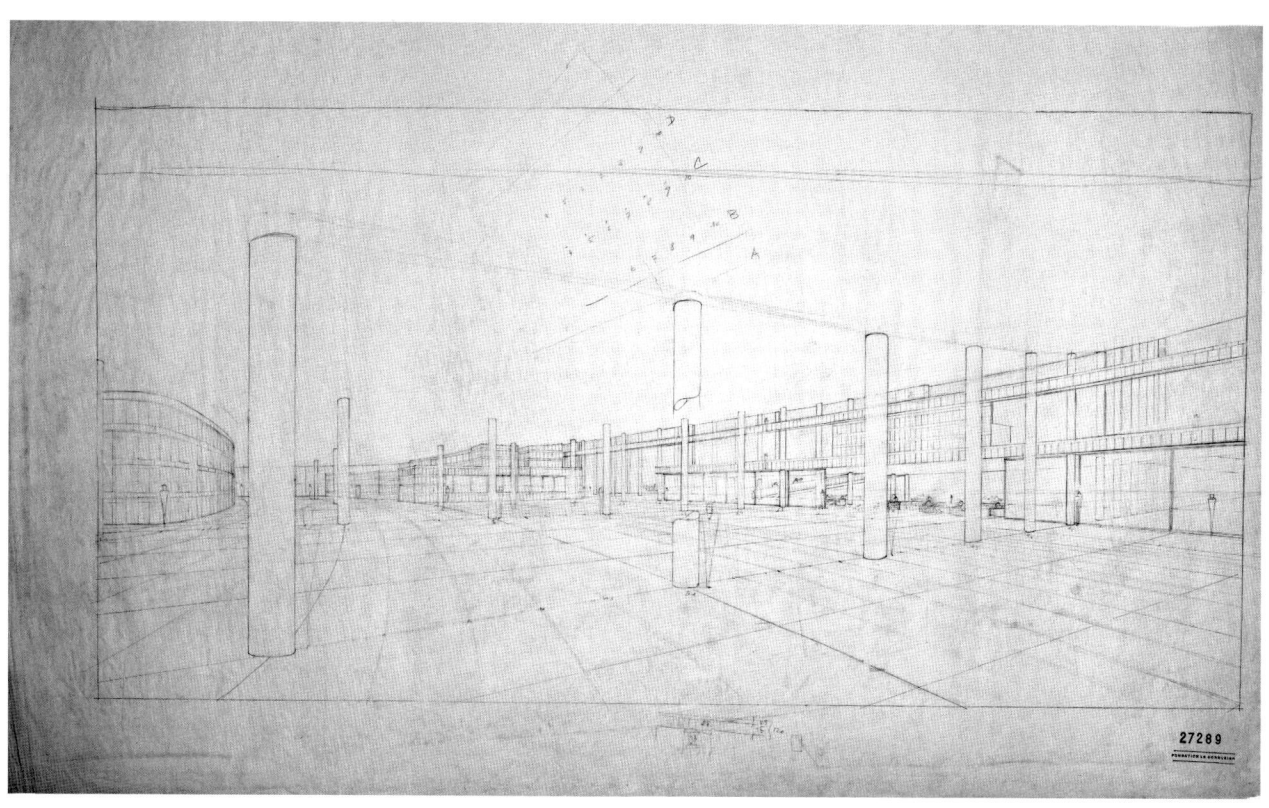

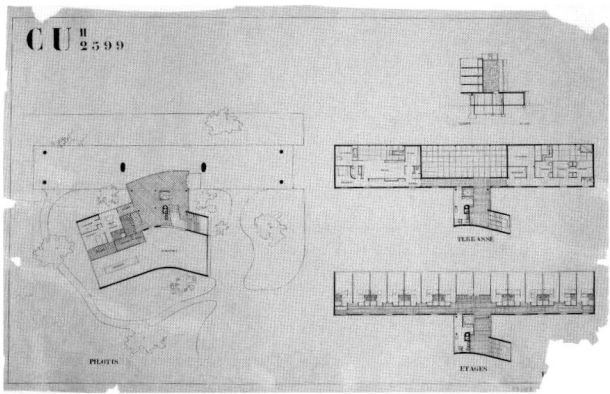

The curved façade of Maison Suisse.

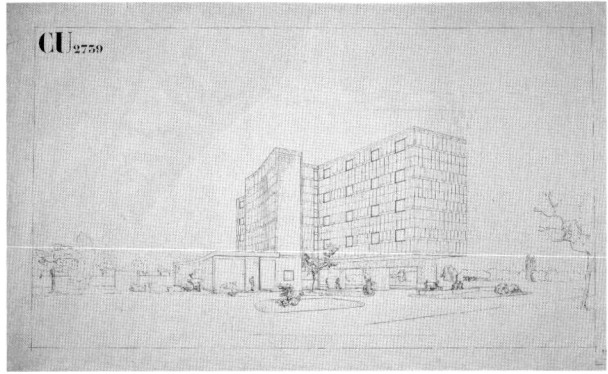

consequently employ only the cheapest of materials. To all these attempts at classification he remains apparently indifferent. It is the problem, the solution, that interests him. To reach his end he will go to work–in this there can be no compromise. I once mentioned the word "façade" in connection with something he said. It set him off. "Architecture is not a collection of fragments, of façades, of interiors. It is an organism." An organism–it is the key to his whole work. His buildings, good or bad, are inevitable results of his whole attitude towards life. They are more than dreams with him–they are his very life. They are the crystallization of an ideal, an ideal of living under conditions which will permit the liberation of a people from drudgery which is as useless as it is degrading.

His last remark was characteristic. As we left the café and wandered out into the hot street, a group of young priests passed. He gazed after them in silence for a while, then said, "There are too many *curés* here. Their black costumes are depressing." There was nothing to indicate that he was even conscious of the fact that they represented the faith of the Eternal City. Their clothes were dark, gloomy. He has no use for darkness or depressing colors. It was his eternal cry: "Light, more light."

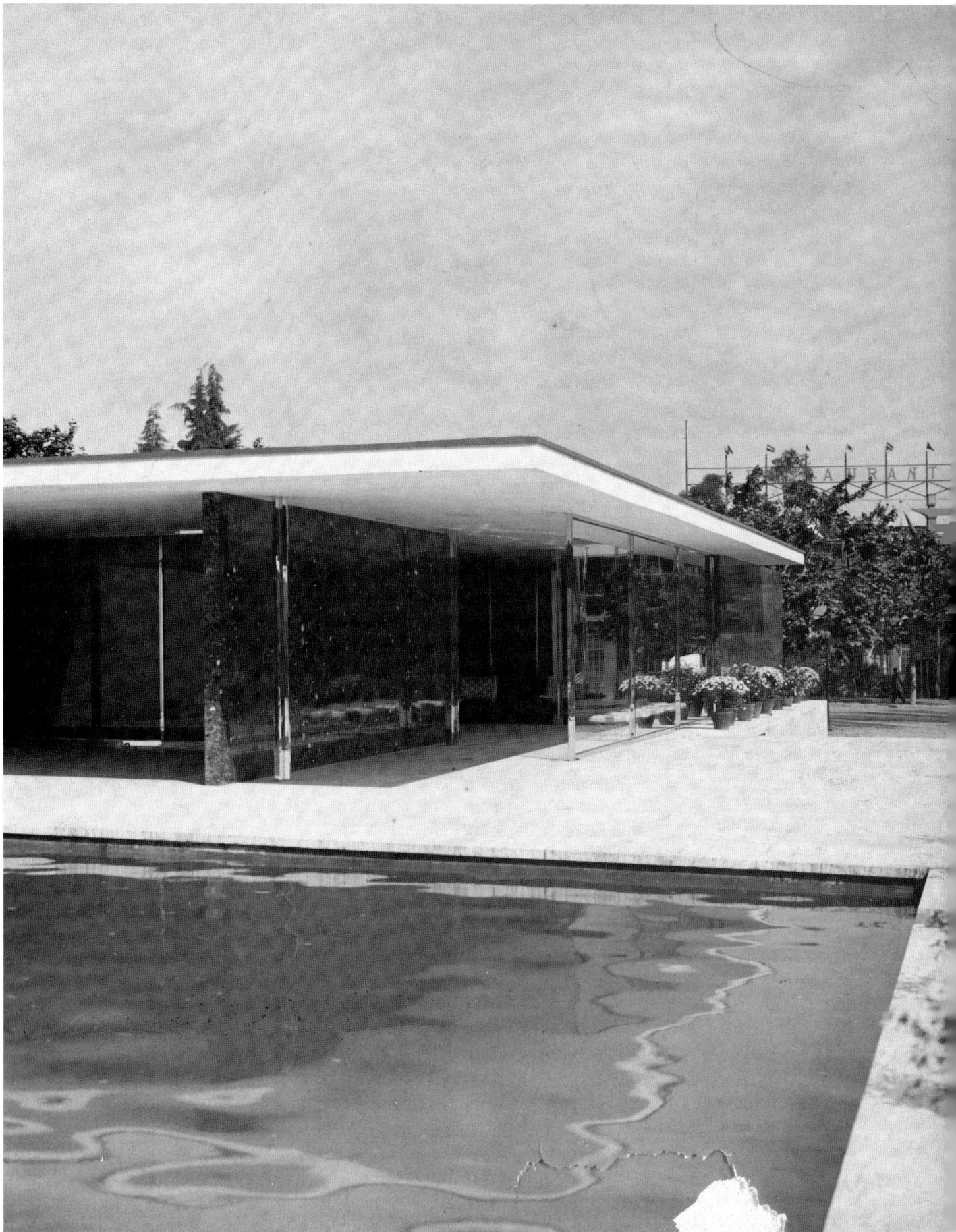

MIES VAN DER ROHE
GERMANY

FROM
PENCIL POINTS
SEPTEMBER 1935

On the top floor of a rather dowdy old house in Berlin there lives a man who, in spite of having built little, spoken less, and written not at all, has somehow come to be considered one of the greatest architects of his time. Such is the power of personality and an idea.

Up to ten years ago he had built virtually nothing of his own, and it was only in certain groups in Germany that his influence was making itself felt. Today he occupies a position which is unique–even in Germany–and he is almost as well known as the more widely publicized Le Corbusier. In spite of his unwillingness to dramatize himself, Mies is no dreamy recluse to whose garret door the world has beaten a path: the luxuriously simple apartment in Berlin is in no sense a garret, and for this ample, well-fed German the meagre life holds no attractions. He likes his food and knows his wines, and with a sufficient quantity of both inside of him he can become a charming and mellow conversationalist.

It has been my purpose in this series to show the work of some of Europe's outstanding architects, not as the automatic results of those vast and vague influences known as "economic pressure" and "social trends," important as these are, but rather as the creations of definite and mature personalities expressing themselves according to the possibilities of their time. And if this is borne in mind it will be seen that Mies' work, culminating in the Tugendhat House, which in one stroke crystallized the ideas and aims of designers the world over, could never have been conceived, let alone built, had this man been a dour dyspeptic for example, or anything, in short, but what he was.

Of all the possible architects Mies was the hardest to interview. He was polite but very frankly bored by the prospect of talking with a stranger, and he did nothing whatever to help out when his interviewer became enmeshed in the abominable intricacies of German grammatical construction. Catch questions, which had set off Le Corbusier on interminable orations, Mies disposed of with an indifferent phrase. When I mentioned the attacks on Le Corbusier for his frequently excessive use of glass he brushed the matter aside with the comment, "The glass façade is not modern architecture." He had known the fiery Swiss in Peter Behrens' office, but it is not likely that they had much to say to each other. A certain intelligent skepticism and breadth of view are characteristic of Mies, and it is very probable that Le Corbusier's tendency to carry theory to extravagant limits might well leave him cold. On the subject of Frank Lloyd Wright he was more willing to talk and, like most of Wright's European admirers, found it hard to understand why he had had so little influence is his own country. Wright, said Mies, was the greatest artist in setting buildings in a given landscape who had ever lived. So much for the prophet without honor in his own land! As the conversation progressed to matters of mutual interest, Mies gradually unbent and we both had a much better time. I left enormously impressed by the keenness and extraordinary personal force of the man.

Mies van der Rohe was born in Aachen, in 1886. His father, a stone mason, had hopes that the boy would

Glass skyscraper designed by Mies but never built.

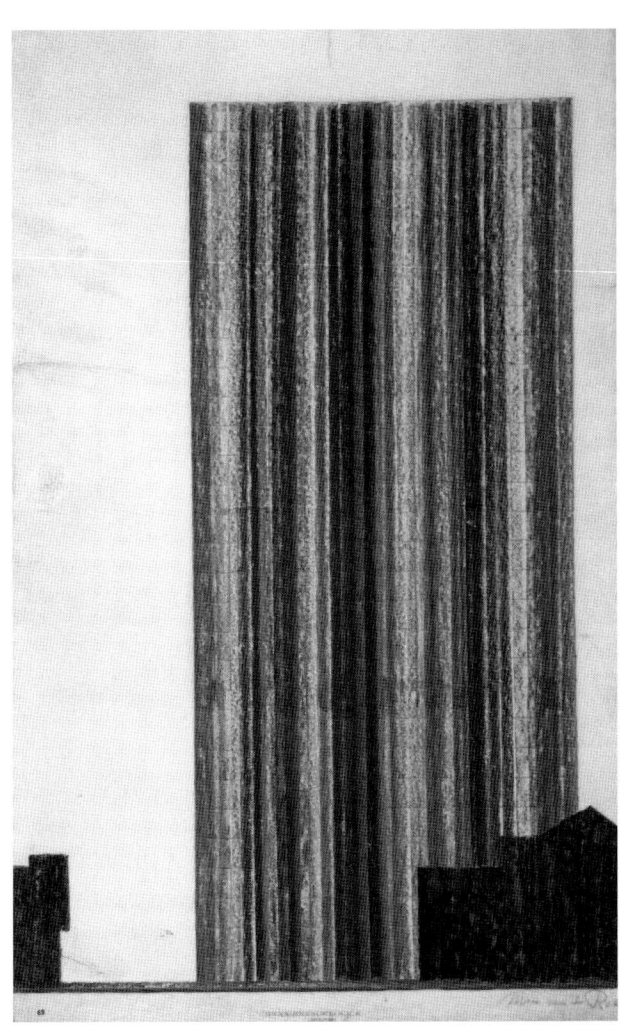

continue in the business, but there was a certain quality in his son that he mistook for stupidity. He apprenticed him to an architect, thinking that in this way he might acquire a certain amount of business acumen—curious idea! A story which Mies himself tells of this time indicates with what unconscious accuracy his father had selected his profession for him. It happened that during the preparation of an important drawing of an elaborate ceiling in the Renaissance manner the head designer fell ill, and there was nobody in the office who could be trusted to finish it. Precisely like the child wonders who appear in the stories of the Italian Renaissance, Mies stayed late one night and finished the drawing. There was a furor, of course, and when it was discovered who had done it Mies was promoted from broom to drafting board. Shortly after this rise in life he went to Berlin, worked with Bruno Paul for a time as a furniture designer, and then went into the office of Peter Behrens. Behrens was the greatest single influence in modern German architecture, and in his effect on his assistants he was very like the late Bertram Goodhue. Here Mies finished his architectural education and was entrusted with work of importance. After about three years of this, however, the association came to a sudden and violent end. Behrens entered a competition, and Mies, of course, worked on it. Apparently unsatisfied with Behrens' solution he did one of his own outside the office, winning first prize with it. The scene which followed, as Behrens swore with mighty Teutonic oaths that Mies had copied his scheme, may well be imagined.

Another unbuilt glass skyscraper designed by Mies.

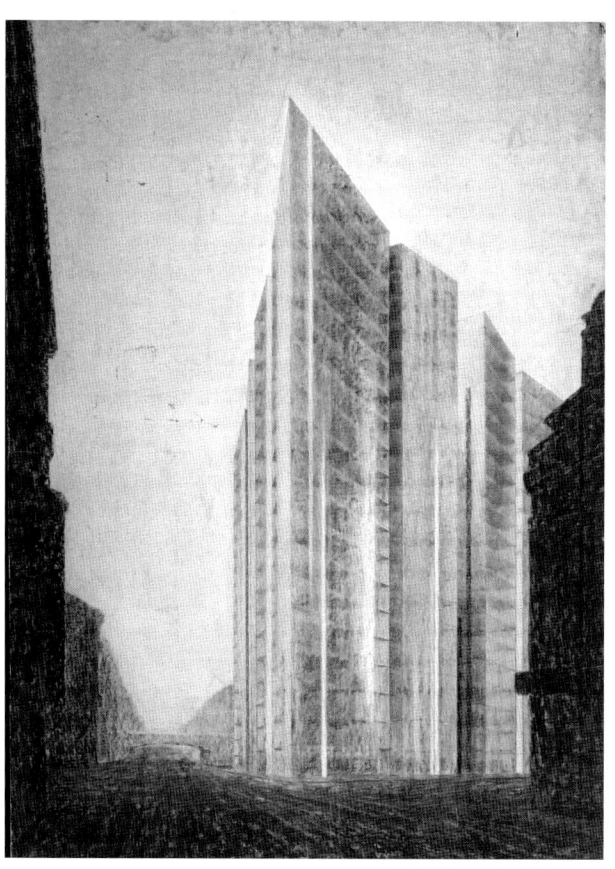

Mies, no weakling himself, did a bit of bellowing on his own, but finally wearying of the argument, announced that he was resigning and going to Switzerland to ski. The resignation was quite unnecessary, but ski he did, for five months. When he returned he opened up an office of his own. Behrens never forgave him.

It was not until several years after the war that he was heard from. In 1921 and the years immediately following he published a brilliant series of studies: the Glass Skyscraper, which proved nothing; a cantilevered office building consisting of alternate horizontal bands of window and spandrel, a scheme used by Mendelsohn with great effect on Columbus Haus in Berlin; and several country house projects. None of these, it will be noted, were ever built; but they were published far and wide, and by means of the printing press Mies entered upon the road to fame.

It was in 1928, however, that he showed, in a fashion that left no room for doubt, that he was no "paper architect." In this year a young lady came into his office, said she was getting married and going to Czechoslovakia to live, and that as a wedding present her family wanted to build her a house. The reason she came to Mies was that someone in her family had a house that Mies had built, and she wanted one exactly like it. The house she referred to was an innocuous Empire villa—Mies' first commission—of which he was bitterly ashamed. To be asked to repeat this house was something of a blow, but swallowing the words which sprang to his lips Mies said he would be enchanted to serve her. Two years later

A design for a cantilevered office building with alternating horizontal bands of window and spandrel.

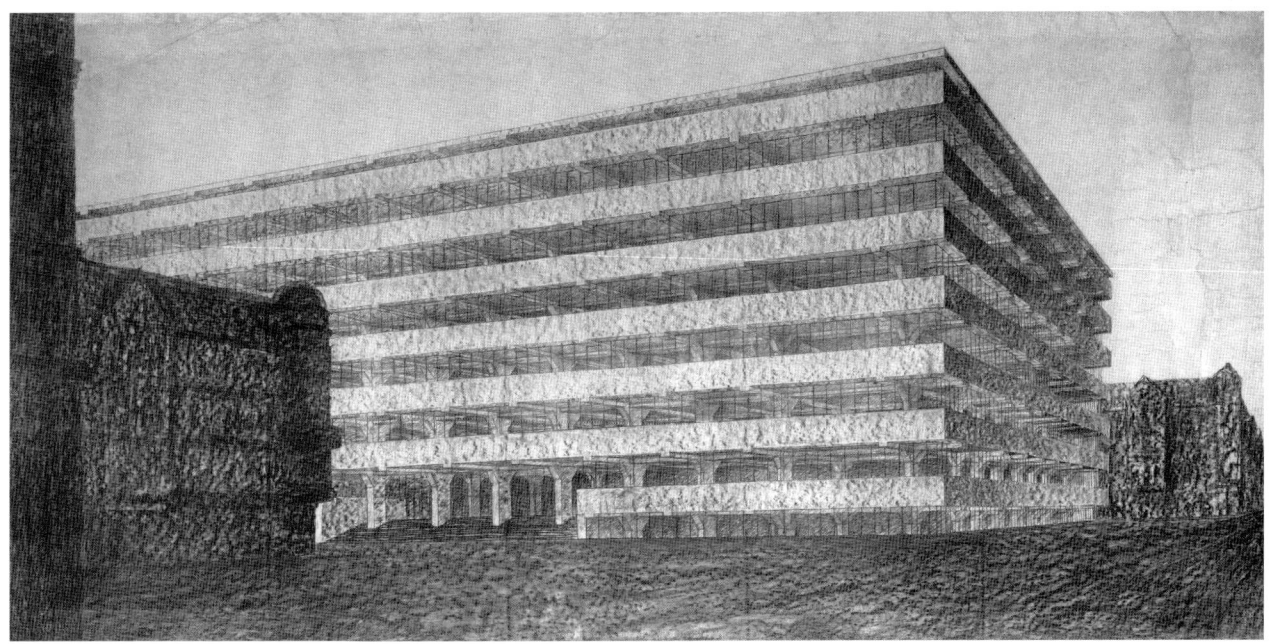

MIES VAN DER ROHE

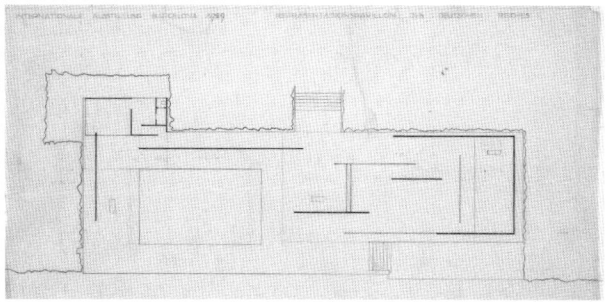
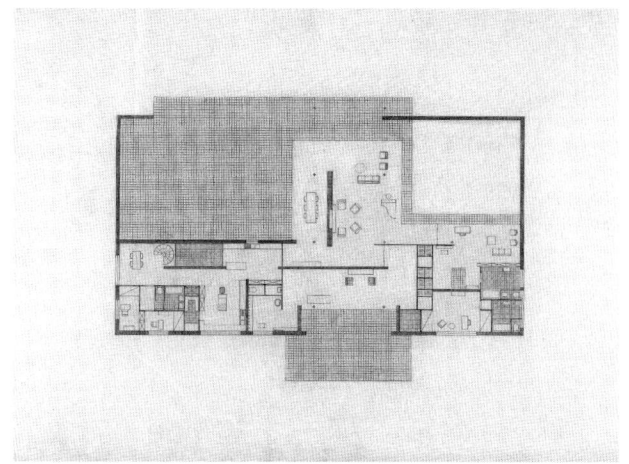

the young lady and her husband moved into their new home—the Tugendhat House.

The Tugendhat House is Mies' masterpiece, justly world famous, perhaps the finest modern house that has been built. But it could hardly be considered even remotely like the Empire villa his client thought she was going to get. What marvelous powers of persuasion the man must have used, what telling arguments he employed can only be guessed at; it was in any case a magnificent piece of salesmanship. The clients, incidentally, were delighted with the house, and they have shown it with pride to the throngs of visitors who have come to see it. In this connection, the remark of one of his associates is interesting: "All his clients are still his friends." What higher praise could there ever be anywhere for an architect?

The Tugendhat House is too well known to justify any extended discussion of it here. Its chief interest to us is to note how closely it reflects the personality and idiosyncrasies of the architect. Mies' fondness for space, for simplicity, for rich materials all find expression here. In the glass-enclosed downstairs portion space literally flows, interrupted by an occasional partition, but [is] never enclosed. The dining room is not a room at all in the conventional sense, but a portion of the living space; the same is true of the so-called living room. The feeling of movement that this type of arrangement gives, and its ample vistas, are enormously stimulating. Mies hates and despises cheap materials, but for once he indulged his tastes. An onyx wall, selected after months of searching for the right material, the curved macassar wall, the hundred feet of plate-glass window and silk curtains to cover them—all these were things he really enjoyed working with. Into his search for the onyx he put a fantastic amount of time and money, demonstrating once again how well founded were his father's fears—but in the end he got his wall, which was all that interested him. Today, when he makes an occasional visit to Brno, he settles his bulk into one of the comfortable metal chairs, looks at his creation with content and says, "Now there is a *wall!*"

Mies designed the first metal chairs in Germany. Others were working on them, and that he did any at all was accidental. He designed a silk exhibition room in Berlin with Lilly Reich, his collaborator on most interiors, and when the room was finished he suddenly remembered that there no chairs. Unwilling to put common chairs in this rich setting, Mies went back to the office and in one evening designed the chair that has since been copied all over the world. Four days later, when the exhibition opened, the chairs were there. They were a great success, and a manufacturer made arrangements with Mies to produce them. He made a slight variation in them, however, and Mies in a rage canceled the contract and bought up all the chairs that had been made. Anything that went out under his name, he stormed, had to be perfect.

If Mies has built few things, he has by no means been inactive. He was one of the founders of the Deutsche Werkbund, that powerful combination of designers

opposite from far left and below:
Plans for the German Pavilion, Hubbe House Project, and Tugendhat House. These plans clearly illustrate Mies' strongly personal conception of a building. Walls are isolated planes which divide but do not enclose spaces. The same relation between inside and outside exists as between the interiors themselves—there is rarely a definite break separating house and garden. The façade in its usual sense does not exist.

below right:
The Tugendhat House represents Mies' closest approach to the conventional modern façade. A hundred feet of plate glass windows on the ground floor can be lowered by electric motors into the walls, opening the entire house in good weather and making the living spaces practically one with the out-of-doors.

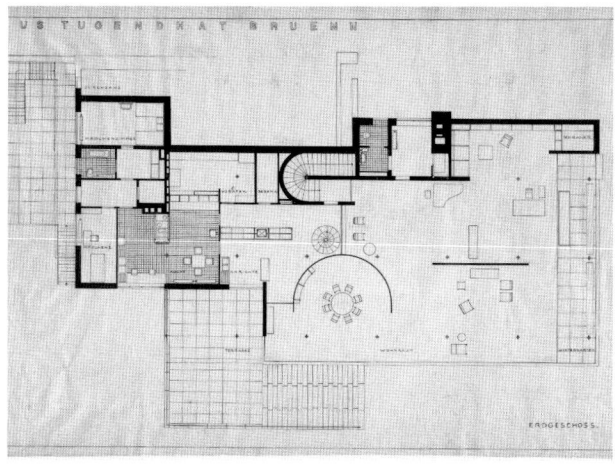

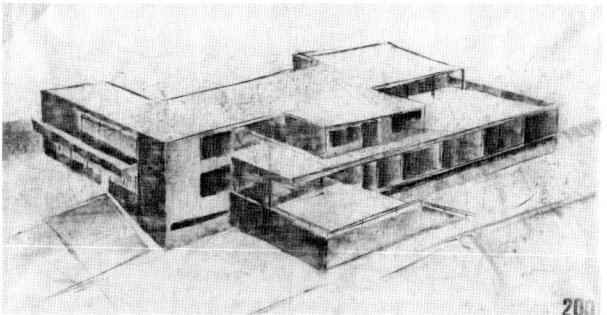

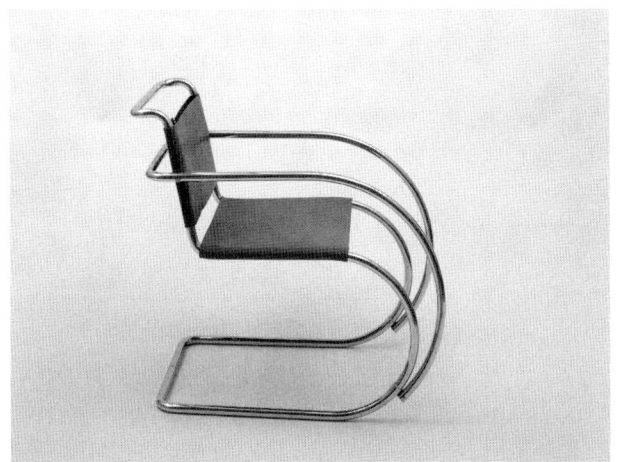 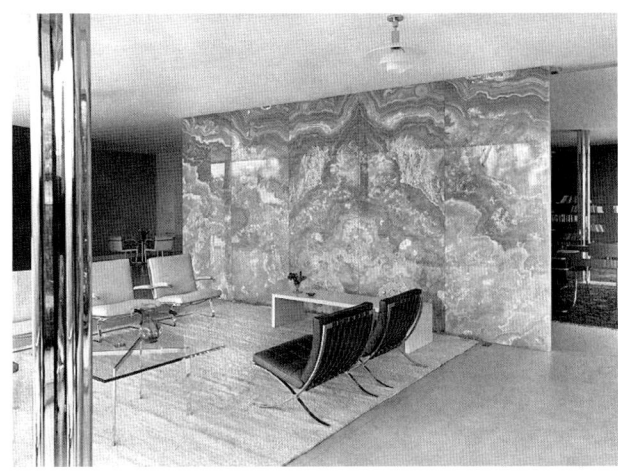

and industrialists, and throughout its existence was one of its leaders. In 1927 he was put in charge of the Housing Exposition at Stuttgart, as the only man who could talk the conservative representatives of that city into allowing modern houses to be built. Two years later he was head of the German section in the Barcelona Exposition, and the pavilion he built here was one of the finest things he has done. His strong tendency to make the roof an independent member, under which partitions are set where he wishes to put them, is even more evident here than in the house in Brno. A roof, to Mies, is not the lid of a box; it is a shelter under which partitions, columns, and living spaces are arranged. On the strength of this work he was made director of the important Berlin Building Exposition. Here he had sufficient power to select as architects the younger men in the Werkbund, and thereby incurred the enmity of most of the more established architects. A movement arose to remove him from the office at the next election, and at the meeting Mies had perhaps twenty people in the large audience who were for him. Before a vote was taken he got up and made one of the longest speeches of his career—fifteen minutes—and when he had finished he was reelected with one dissenting vote—his own. Shortly after this he retired, however, and it was rather fortunate, because six months later the Nazis came in, and that ended the Deutsche Werkbund.

Another phase of his career is linked up with the Bauhaus. Gropius built it and was succeeded as director by Hannes Meyer, a functionalist and a communist to boot. More interested in communism than architecture, apparently, Meyer changed the character of the school radically. It must have been a rather hectic place, with a wild group of students agitating for one thing and another, and turning out a large crop of illegitimate babies, much to the horror of the staid citizens of Dessau. So bad did things become that Gropius was invited back, but he was busy and suggested Mies, who accepted. Mies was completely indifferent to communism, or any political system, for that matter, and his students objected to him violently, calling him a reactionary. He stayed a year, however, doing some interesting work. Gropius had just finished a study of a tract of land in Berlin, proving that the solution of the housing problem was to put everybody in twelve-story houses, set a considerable distance apart. Mies, never much taken in by this sort of thing, put his students to work on the same tract of land, and proved that the same number of people could be settled for the same amount of money in little two-story houses. This little experiment showed exactly what Mies wanted it to show, that there are several ways of doing almost anything. Most of his students were too busy talking to get the idea.

At the present time, oddly enough, Mies is on the upgrade. Hitler and his aides have condemned modern architecture repeatedly, evincing a preference for a kind of bombproof Nuremberg style, but Mies, who has never shown much love for pitched roofs, has been made head of the architects in the German Academy. And only a short while ago his competition drawing for

opposite left:
First of the famous metal chairs, designed overnight by Mies and since freely copied all over the world.

opposite right:
"There," says Mies, "is a wall." In his realization of the enormously rich decorative possibilities of natural materials, Mies is unique among modern architects. Unlike his more ascetic confreres he argues that something has to be done to relieve the harshness of the bare interiors found in today's work.

below:
The silk exhibition room in Berlin designed with Lilly Reich.

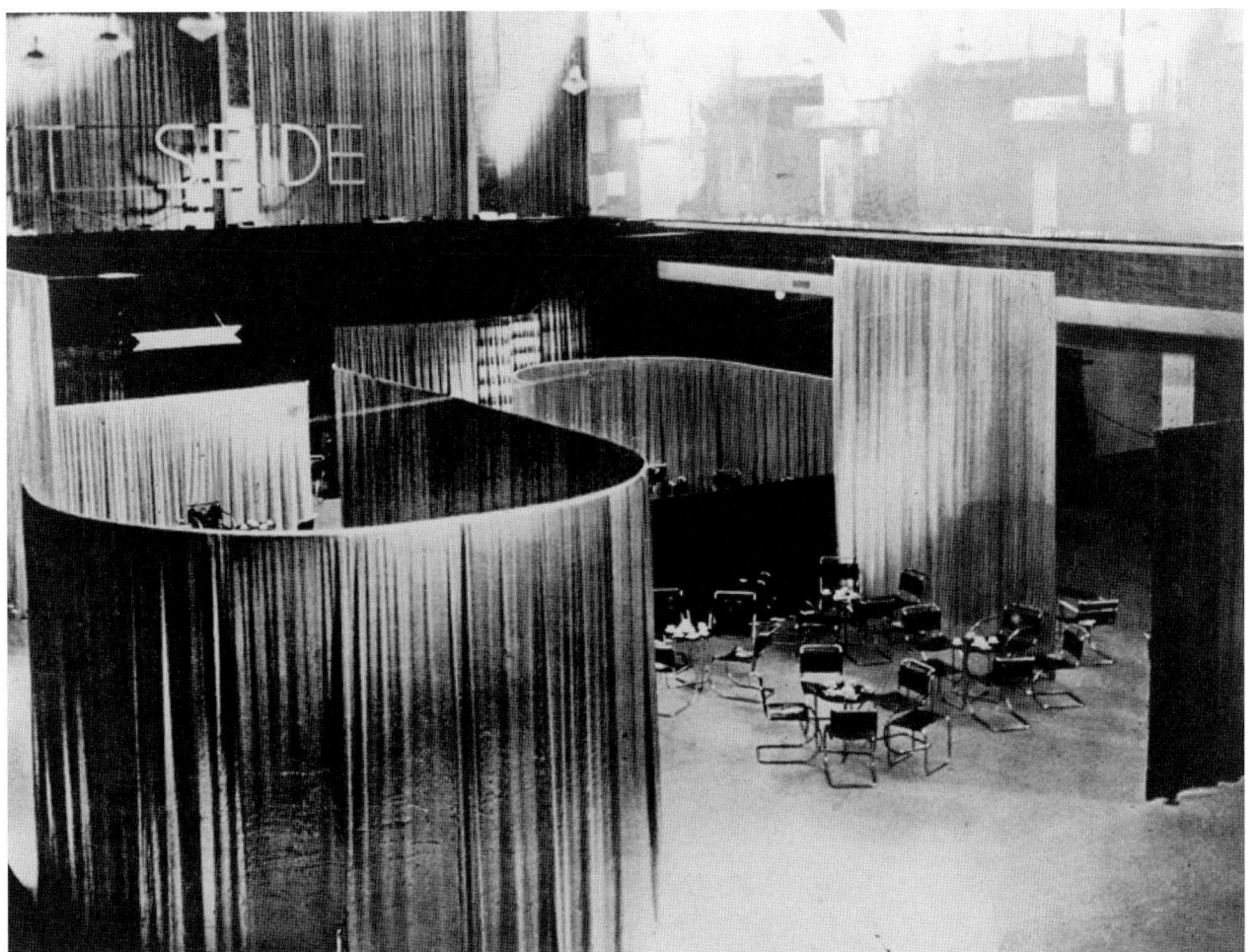

Apartment House—Stuttgart—1927. In this, his first steel building, Mies showed how clearly he understood the basic principle of its use: repetition of a unit. The construction system is simplicity itself. The regularity of the plan is reflected in the exterior. Only in the arrangement of individual apartments do his personal preferences find expression.

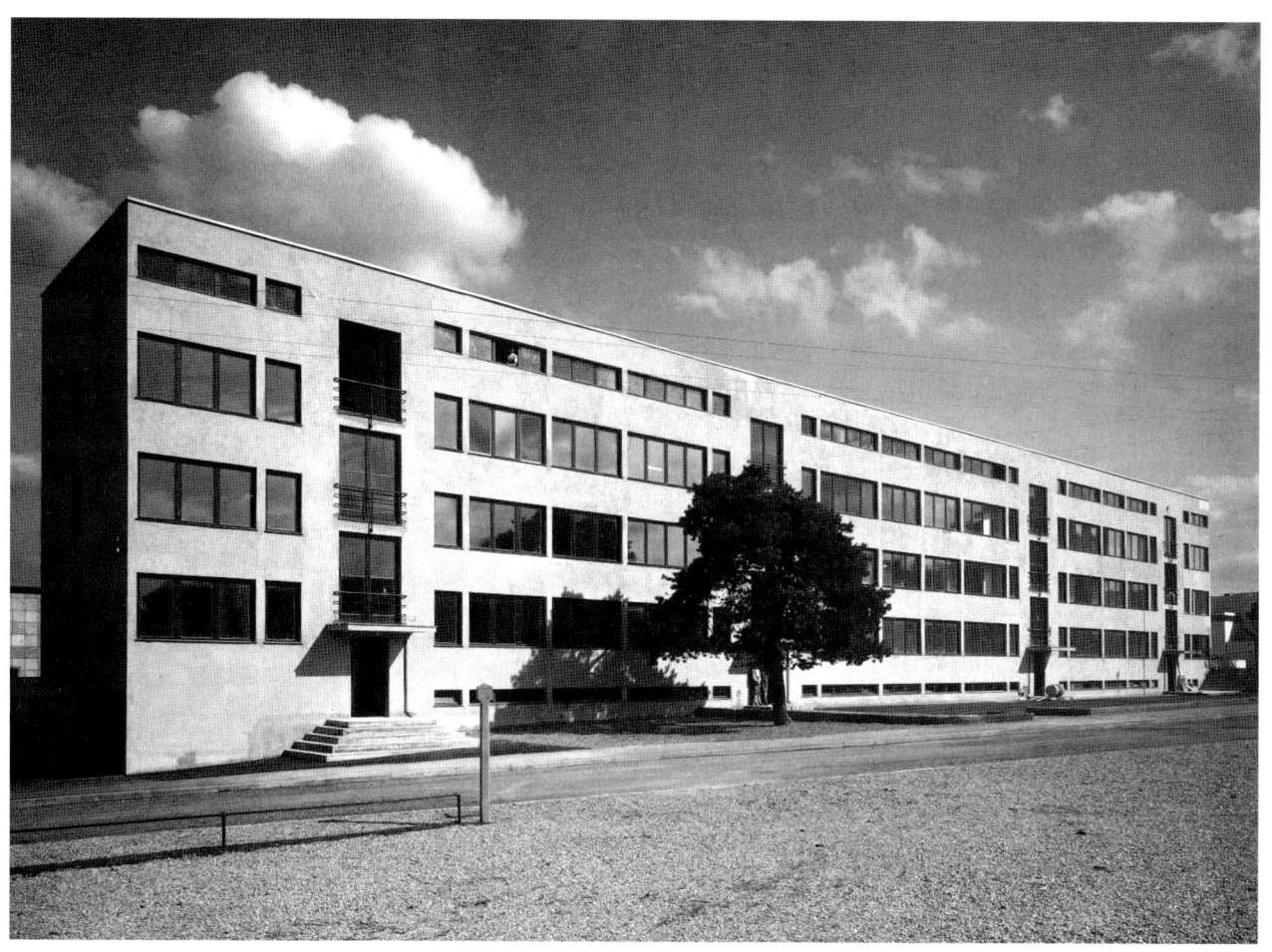

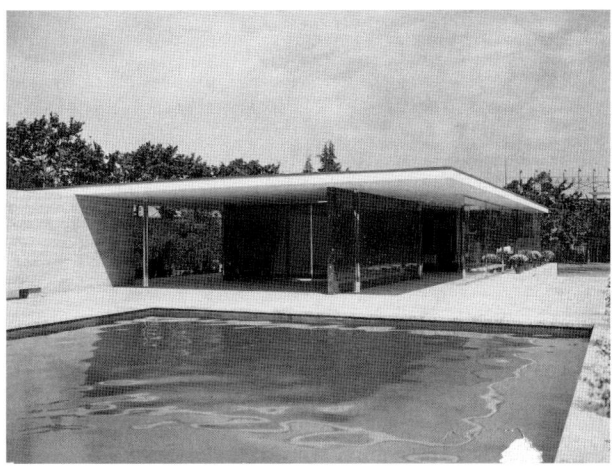

The German Pavilion–Barcelona Exposition, 1929– a brilliant composition, notable for its proportions and use of materials. The conception of the roof as an independent slab is emphasized with great effectiveness by the use of different materials in the vertical planes which meet it.

a new Reichsbank won first prize, although his design will not be built. Whatever it is that accounts for his enviable position, it is hoped that he will get some jobs out of it. With Mendelsohn, the Tauts, and Gropius out of the country, there surely ought to be a commission or two for those who remain, and it would be interesting to see what Mies would do on an important building.

If this picture of the man is incomplete, it is because his career, more than that of any other living architect, has been one of great promise and little realization, and the story of it leaves one with the feeling that more must be forthcoming. This is only a feeling, however–he is living in an uncertain country under an unpredictable government. He has done the Tugendhat House, to be sure, and his pavilion in Barcelona was a major achievement of a kind of abstract architecture, and the sum total of his work, if small, is important. As for the man himself, he is a sure, sensitive artist, and in his handling of space and feeling for material he has no superior. He is brilliant, slow, affable, and vain. Impractical, utterly uninterested in politics, the social or economic aspect of architecture, he is paradoxically the only one among Germany's great modern architects who has anything like a sure position in the country at this time. Quiet and reserved, he nevertheless could fly into a tantrum like a petulant child when a manufacturer made a minute change in the design of his chair–an attitude not unlike the "Art for art's sake" of the nineteenth century. At the present moment he refuses to release any more of his photographs for reproduction in America because it seems that someone copied something he did and he is determined not to let it happen again. Such conviction of his own importance is a curious but not inconsistent part of a complex personality. Physically he is strongly and heavily built, but lazy. A fine draftsman, he prefers to have his drawings done for him, and if sitting is the final test of a chair, the metal chairs in his office leave nothing to be desired. Mies, the academician, and former professor in the Bauhaus, has no use whatever for schools, and delights in listing the outstanding men in architecture who never saw the inside of one. His reaction to a remark about the Beaux-Arts was brief and to the point. "It's dead," he said.

As I got up to leave I noticed a beautiful engraving of an Ionic capital, prominent in the modern room, and asked what it was doing there. Mies looked at it seriously for a moment before replying. "The old architects," he said finally, "copy this sort of thing. We appreciate it."

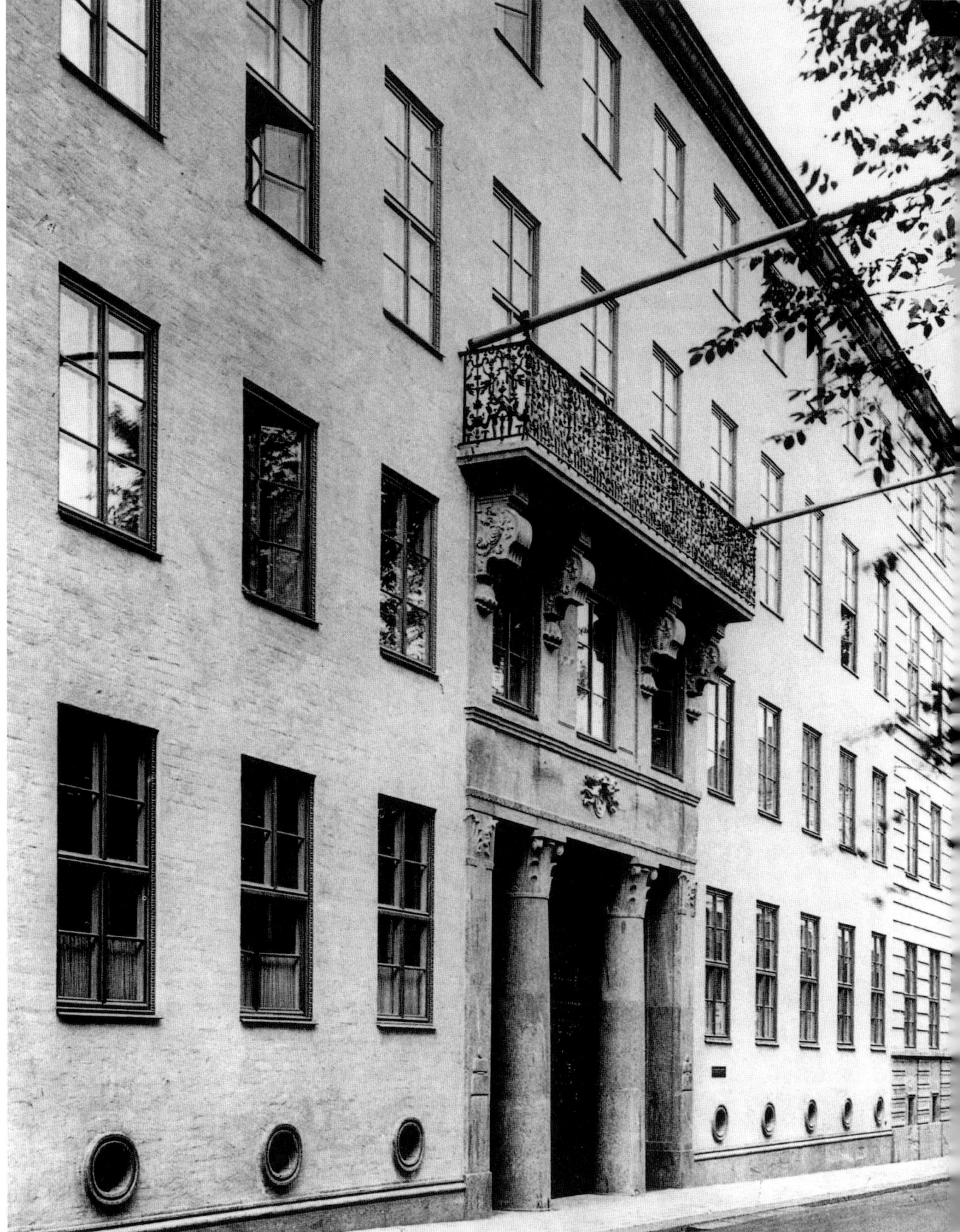

IVAR TENGBOM
SWEDEN

FROM
PENCIL POINTS
NOVEMBER 1935

An interior view of the greatest of modern Swedish churches, the Hogalid Church in Stockholm, designed by Ivar Tengbom.

As the train pulls into the station at Stockholm the traveler can catch an occasional glimpse of the tower of the Town Hall, alternately framed and blotted out by ascending clouds of steam, by blank warehouses and the other familiar objects of station yards. It is a very fitting introduction to the city, the curious dark pile whose heavy ornaments of bright gold gleam with barbaric effulgence against somber masses of brick and the pale brilliance of a northern sky. This prodigious monument, which has already taken on a character of agelessness, is, as much as any organized collection of sticks and stones can be, the complete summing-up of a culture. The infinity of traits which go to make up that thing called national character here find concrete expression, and to one sensitive in such matters, the very walls reveal those influences that through countless generations have molded and emphasized the Swedish character. Today this building stands for other things as well: the multitude of forces battering against the old order in architecture–the machine and mass production, new ways of living, a growing need for simplicity–have precipitated a conflict not unlike that going on elsewhere in the world, and Stockholm's Town Hall emerges as the swan song, the final expression of an architecture that is changing beyond recognition. In this sharp division between the old and the new, one man comes to mind as preeminent in both, his essentially realistic point of view effectively preventing a fanatical adherence to one school or the other. This is Ivar Tengbom.

Among the men who have appeared in this series, all outstanding in a greater or less degree, there has been an extraordinary divergence of personalities: a fiery Swiss with visions of a new social order, a crafty Italian politician, sliding from one architectural mannerism to another as expediency dictates, a fleshy German, dreaming dreams of buildings closer to pure geometric abstractions than anything since the pyramids, all of these have stood out as forces instrumental in the forming of a new architecture. Tengbom, totally different, is nonetheless a dominating personality. This man, whose distinguished bearing stands out in any group, has been from the beginning a superlatively able and practical architect whose mastery of the traditional modes of building is best illustrated by the liberties he has taken with them.

He was born in 1878 to a family which had numbered many soldiers and ecclesiastics among its members, but no architects. There does not appear to have been any specific event that led to his adoption of architecture as a profession, but it was settled while he was still in his teens, and when barely twenty he entered the Chalmers Technical Institute in Gothenburg. This institution was described as "a private college, but very good none the less"–an interesting comment on the importance of government schools at the turn of the century. After completing the course, which gave a thorough training in all practical matters relating to architecture, he went to Stockholm, entering the Royal Academy of Arts, which occupied somewhat the same position in Sweden

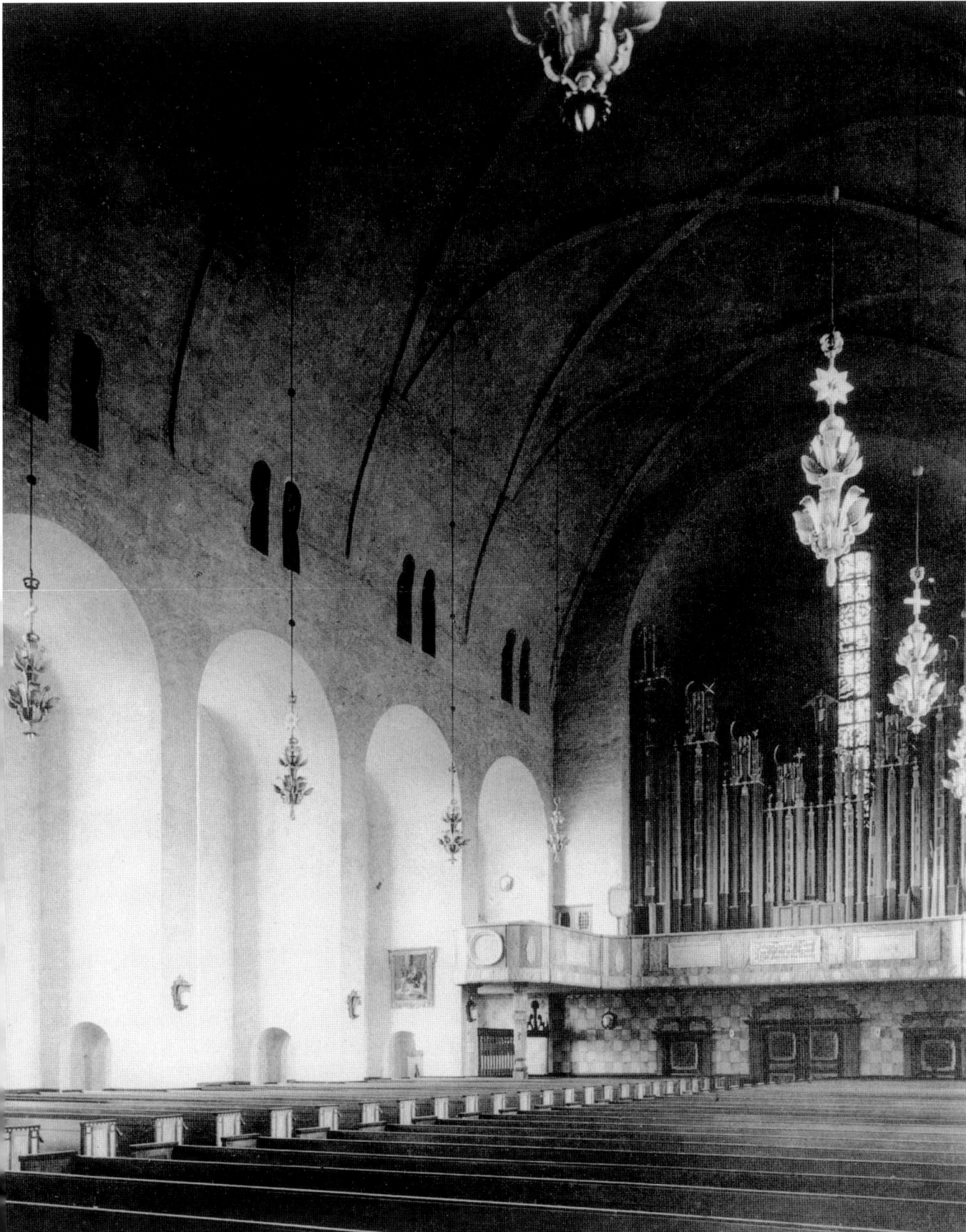

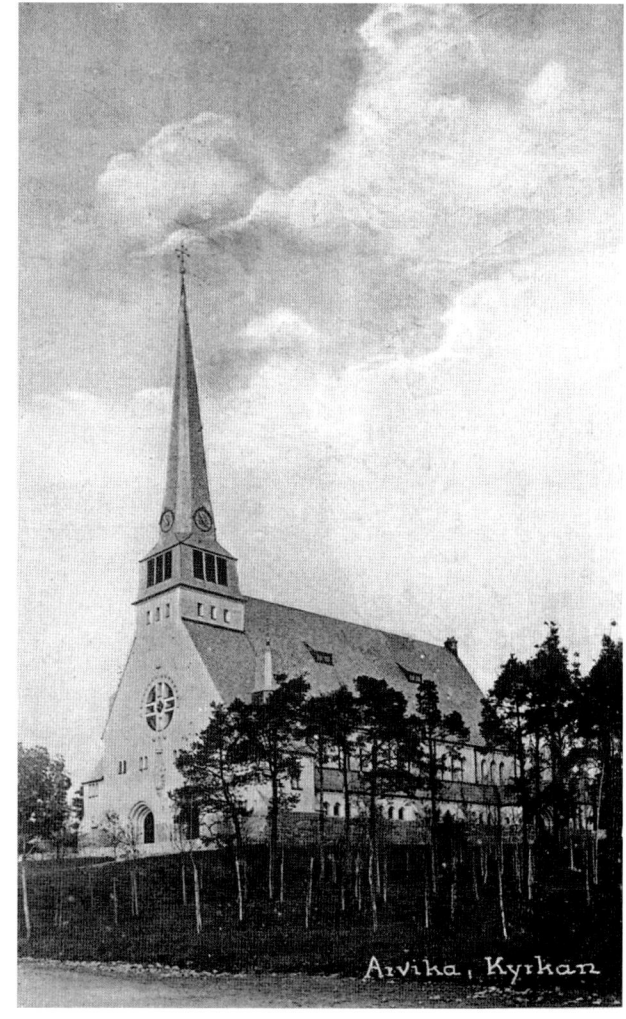

Arvika Church, designed with Ernest Torulf.

as the Ecole des Beaux-Arts in France. He immediately became one of its most outstanding students, and his work gained for him the highest award that could be won: the Royal Medal, which carried with it the privilege of study and travel in foreign countries for several years. Tengbom went to Paris, then as now a mecca for students, and he studied there for a considerable time, coming into contact with the best men in the Beaux-Arts, whose influence on him, while later greatly transformed, was nonetheless important. Before returning to Sweden he traveled all over Europe, observing, sketching, acquiring a new sense of values, and learning much about the old styles which were to appear in such surprising forms in his later work. When he went back to Sweden it was not to the capital, where he had so distinguished himself as a student, but to Gothenburg.

Practicing in Gothenburg at the time was Ernest Torulf, one of the leaders of his profession, and it was with him that Tengbom became associated. Torulf had commissions of considerable importance, but it was during the five years that they were associated that some of the greatest competitions ever held in Sweden were announced, among them the competition for the Engelbrekt Church and the one for a new Town Hall for the city of Stockholm. That they took second place in each of these competitions in face of the stiffest opposition Sweden could offer was no doubt due in large part to Torulf, but nevertheless it was no small feather in the cap of a student recently returned from abroad. They had better luck on their other attempts, and among their winning designs were the Town Hall for Boras and the Arvika Church. Growing ambition, based on confidence gained from these successes, and the urge to go to Stockholm led him finally to sever his connections in Gothenburg. In 1912 he arrived in the capital and opened his own office.

Tengbom brought with him more than the invaluable lessons he had learned from Torulf, more than the experience gained in the carrying out of actual buildings: a most engaging personality and excellent connections were by no means the least of his equipment. In 1915 these things bore fruit; he was given his first important commission, the Enskilda Bank of Stockholm. Here for the first time appeared those characteristics which gave his work so definite a flavor. It will be seen that the effect of this building is that of an Italian palace of the Renaissance; on second examination it becomes apparent that the entire composition has been treated with a disregard for stylistic correctness that approaches the monumental. The ponderous rhythm of the typical Italian rusticated base is interrupted by four groups of engaged columns, above which are set figures almost a story in height. The windows of the upper floors are the common windows of the country, and no attempt has been made to ornament them with frames and pediments; the cornice consists of a bold fascia and plain blocks below. The whole of this unusual design has been handled with such skill and strength that only study reveals its complete lack of conventionality. Note, too, that the design is in excellent character: the bank is a private one, as might almost be guessed from the exterior, and the work spaces above are well expressed by the severely utilitarian façade and plain windows. At the present time, when most of its contemporaries are acquiring a "dated" look, this building is quite as satisfying as when it was erected. An event of importance is marked by this work: it was the first of a series of collaborations between Tengbom and the greatest of living sculptors, Carl Milles. Haakon Ahlberg describes the building as a "substantial structure . . . a modern arrangement with old-time distinction." One might quarrel with the "old-time" but certainly not with the "distinction."

Work came in increasing quantities after the completion of the bank. Most of the commissions were for private houses and villas of more than average size, and Tengbom, by virtue of this work and the circles in which he moved, soon acquired the reputation of a deluxe architect, the man to whom one inevitably came for work of the most expensive sort. He did not allow himself to be pigeonholed, however; a person of rare energy, he designed factories, hospitals, schools, churches, and sanatoria. But it was not until 1920, five years after the completion of the Enskilda Bank, that he had an opportunity to display his rapidly maturing talents in a monumental work. It was in this year that he won the competition for the Stockholm Concert Hall.

The problem was to design a building for a plot almost square in shape, one side of which was on a street, while the main elevation faced an open marketplace. Two

The Enskilda Bank, in Stockholm, Tengbom's first important commission, shows the freedom with which he characteristically treats traditional forms.

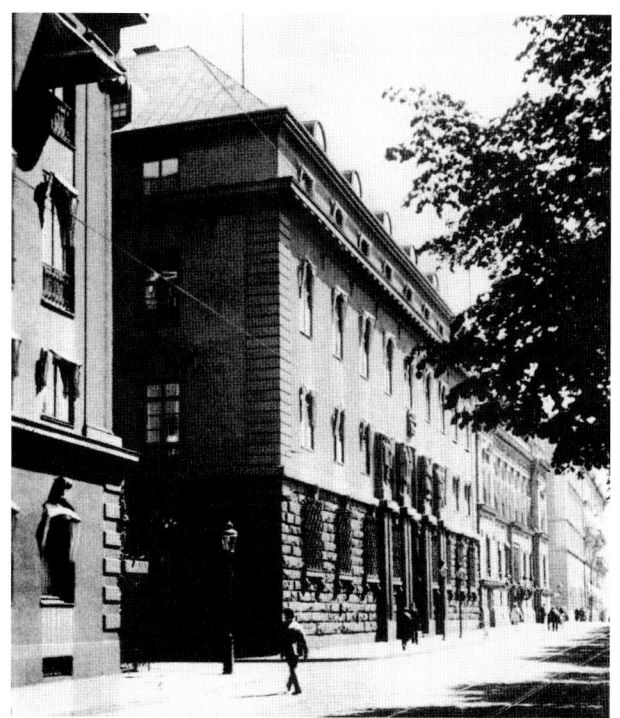

halls were required, and Tengbom placed one in the center of the mass, as in the typical French plans, and he tucked the other away behind an enormous noncommittal façade, providing it with separate stairways. His design shows the strong leaning towards the antique, which characterizes much of the Swedish architecture of the time, but the treatment, as in the private bank, is anything but classic in the archeological sense. The elongated columns, the decorative scheme (which is an arresting combination of rigid geometry and the freest naturalism), the playful handling of the interior of the large hall, these are the work of a man who had preferences for certain types of traditional architecture, but whose tastes were so strongly personal as to produce something unlike anything seen before.

The Hogalid Church, finished a few years later, shows a shift from classic influence to native styles, but here, too, the bold freedom of treatment is the same. The great barn-like mass, with its twin towers, encloses what is perhaps his finest work. There are few church interiors of the past three or four hundred years which can be compared to this for moving simplicity, deep religious feeling, and consistent design, nor is it necessary to point to the expensive dream of a bygone day which will someday be the Cathedral of St. John the Divine, or to that masterpiece of architectural anachronism, Grace Cathedral in San Francisco, to further bring out this fact. When Tengbom indulges in a bit of architectural recapitulation, he invariably handles his theme in a manner which leaves no doubt in the mind

Here, in Stockholm's Concert Hall, the inspiration is obviously classic, but so changed are the proportions and details, so personal the approach, that the building attains an authentic character in no way dependent on the traditional criteria of "correctness." Swedish craftsmen contributed to its success.

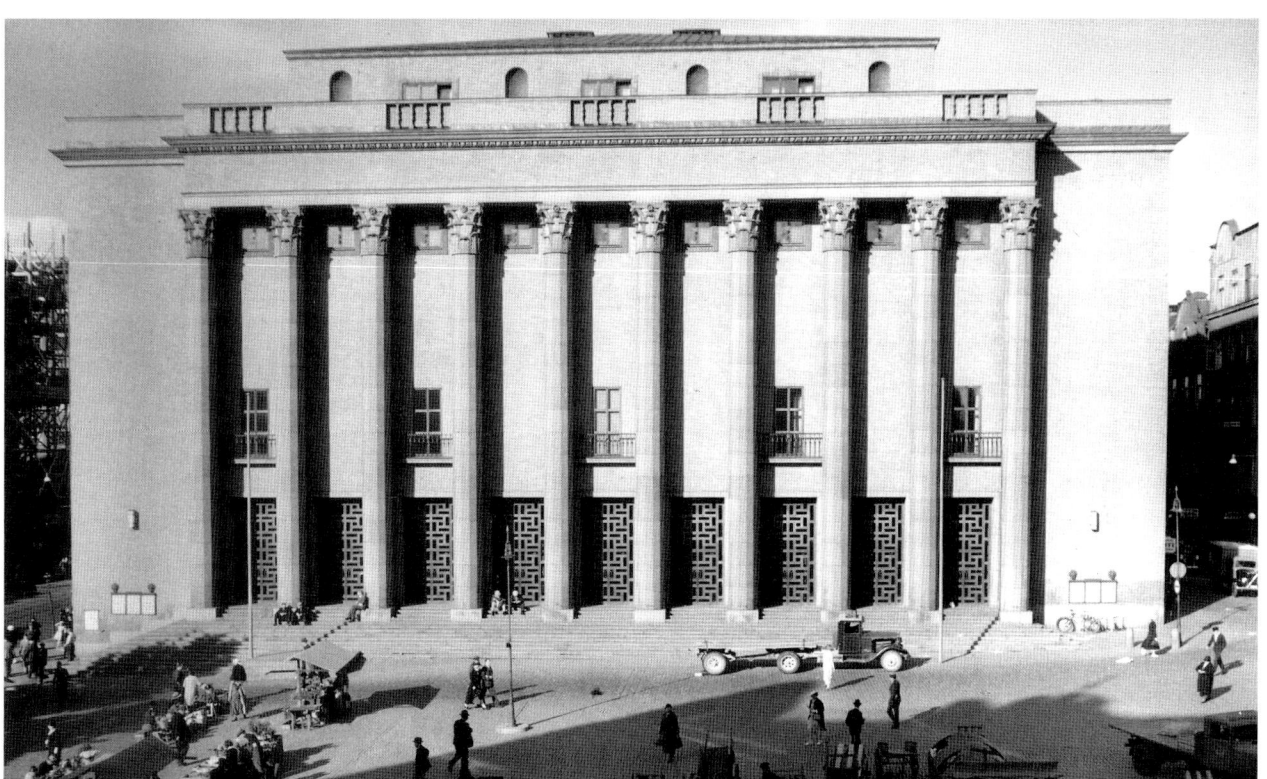

IVAR TENGBOM

below, opposite:
The distinctively national character of Tengbom's work is well illustrated by the Hogalid Church. The form of the main body of the church, the fenestration, and the handling of the towers all show the influence of earlier Swedish architecture on that of today. The interior shows the same quality of design, its splendid proportions and knowing simplicity placing it among Tengbom's most satisfying creations. Note the decorative lighting fixtures.

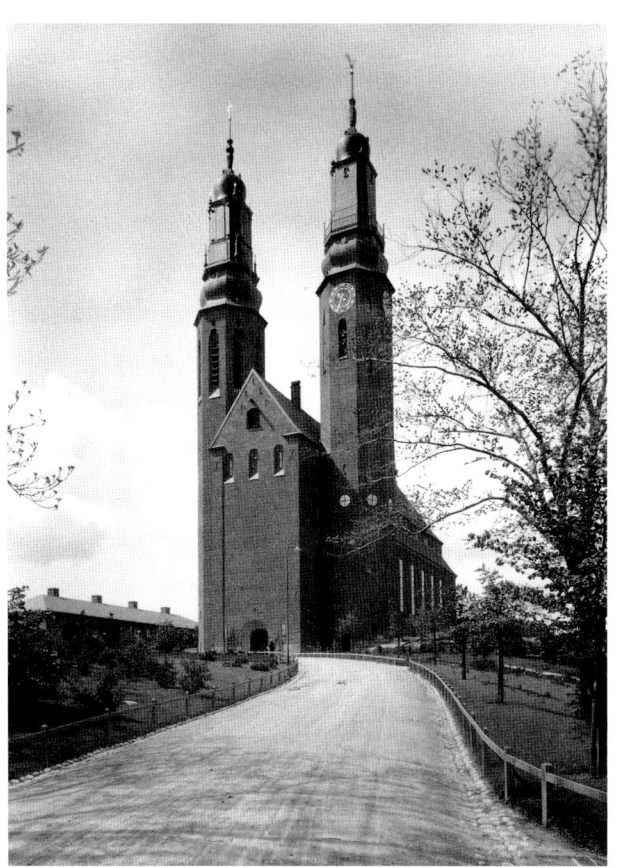

of the beholder as to whether the architect knew what century he was living in or not.

It has already been remarked that Tengbom early in his career acquired a reputation as a designer of elegant and expensive buildings. It was the late Ivar Kreuger who gave him a chance to show what he could do when given absolute carte blanche. He proposed to move the quarters of the Swedish Match Company to one of the fine old streets of Stockholm, and he appointed Tengbom as the architect. Tengbom's summing up of the problem as he saw it is most revealing. He said, "The site for this building is steeped in tradition. Once one of Stockholm's finest residential streets, there remain today a few mansions that have been able to defy the onslaught of a new age. The street has characteristics, however, which made possible the preservation of its quality. The old houses were built to the same height as allowed by the present laws. Nor, in this case, was there any special necessity to disturb the street's physiognomy. The task was simply to build an office, and there were no room requirements of any special kind which could necessitate exterior peculiarities. It was the old and usual request for rooms of normal size and window space, the same requirements that had been fulfilled in this street for several centuries. The usual modern office need for large rooms with walls of glass was not present here. There was nothing to prevent the newcomer from fitting in happily in the old street." Here is the conclusion of a practical architect, not a dreamer seduced by some beguiling idea of how a modern building should look.

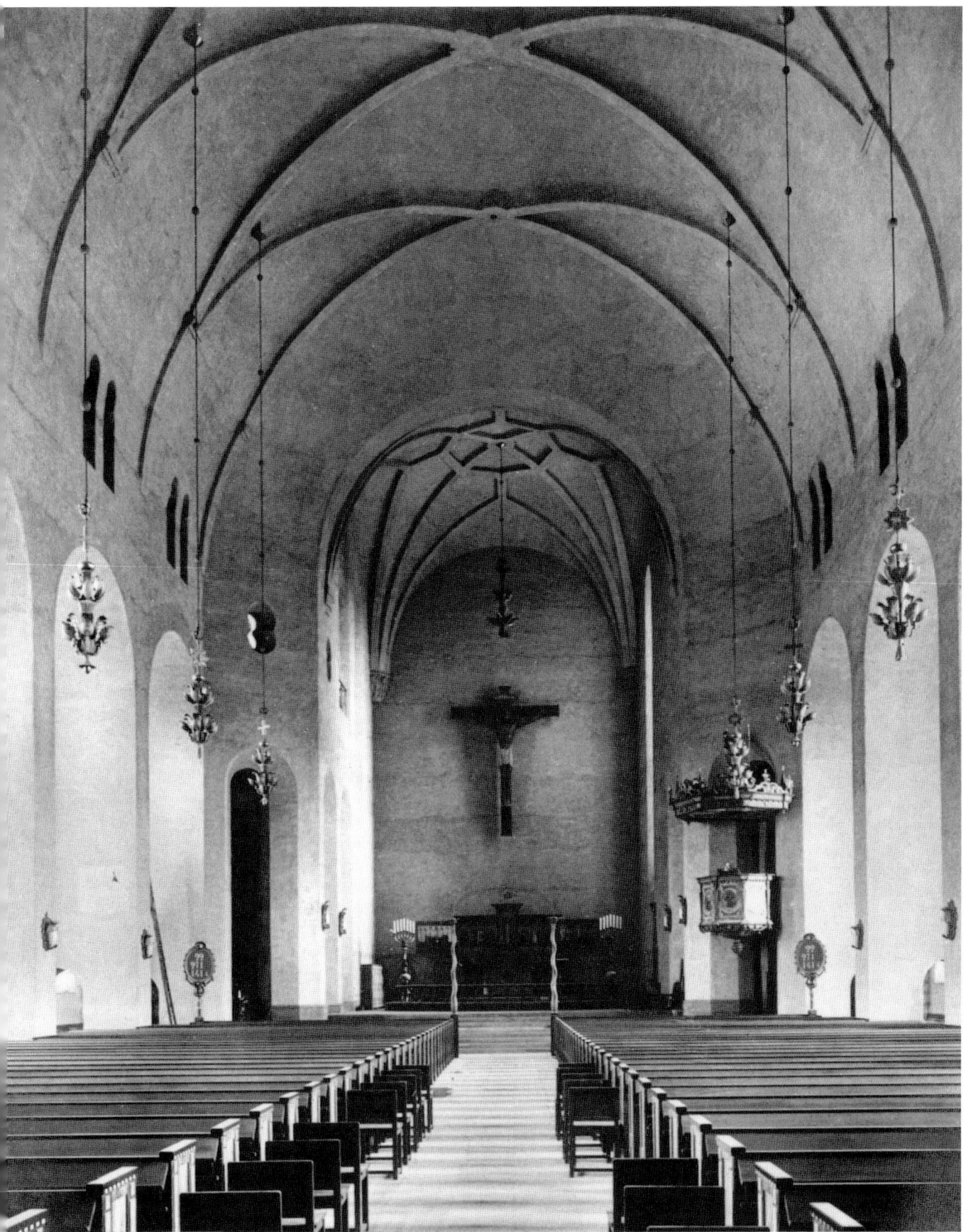

The Swedish Match Company's head office in Stockholm. The old buildings on either side show what care was taken not to destroy the harmony of the street—care not commonly exercised. Bold, distinguished design and superb craftsmanship characterize the Swedish Match Company Building. The formality of the building is in striking contrast with the free design of the wrought iron gates and balcony railings. The ironwork on this building is among the finest examples of modern times.

It was designed by Robert Hult and Gustaf Cederwall, the former of Tengbom's staff and the latter the sculptor for all the details.

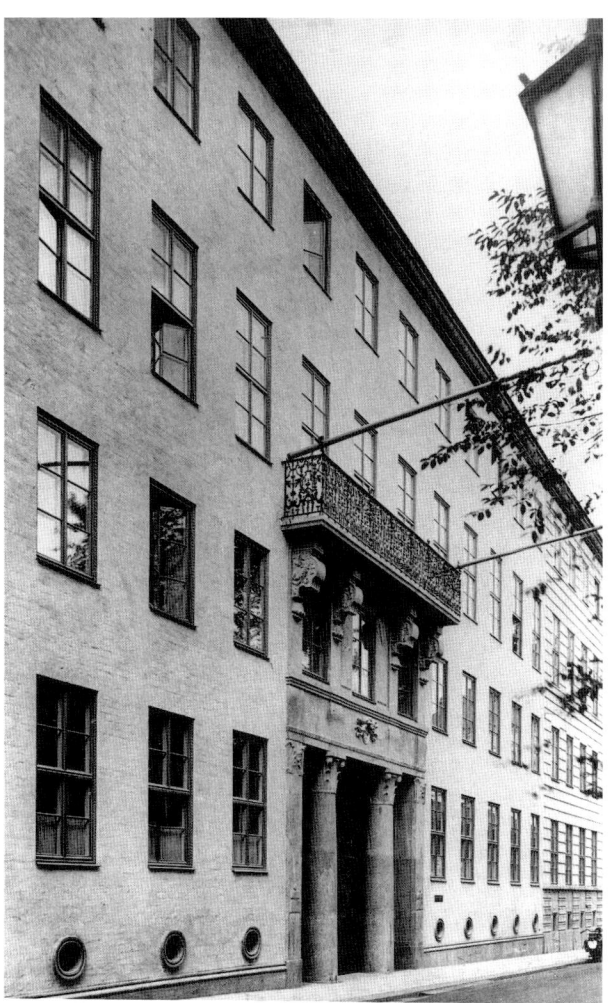

The Swedish Match Company Building is the final development of Tengbom's personal style as based on an originally classic inspiration. Here the familiar motifs are so changed as to be almost unrecognizable, and the freedom of his design is equaled only by its tremendous vigor. The list of craftsmen who collaborated with him reads like a roll call of the great names in contemporary Swedish art. Carl Milles did the famous Diana fountain in the courtyard and other sculptures; Carl Malmsten designed and built all the special furniture; Simon Gate of the Orrefors works did the lighting fixtures. The materials were splendid native marbles and finely grained granite; textiles, wood, and metals were all specially selected or designed. The craftsmen who worked on the job were limited only by the requirements of the problem, and Tengbom coordinated their efforts in a building worthy of the best they had to offer.

A sudden and radical change took place in his work in 1933. Two projects came up, one for a bank and hotel building, the other for a large printing company, and in both of them Tengbom "went modern." A preponderance of window area, horizontal lines, total absence of exterior ornamentation characterize both of them. To queries as to what caused the apparently revolutionary change in design his answer is brief: "I never had buildings of this type to do before." And in the light of past performances, it is convincing. It is notable, however, that in neither the "City" building nor the printing plant did he adopt the more pronounced mannerisms of the International School. The former, for example,

Two views of the interior courtyard of the Swedish Match Company Building, of which the Diana Fountain by Carl Milles is the main feature.

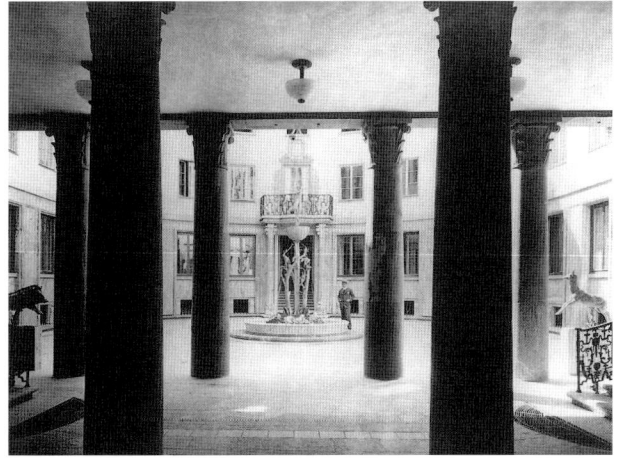

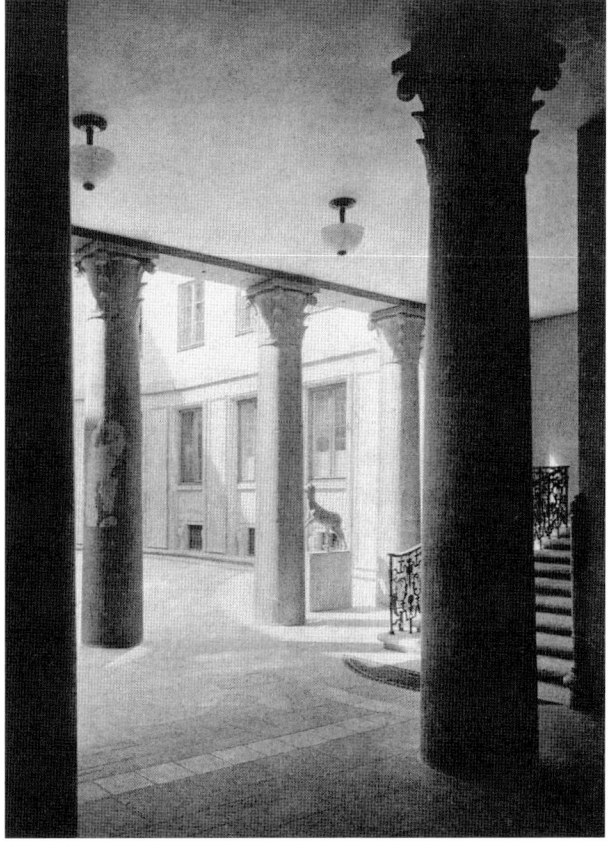

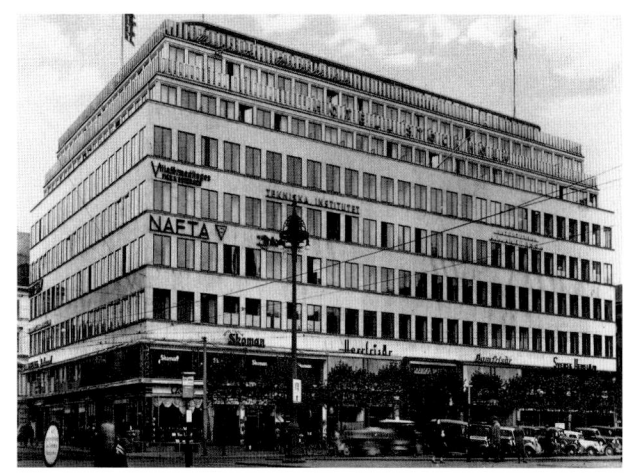

has many large windows; they are not forced into horizontal strips for an effect. They are simply openings in a wall of the size which was required. The wall, incidentally, is not of stucco, but is made of large slabs of fine white stone, and the railings at the top are anathema to extreme modernists because instead of being made of pipes they consist of rows of vertical members whose purpose is obviously decorative. The interiors, similarly, have a typically personal character which even the severity of the design could not entirely conceal. One can only come to the conclusion that between Tengbom's traditional and modern work there is no essential difference; the whole is always given consistency by a basic and sound approach.

Of his attitude towards architecture there still remains one point of major importance. To Tengbom, architecture is more than the bare building; it of necessity includes the correlated efforts of craftsmen, who, working under the guidance of the architect, the master builder, produce a finished and complete work of art. These efforts he describes as a "great union of forces working towards a common aim." Of recent developments in architecture he says, "They are the result of the social upheavals that followed the War. Social and mass problems have become the chief interest, and the cult of machinery has found fertile soil. In this age of standardization, however, it ought to be worthwhile to foster the individual contribution, to leave some room for beauty and charm, if we wish to avoid mentioning such a fantastic idea as beauty." Always realistic in his approach, Tengbom will do a "modern" building when the program calls for it—he would not put Gothic buttresses on an engineering laboratory as a protest against the new order—but to him there is a fundamental difference between architecture in its noblest sense, and the commercial building of today, so aptly described by Christian Barman as a "collection of cubic feet."

This insistence upon the broadest and most comprehensive aspects of architecture at a time when problems of a very special and complicated sort are clamoring for solution is not a popular point of view, and he realizes the situation and accepts it. Once, when referring to the Swedish Match Company and the craftsmen who worked on it, he said, "Without their help the result would have been a soulless construction." This strikes the keynote of his life's work, summed up in a sentence.

opposite:
The City Building is a notably clean design, dependent for its effect only upon its proportions and materials. The absence of the more pronounced mannerisms of the International Style is clearly apparent.

below:
A view of the Esselte Building in Stockholm. It houses printing company offices and equipment.

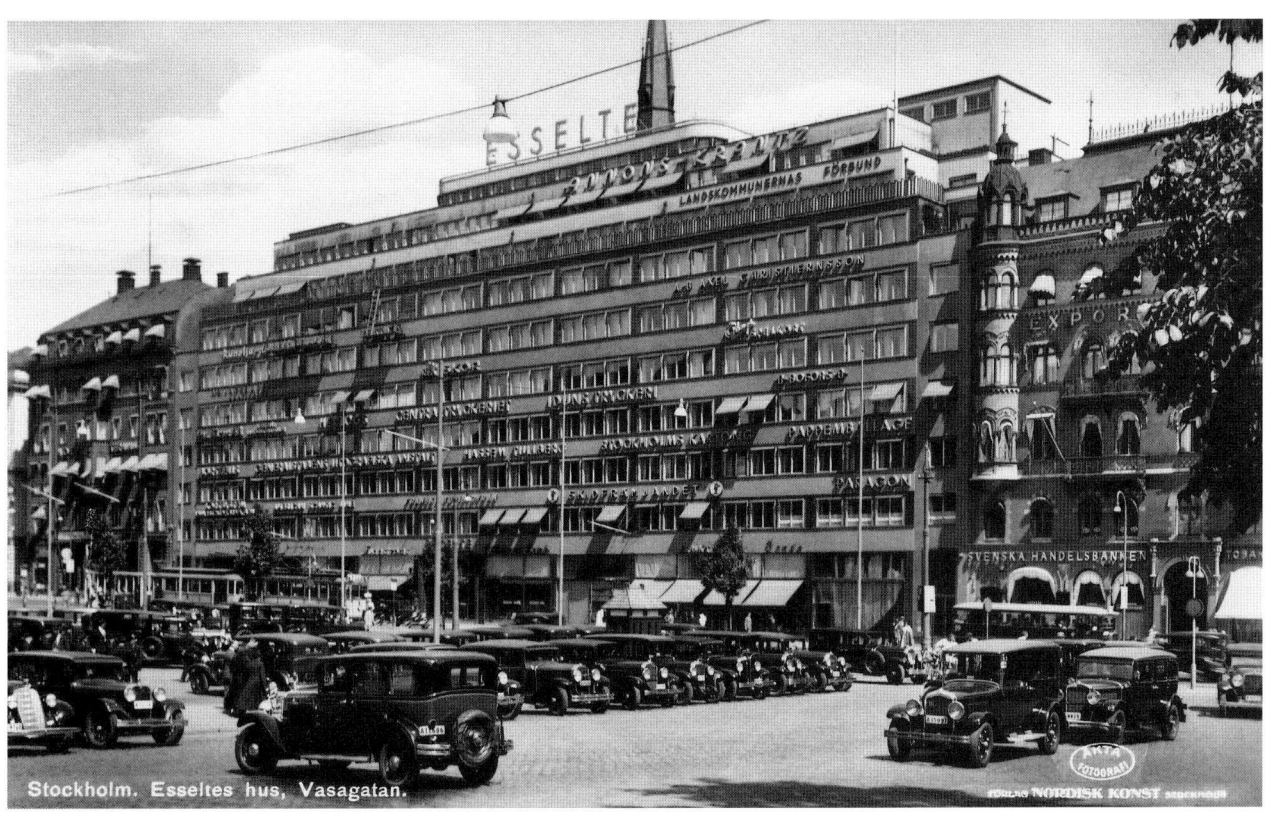

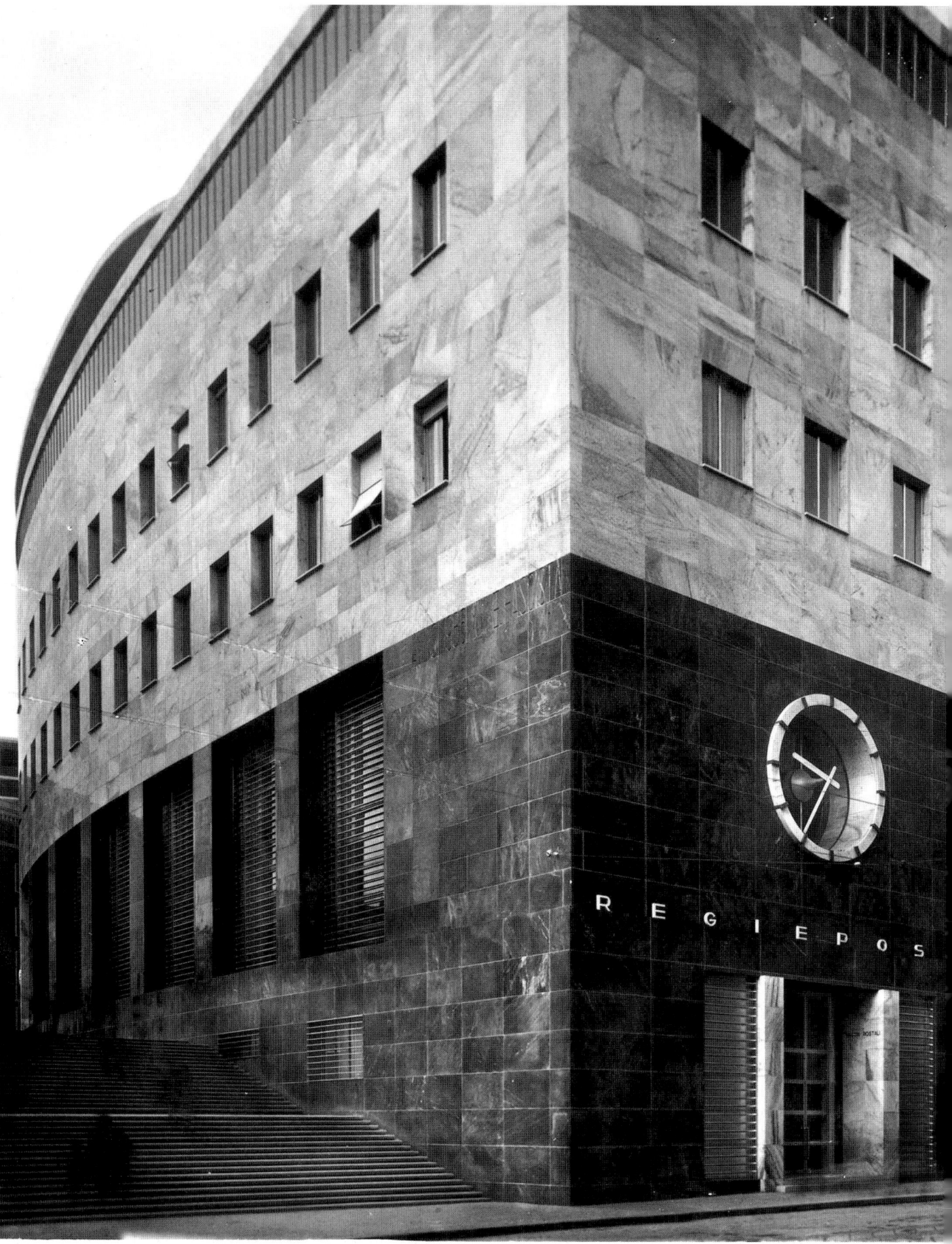

GIUSEPPE VACCARO

ITALY

FROM
PENCIL POINTS
JANUARY 1936

While present-day developments in architecture in most European countries are along lines closely related, the movement in Italy differs so greatly in many of its essentials that it might be well to take some note of them before going on to consider one of its exponents.

Unlike the postwar movement in Germany, which was due to an enormous economic pressure combined with a popular determination to make a clean break with forms reminiscent of a distasteful past, the Italian attempts to solve the aesthetic problems raised by new and radically different methods of construction are comparatively recent and due in large part to one man. It is true that before the war there were architects like Sant'Elia whose forecasts were startlingly accurate, but whose influence at that time was practically nil. Also the various factors in operation throughout the world have combined to make a break with old forms imminent. But it was not until Mussolini put his official stamp of approval on the so-called new style that it made any progress worthy of the name. He may or may not have acted from aesthetic convictions, but the fact remains that it was an excellent political move. Augustus, by calling attention to the great improvement he had made in the appearance of a Rome he had found built of brick, got much good advertising for his regime, and the wily Duce is following in his footsteps. That Mussolini will leave his Rome in red stucco instead of marble is beside the point, and whatever its color, the new style fits admirably into the program of his party and goes well with his highly advertised predilection for youth. And at the present moment, since the only game in favor is "follow the leader," one finds even the virtuosi of the old school having a try at the style so arbitrarily decided upon.

Obviously there are certain difficulties; a new style of architecture cannot be created out of whole cloth, regardless of how well it suits party aspirations, and we find Italy following the only course indicated in such a situation: it looked around to see what its neighbors were doing. A bit of German influence, a spot of Scandinavian, a large dose of Le Corbusier, all modified by the Italian sun, a lack of comprehension of the structural meaning of the new forms, and a constitutional inability to forget their beloved Barocco, and you have a new style under way. A parallel between this process and what went on a few centuries ago when Gothic was imported with the same lack of understanding of its essential characteristics is rather striking. Today a new element complicates matters. The dangerously intense spirit of nationalism which is sweeping Europe has nowhere reached a higher pitch than in Italy, and architecture has not been spared. Yesterday, perhaps, it was clever to borrow a trick from Holland, let us say, to help solve a difficult corner–today it is high treason. All corners must be Italian, Fascist if possible. Another thing: Italy, alone among European countries, is doing a vast amount of monumental building. Now it is one thing to do a commercial or industrial job: the practical aspects are so compelling that often a thorough understanding of them is the solution. The building that is also a

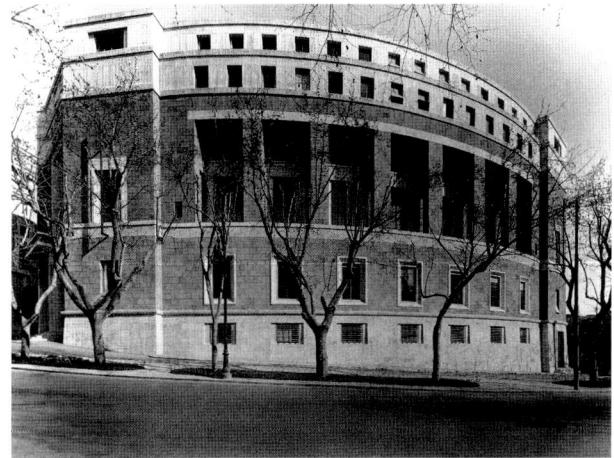

The Ministry of Corporations in Rome, first of the "modern" Italian government buildings.

monument presents problems infinitely more difficult, especially at just this time, and here we find the greatest interest and strongest individuality of modern Italian architecture.

In such a situation as the one described there is a good bit of confusion, inevitably. The architect must work in an imperfectly developed style; the problems are not unlike those of other countries, but his solutions must be different. Particularly in the monumental work, where he is guided less by necessities of plan and construction than by a desire to do something distinctive and arresting, it is small wonder that he has produced buildings more remarkable for their fantastic qualities than anything else. The work of Vaccaro is especially interesting at the present time because in it one can find the best characteristics of contemporary Italian architecture in their clearest form. Moreover, he is fortunate in being old enough to have been through first years of change but is still young enough to have his sympathies definitely with the new order.

He is fortunate in many ways, this man. He has an inexhaustible fund of energy, which during our interviews kept him restlessly pacing up and down while he expressed his ideas in rapid-fire Italian, each word of which landed with the impact of a bullet. And he has considerable personal charm and a frank manner which inspires confidence. He is the only man I have ever met who decided upon architecture as a career before going through the stages of wanting to be a sailor, fireman, or painter. By the age of six his mind was apparently made

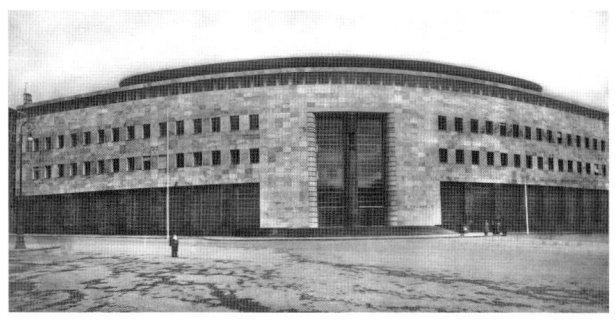
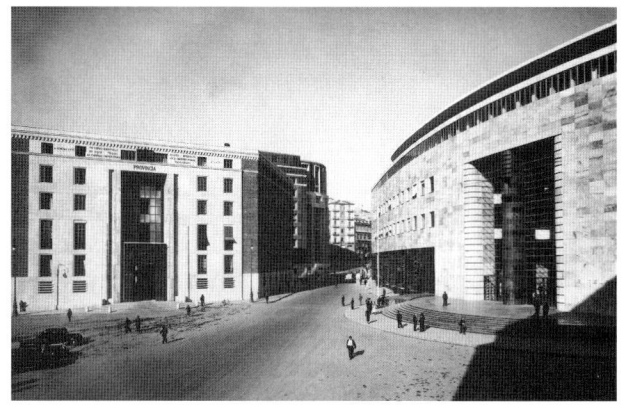

up once and for all. He began to draw at a phenomenally early age, but the most remarkable thing about these early efforts is that they concerned themselves with buildings, not the more dramatic objects that ordinarily engage a child's attention. He made huge quantities of sketches. The prevailing taste at the time was atrocious, but there was no excess of ornamentation, no multiplicity of parts that was too much for this boy. He showed me many of these sketches over which we both laughed, but there was nothing laughable in the power of draftsmanship displayed. None were in elevation; he seems to have felt the building as a three-dimensional form and drew it that way. In due course of time he entered the school of engineering at Bologna, found that his mountain of sketches had given him more than his courses in design could, and he concentrated on acquiring an excellent technical background. He did very well indeed, and in 1921, the year after his graduation, he was back on the faculty. A year of this was enough. Teaching was no job for an ambitious young man, and he hurried down to Rome. There, with the sure instinct of the man predestined to success, he entered the office of Marcello Piacentini, later official architect for the government. Here again he stayed only a year. He had gone in to learn how an office functions; he learned, left, and opened one of his own. Five years later he and Piacentini were collaborators on the great buildings for the Ministry of Corporations in Rome.

Such a rise would be considered rapid anywhere. In Italy it was meteoric.

The path of the young Italian architect starting out on his own is rather definitely marked. Private commissions are scarce and, in any event, go to the older men. So, unless a beginner has phenomenal luck and exceedingly influential backing, his only course is to try to get one of the numerous government commissions which are given out on a competition basis. It is not easy. Added to the normal difficulties of competitions there is the fact that many of them are anything but straight. But a young man with nothing to lose can take the chance, and if he gets one or two of the unimportant ones he begins to acquire a certain prestige which will help in the larger ones. This was the course Vaccaro followed. The first year out he won a small competition for the redesigning of a piazza in Rome. The next year it was a war memorial in his native city, Bologna. In 1926 he was taken in by some older men to compete for the Palace of the League of Nations. They won a first prize. In 1927 he was judged co-winner with Piacentini of the competition for the Corporations building in Rome.

This building underwent some rather curious changes which show in a particularly illuminating fashion how buildings sometimes reach their final form in a country where speed is not of prime importance. The winning design was liberally sprinkled with the various architectural accessories considered so necessary by juries at the time. The finished building, on the other hand, is of striking simplicity. Most of the changes in the design were made after the concrete framework was up. For example, the main façade, a long curved affair, consist-

Naples Post Office. The curious split entrance is a typical example of the persistent use of the Fascist symbol in new Italian government architecture.

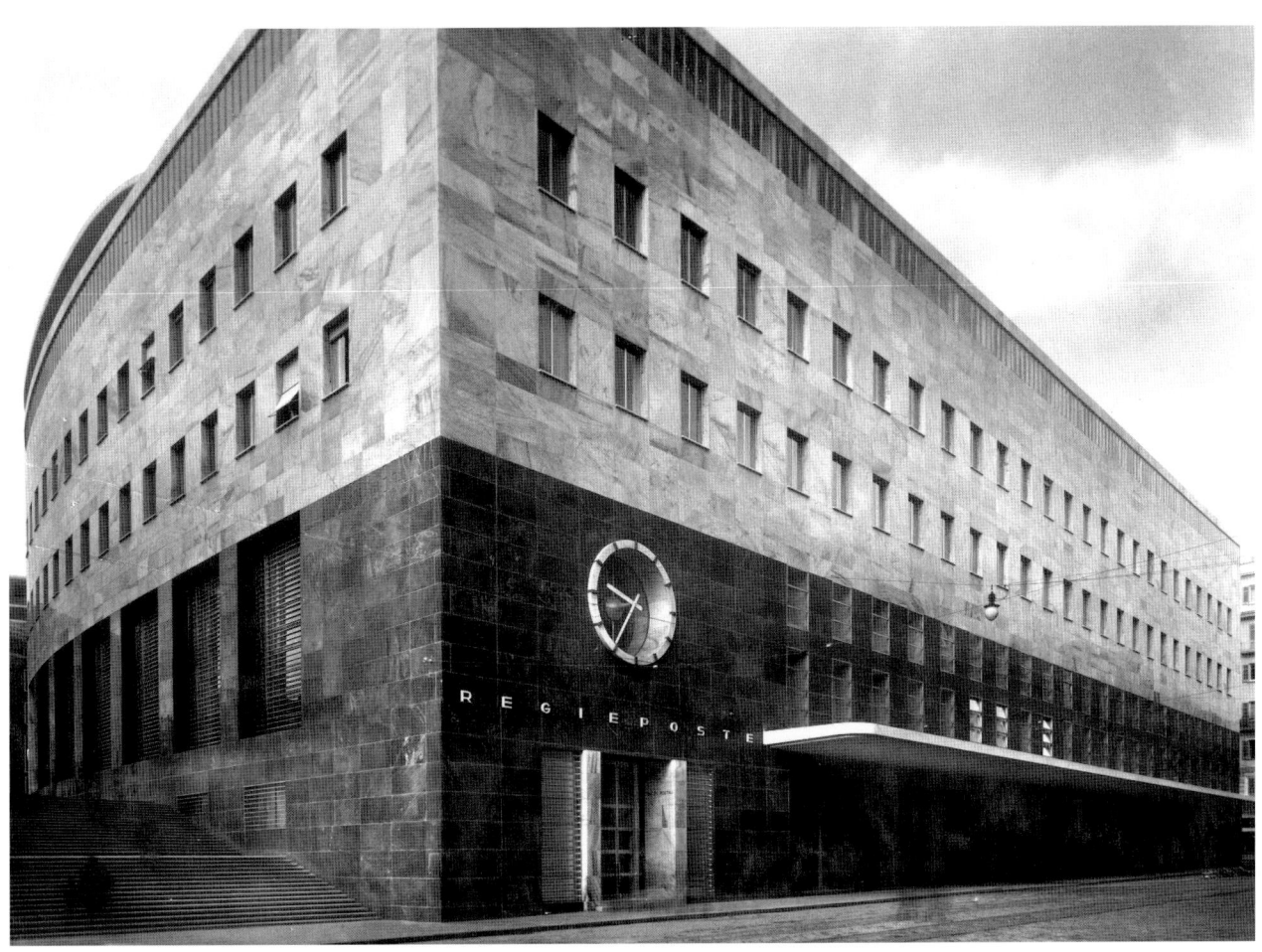

GIUSEPPE VACCARO

below:
A view of the square, Lugo. In the center is the usual memorial tower and speaker's stand, with Fascist headquarters behind it. The bank, with its row of windows under the loggia, shows the effect of climate.

opposite:
Perspective sketch by Vaccaro of his competition design for the Palazzo del Littorio in Rome. Its author, whose design was more severe and formal than most designs submitted, was selected as one of the fourteen finalists.

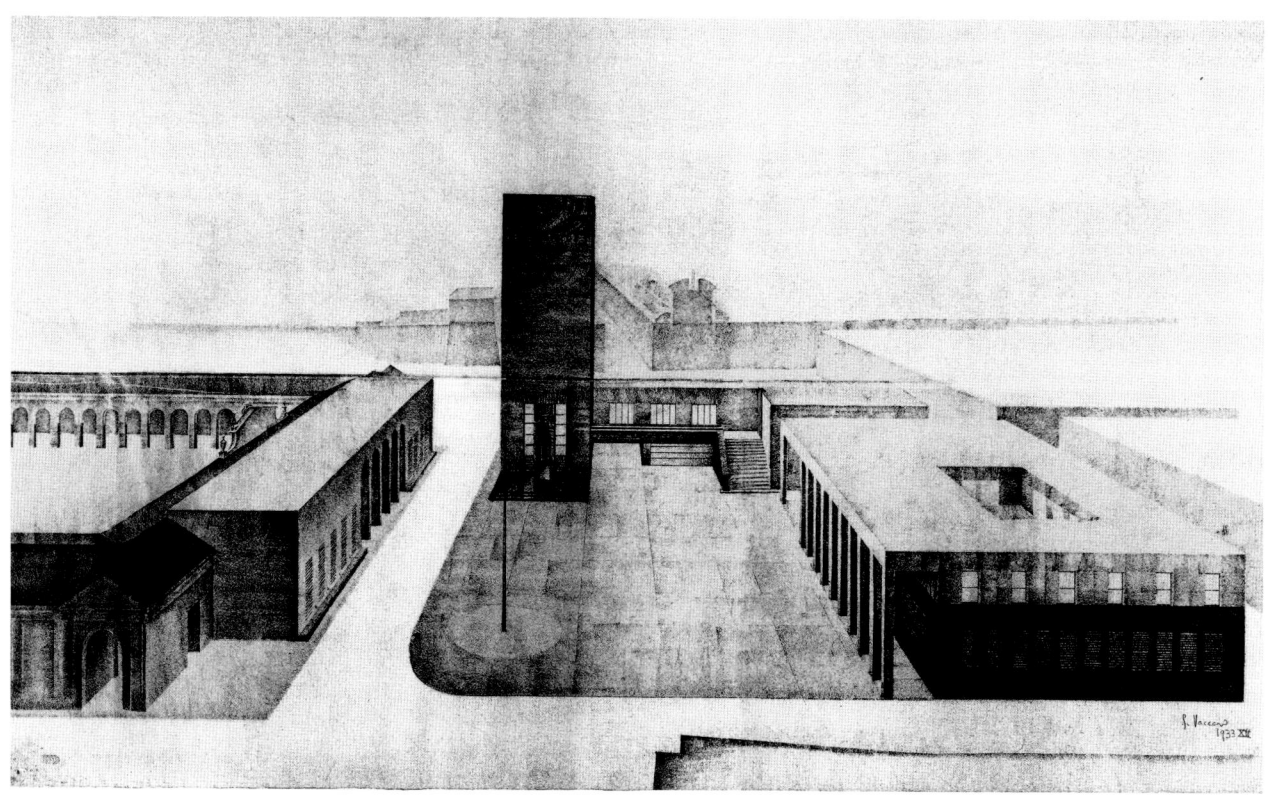

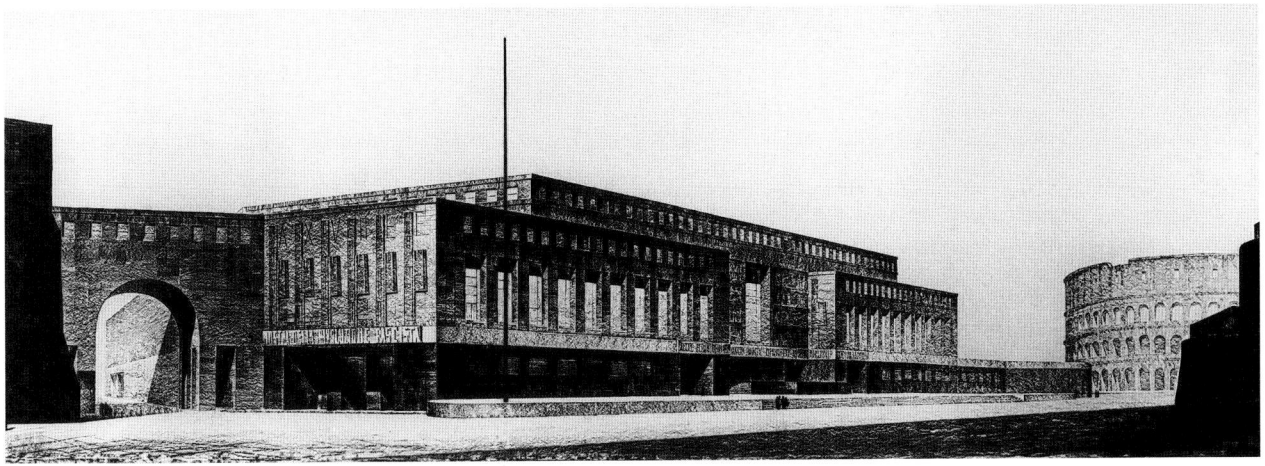

ed originally of a series of fairly gaudy arches, while the framework was a pier and lintel construction. Vaccaro, while on the job one day, was so struck by the power of the naked forms that he had the useless arches eliminated, much to the improvement of the building, and once started, other similar changes followed. It was a good lesson—since then he has designed no hung arches.

His last successful competition, the large new Post Office for Naples, is his biggest job to date. Once again, knowing his jury, he turned in a design that satisfied the more than slightly decadent Neapolitan tastes, [then] scrapped it as soon as he won. On publication of the final drawings the howl of surprise and rage that went up from the startled citizenry turned into a storm of protest so overwhelming that he was completely stopped. He cut through the opposition characteristically enough.

"I asked for an interview with the Duce, and it was granted," he said. "I brought the old designs and the new ones. He instantly grasped the situation. A post office is not a monument, primarily; it is a highly complicated mechanism. It can't be hidden behind a fake palace façade." Going to the head of the government to settle the dispute may seem odd to citizens of a country noted for indifference in such matters, but it wasn't the first time Mussolini had intervened, and he showed great interest. Perhaps it was the opportunity to play the benevolent despot, giving the misguided Neapolitans what was good for them instead of what they wanted. Perhaps he liked the respectful but vigorous arguments of the young architect. Or it might have been the building. In any event his decision was definite and rapid. "Go ahead," he said. "The Neapolitans will like it!"

Other jobs now began to come by themselves. Bologna gave him the new School of Engineering to do. Showing a strong influence from the north, it nevertheless fits its surroundings very well. The loose open plan was adopted to save the trees on the site, and the tower is not out of place among the magnificent towers that have come down from the middle ages. Of late he has been working on small houses, trying to develop a simple and cheap fireproof construction. His latest and most ambitious attempt is the competition for the Palazzo del Littorio, a huge building set down in the Roman Forum, destined to become the center of Fascist activities. A typical gesture on the part of the Duce, who likes to visualize himself as a true descendant of the Caesars, it is one whose wisdom is dubious. Questions of appropriateness aside, however, it is the greatest of a series of important competitions, and Vaccaro's sound, unsensational design was selected as one of the fourteen permitted to enter the final competition. There is no predicting the outcome, even whether the thing will ever be built or not—Italy has plenty to worry about besides monuments at the moment—and whether Vaccaro's personal influence and increasing prestige will have sufficient weight against his more experienced opponents is questionable, but in any case, one may be sure that his project will have few superiors in directness, dignity, and strength.

GIUSEPPE VACCARO

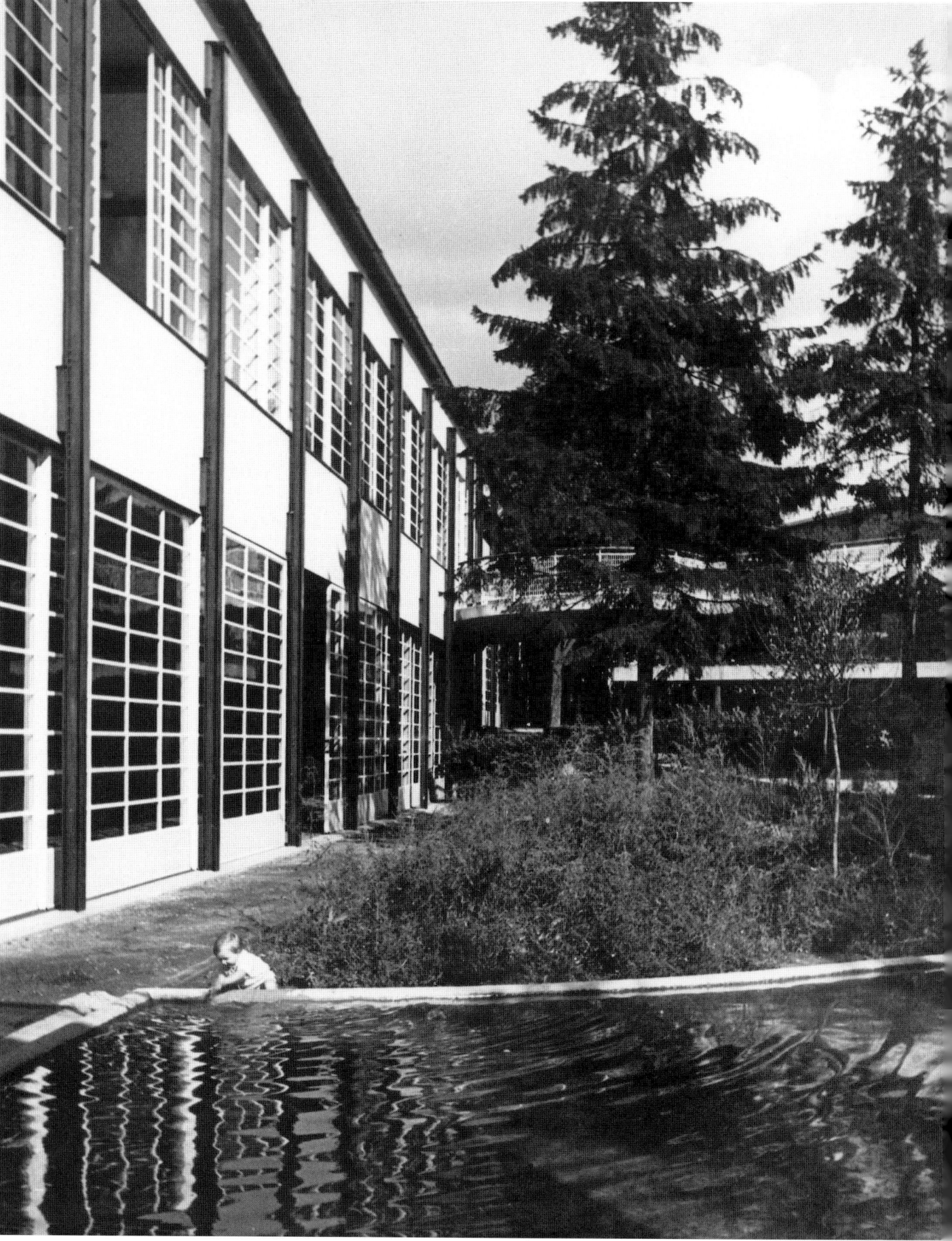

EUGÈNE BEAUDOUIN
FRANCE

FROM
PENCIL POINTS
MARCH 1936

"The Beaux-Arts," once remarked Mies van der Rohe, with a certain amount of asperity, "is dead." One does not take issue lightly with the Grand Mogul of modernism, and Beaudouin may be an exception proving the truth of Mies' assertion; but as long as the school turns out men of this caliber, it might perhaps be safer to replace the "dead" with "dormant"—and to realize that there is probably more than one way of training men to produce good architecture. For Beaudouin possesses to a remarkable degree the qualities that go to make an outstanding modern architect; few of his contemporaries show more promise, and none have done more significant work than this young Frenchman who has still some time to go before reaching his fortieth birthday.

What makes a modern architect? Those readers who have been repeatedly irritated by the series of buildings which have illustrated this series might select a combination of knavery and imbecility as the most likely qualities. It is hard for the confirmed traditionalist to admit that the men whose creations apparently violate every established idea of what constitutes beautiful building, are continuing in the great tradition of architecture. The ugliness of certain modern buildings, so often advanced as an argument against the entire movement, differs only from the ugliness of the buildings around us in that it is less familiar. A Westchester suburb is probably the most pretentiously hideous sight in the world; yet its inhabitants, blithely unconscious of the ghastly mixture of fake French, Italian, Spanish, and Early American houses that surround them, will squeal in righteous indignation if a modern house be added to the potpourri. Architecture, to the vast majority, is still the elegant pastime of erudite amateurs, and work that is different is disturbing because it has no copybook ancestry. The revolution brought about by the machine, and its unmistakable effects on every part of the social structure, may not be news; few recognize it, nevertheless, when they see it in steel and stone. Beaudouin is a modern architect, but his buildings and his expressed ideas reveal no qualities that could not be possessed by the true builder of any period. If his work seems odd to the style-minded, let it be remembered that he has been solving problems that were not in existence fifty years ago, and structurally his resources are of even more recent development. Three characteristics in particular mark Beaudouin as one of the leaders of his time: a keen historical sense, a brilliant grasp of the structural and aesthetic possibilities of modern techniques, and a profound social consciousness.

He began respectably enough: a conventional education, the decision to become an architect, and entrance into the Ecole des Beaux-Arts in Paris. His work from the beginning was good, and after he moved up from the elementary classes his *projets* began to stand out. He had tremendous vitality, a capacity to think to the point, and discrimination—and his solutions, good or bad, were invariably worked out with a freshness and finish that was almost unique. By the time he was in the first class it was practically a foregone conclusion that he would win the Prix de Rome. And he did, with a series of drawings that left no doubt in the minds of the jury.

Rome made a tremendous impression on him. While still a student at the Ecole he had already become interested in town planning, and Paris in itself was an inspiring example. But Rome, first city of Latin Europe, had a story to tell that no architect could ever forget. Buildings of every period remain as evidence of thousands of generations of building; layer upon layer, city on city, with each style "modern" in its time, it presents a cross section of living architecture unequalled by any city in the world. Rome is no place to breed rebels: the picture of a splendid architectural continuity is too vivid. Beaudouin, knowing his styles perfectly, now builds with prefabricated sections—but not as a gesture of futile revolt. The effect Rome had on him can be seen in his choice of a study of the Vatican City for his first year's *envoi*. What interested him, as he stated, was "the development of an independent urban organism through the ages, particularly worthy of study because of its link with ancient history and its spiritual influence on our own time." From this time on, he left no doubt as to his interests in the larger aspects of architecture.

Beaudouin has a number of traits not common to his race; among them is a passion for traveling. The customary itinerary of a student in the French Academy includes Italy, Greece, occasionally Egypt and North Africa, but not much more, and the popular procedure is to spend most of the year in a pleasant villa on the Pincian and then run up to Paris for a change. Beaudouin would have none of this—he wanted to go places. One of his little jaunts, taken during his last year at the Academy, involved nothing less than a motor trip to Persia, where, with his infallible instinct for finding town plans on the grand scale, he made a beeline for Ispahan. On this trip he had the company of his wife and Paul Herbé, a friend who had been working in Paris. It is rather typical of Beaudouin's personal charm and the admiration he aroused in those who knew him that Herbé would throw up a perfectly good job and travel hundreds of miles over deserts and mountains just for the pleasure of helping Beaudouin measure a forgotten city in an inhospitable country. The trip, according to Herbé, was something to remember with mixed feelings. At Ispahan they remained for two months, measuring mosques, bazaars, palaces, ending up with a plan of almost the entire city. Persian art reached a high point during the seventeenth century, and Ispahan is its finest architectural expression. In fact it is one of the great architectural creations of the world; Beaudouin, knowing this, did not care how far he had to go to see it. When traveling it was the custom to stop at every town that looked interesting, so that he might sketch—not pretty pictures of façades, but plans. Beaudouin's ability to grasp the essentials of a town plan after a seemingly casual stroll is one of his most extraordinary accomplishments; from this practice he learned more about scale and the relation between buildings and open areas than any number of books could have taught him. Later, in a housing project outside of Paris, he was to show the result of his town planning studies in a most unexpected fashion.

A man who has won the Grand Prix in architecture has little to worry about in France; an honorary government post is usually given him after his return, carrying with it a modest stipend. To Beaudouin, who was already moderately well off, the post meant not security but a chance to get important work. And he got it. One of his first jobs was a housing project at Bagneux, containing a thousand apartments. With his partner, Marcel Lods, he worked out a simple arrangement of four- and five-story walk-ups, leaving ample space for recreational areas. While the arrangement was not unconventional, the construction was. The factory, insisted Beaudouin–not the field–was the place to do the building, and every possible means was employed to arrive at this ideal of prefabrication. A light frame of standard steel members, not sufficiently strong to carry the entire load, was erected. Then walls and floors of precast concrete units were attached, joining with the frame to form a rigid, economical structure. On the strength of this performance he later obtained a much larger commission at Drancy, where he and Lods produced the most talked-of series of dwellings in Europe.

Beaudouin, it might be noted, has a flair for getting himself talked about. His brilliant and lucid study of Ispahan attracted much favorable attention in Paris; so did Bagneux, for different reasons. The tower tenements in Drancy were the first things of their kind in the world, and aroused a storm of controversy in government as well as architectural circles. At Suresnes he added another "first" to his growing collection, this time the first open-air school in France, and he did a magnificent job on it in the bargain. His recent project for a mammoth exposition building of steel and glass received no award from the jury; it caused more excitement, however, than all the other submitted designs put together. Beaudouin does not go out after this publicity: solutions are what interest him; his keen intelligence and a fresh outlook have produced some startling solutions, but these are always a result, never a deliberate attempt to attract attention. Personally the man is completely unassuming, entirely absorbed in what he happens to be doing. He has certain peculiarities, to be sure; he likes exercise, is interested in sanitation, wears no hat, approves of America, and lives all year round on a houseboat on the Seine. But in Paris, where personal idiosyncrasies are generally accepted without comment, no measure of Beaudoin's reputation can be laid to his habits.

The open-air school in Suresnes is a particularly interesting piece of work; it fascinated Beaudouin, who has strong convictions on the subject of architecture as an instrument for social betterment. The school was built for children who were physically under par, but not actually sick, and occupies a wooded slope facing the south and a view of Paris. Beaudouin put his large building on the northern boundary to break the wind, creating in effect a glorified sun-trap. The large building is entirely glass on the south side, and sliding windows allow the classrooms to be opened to the air. A separate octagonal building houses the kindergar-

The purpose of the group needs no description. Open to sun and air, protected from north winds, the school suits its purpose with maximum efficiency and minimum complication.

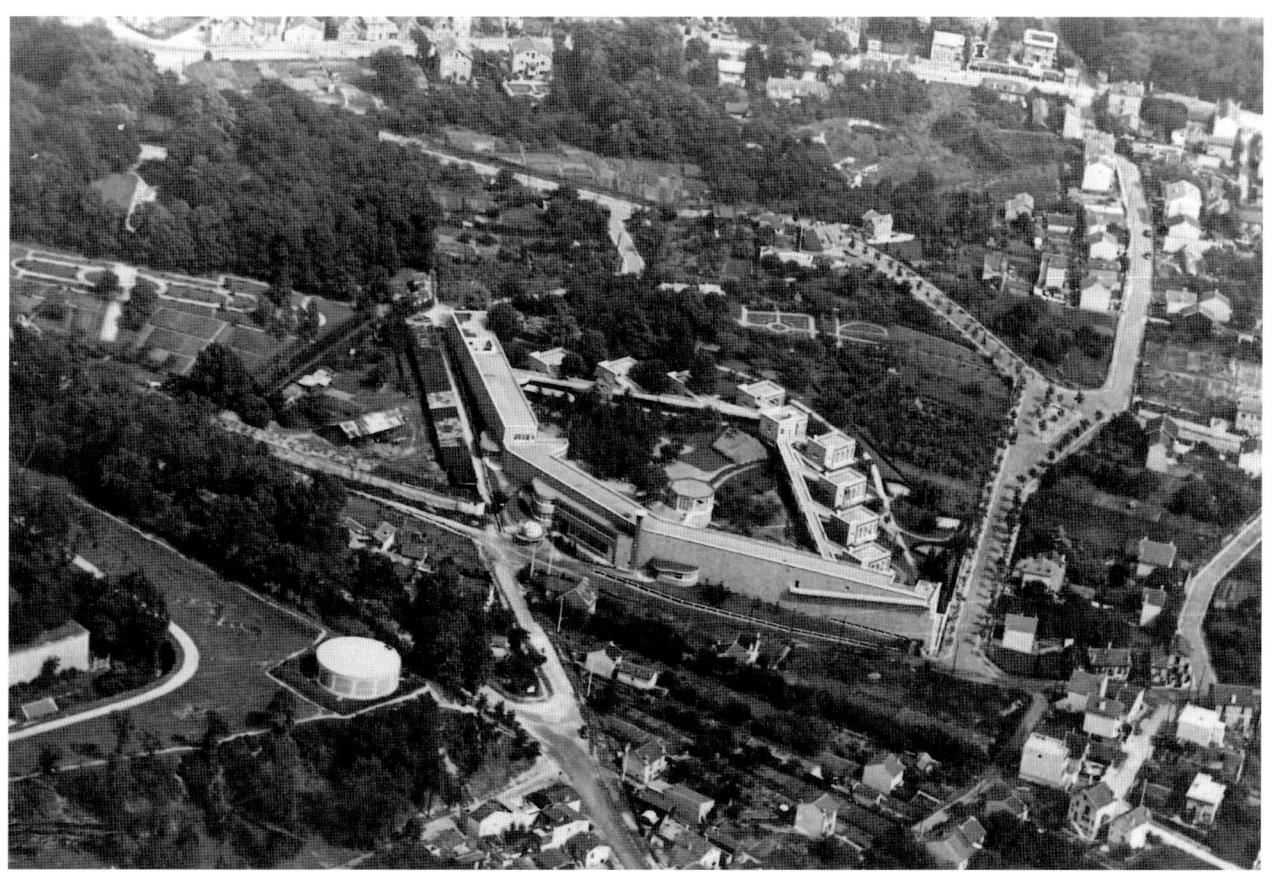

EUGÈNE BEAUDOUIN

Functional architecture in one of its finest expressions, the open-air school at Suresnes derives its undeniable architectural quality from harmonious use of simple materials and effectively repeated elements.

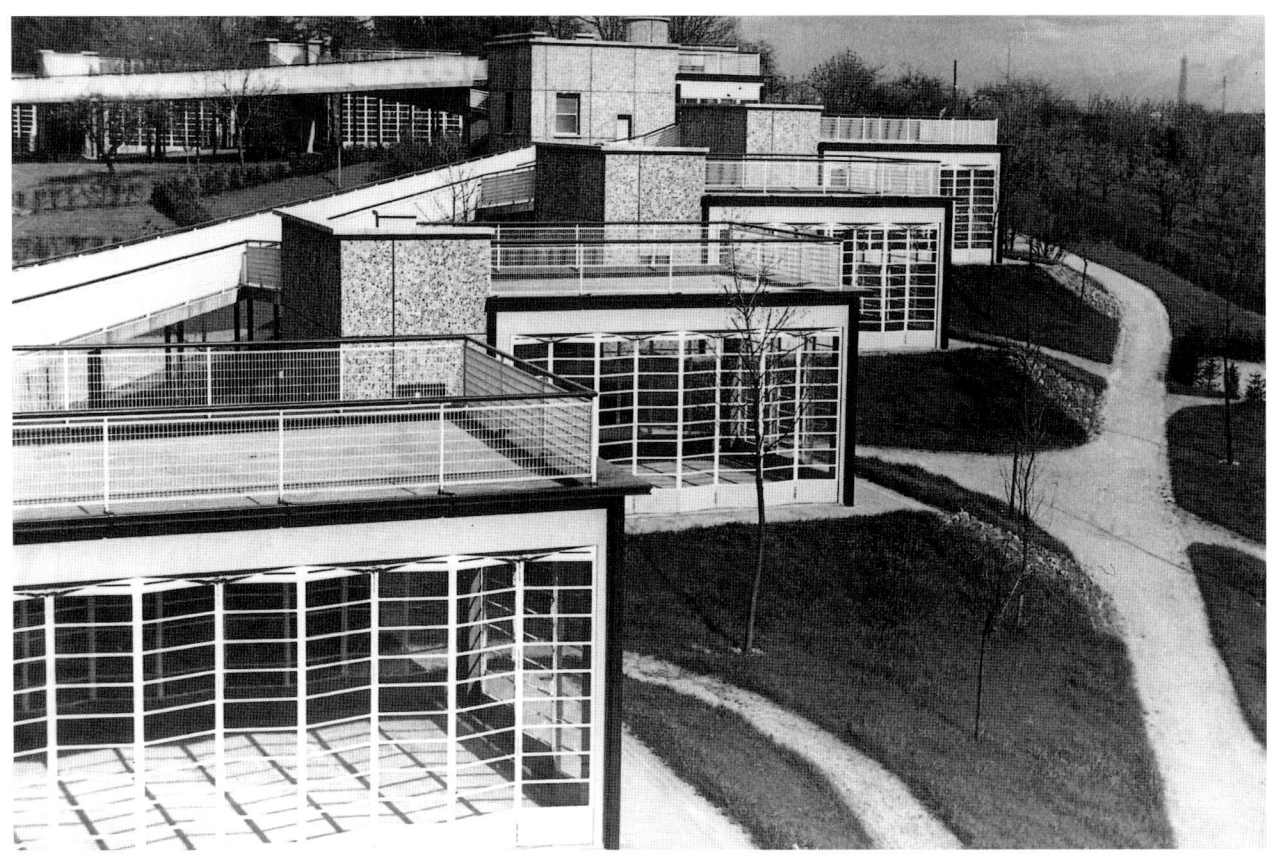

PORTRAITS

ten; here the eight windows drop into pockets, leaving only posts and a roof. From each end of the large building runs a covered passage, off which are classrooms. These also present a blank wall to the north, opening on the remaining three sides. Above the classrooms are terraces where the children can rest and take sunbaths. After the preliminary studies Beaudouin laid out the proposed group on the site, in order to spare as many trees as possible; so loose was his plan that only about a dozen out of several hundred had to be cut down. Among the trees he set a series of clearings; these, in good weather, are used as classrooms, and he even went so far as to design the furniture so that the children could carry it without difficulty.

Architecturally the school is most satisfactory; it has a grace and lightness entirely in accord with the means employed to produce it, and its chief charm lies in the fact that it looks exactly like what it is. Technically the building is a marvel of ingenuity; difficult problems of heating, construction, and the design of equipment such as the special doors and windows were all worked out with patience, intelligence, and a complete disregard of cost to the architect. He even eliminated all stairs, substituting gently sloping ramps to remove another possible source of danger to the children. He has since had schools to do—and small wonder!

Drancy was another departure, this time of a different nature. A factory suburb of Paris, Drancy grew at a great rate of speed—from six thousand in 1918 to forty-two thousand at the present time. Its growth was uncontrolled, and as a result the town now can boast some of the choicest slums in Europe. The problem that faced Beaudouin was the usual one of redistributing the population of a congested town, but it had a special twist: only twenty-seven acres were available for the accommodation of twelve thousand families. Had the usual two-story dwellings been erected it would have meant the creation of another slum area; had a uniform limit of five stories been set, recreational space would still have been inadequate and the appearance of the group far from inspiring. Beaudouin reviewed all of these unsatisfactory possibilities, and then, taking the bull by the horns as usual, he pushed five of his units up to fifteen stories, redistributing the rest in the usual low buildings. Criticism was later made of this separation of the high dwellings into five units, but Beaudouin knew, from a careful study of preliminary models, that this was the only way to assure sunlight for the group. The same system of light steel and precast concrete units was used here that had been employed at Bagneux, resulting here in a saving of 20 percent over conventional structural methods, and this saving was put into equipment and interior finish. Rents range from $65 to $165 a year—not bad for skyscraper apartments! With one of the finest housing developments in Europe in their midst, the slum-dwellers of Drancy are not happy, however. The towers are too high, too clean, too much like New York. Whether they will learn to like them or not remains to be seen. In the meantime, Walter Gropius has given the project his most enthusiastic

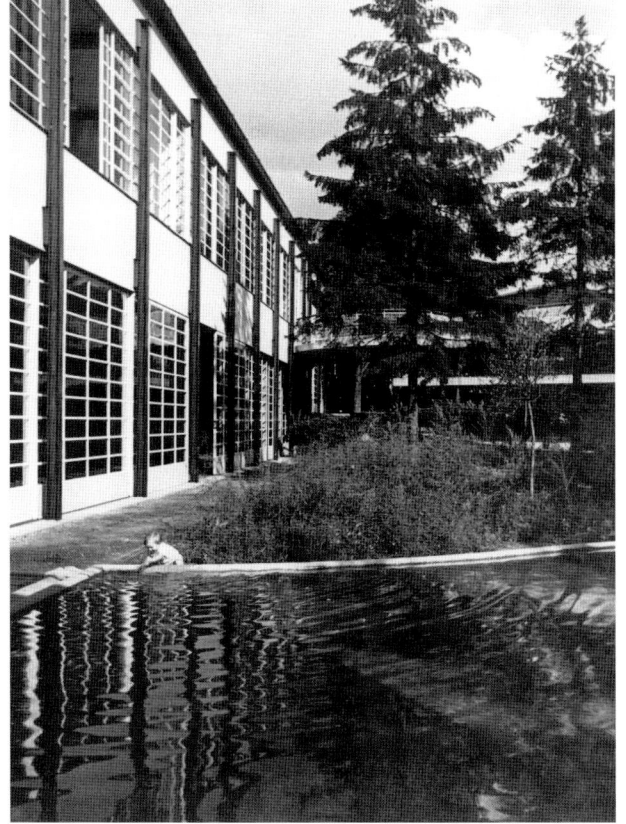

The open-air school at Suresnes, where sliding windows allow classrooms to be opened to the air.

commendation, architects from all over have come to see it, and Beaudouin and his associates find themselves experts on housing as well as schools.

Other work came to the office, although not on such a grand scale, and they did a number of large competitions as well. Among these was a competition for a large hospital group at Lille, which he won. Beaudouin's summary of the problem and his solution is a masterly piece of straight thinking, and it was typical of him that he continually emphasized the importance of hospitals as social functions. A hospital is a monument, a machine with a definite psychological effect on its inmates–these things Beaudouin took as granted and solved the problems they presented. But the important thing is that it is a necessary part of the social organism; for a prosperous young Frenchman, Beaudouin gets very close to the communist ideal at times. Few architects have a stronger sense of architecture as a living part of society; it is not accident that his work has a corresponding vitality. Incidentally, it was quite characteristic of the way his office works that they spent so much studying the problem as to use up all the prize money.

All of Beaudouin's competitions and executed works are of absorbing interest. But in none of them did he make so magnificent a gesture as his project for an exposition hall in Paris. The program was given out by a group similar to the Steel Institute in America, and required that a hall, rectangular in shape and with a flat ceiling, be designed to cover a thirty-acre plot without any intermediate support. This was a sort of thing Beaudouin loves, and he threw himself completely into it. All possible variations were studied, all means of spanning the huge space were investigated, and when he got through he wasn't satisfied with any of them. A steel truss 800 or 1,000 feet in length had to be colossal, and most of its tremendous weight was effective near the center of the span rather than at the supports, a situation demanding a most wasteful use of the material. Beaudouin's studies finally led him to the conclusion that the most logical thing to do would be to use the steel in tension, and he finally arrived at a fantastic result—a ring 1,200 feet in diameter, with cables stretching to another small ring in the center. He knew that the design would be thrown out of the competition, because the program required a rectangular hall, but by this time he was more interested in the problem than in winning the competition, so he went ahead, had a model constructed, figured the steel and all details of construction and equipment with engineers, and worked out the surrounding area to take care of existing roads and to provide for the influx of traffic such an edifice would attract. The design was thrown H. C., as he had expected, but it caused a sensation. The jury of award had no choice in the matter, of course, but Beaudouin and his associates were quite unanimously applauded for having so deliberately departed from the too inflexible program.

At present he is busy with the coming World's Fair, as are many other architects. His sketches for a treatment of the waterfront . . . are lovely, sensitive drawings, recalling forcibly the rich vein of fantasy that is part of Beaudouin's make-up, a part which has found little direct expression in the severely utilitarian buildings which have made up the bulk of his practice. What will come after the Fair remains to be seen. Probably more houses and more schools—but it is not likely that he will settle down and become a specialist. In the meantime, he admits, life is very pleasant. His office has become imbued with his own ideals, and in it he is just one of a group at work. Lods, while somewhat overshadowed by his partner's brilliance, is no silent member of the firm; Bocquillon works out models of everything as studies progress; Henrot, another draftsman, photographs them in his spare time; and Paul Herbé, of the famous trip to Ispahan, does much of the designing with Beaudouin. When work is rushed Beaudouin wears himself to a frazzle, and when it is over goes away on a long trip, usually managing to collect more ideas, more sketches of town plans, and more photographs of exciting buildings. One of his trips took him to America a short time ago. His comments, when he came back, covered everything from mass production to New England cemeteries, and were penetrating and objective—and singularly fair. Beaudouin accepts good where he finds it; his only aim is to produce fine architecture, and success has not diminished his fresh outlook. He is the youngest of the architects who have appeared in this series; there is no indication that he will ever grow old.

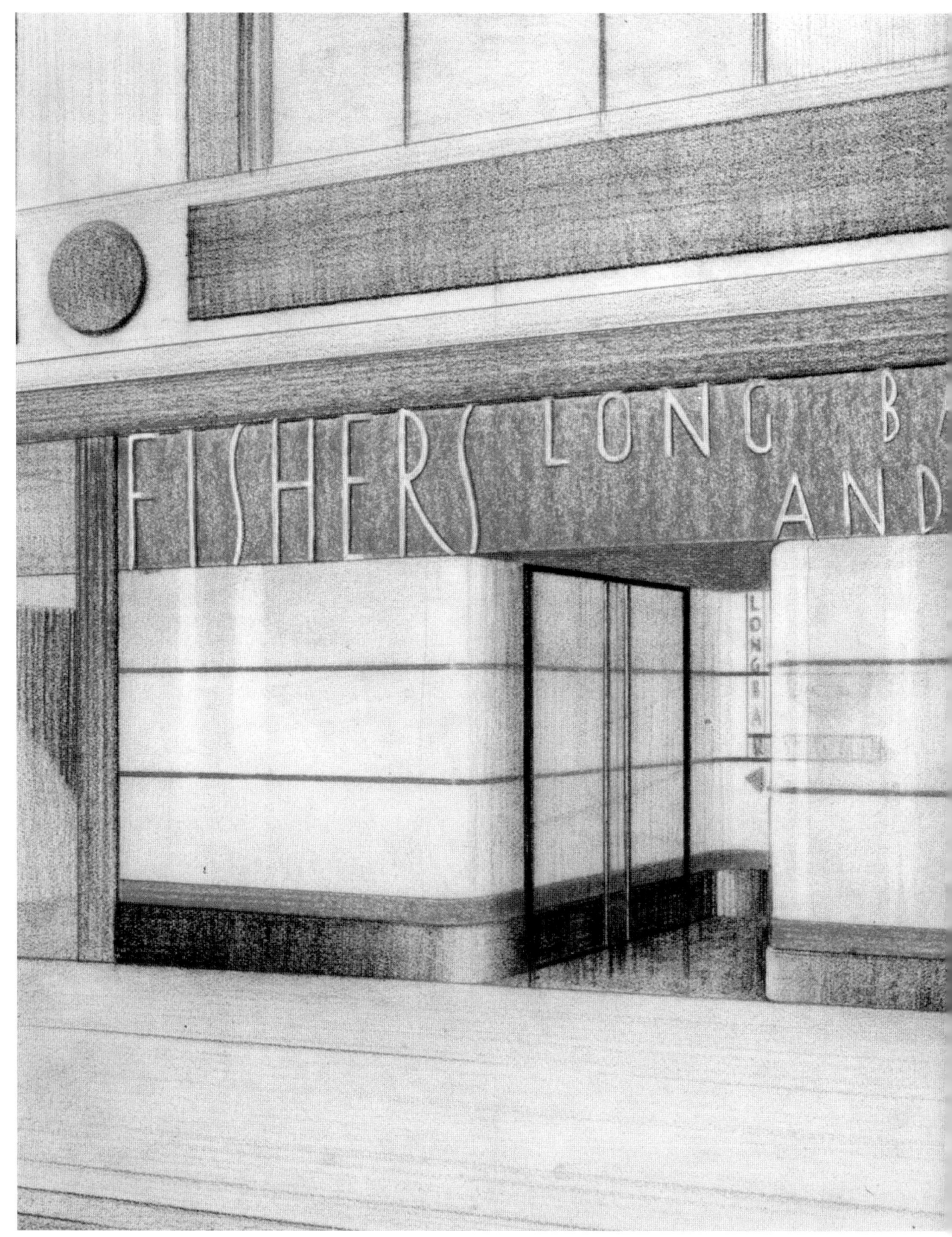

RAYMOND McGRATH
ENGLAND

FROM
PENCIL POINTS
JUNE 1936

Ten years ago Raymond McGrath arrived in London, just another student on a traveling fellowship; today at the age of thirty-three he is one of the most successful of the younger English architects. While McGrath objects strenuously to the word "modern"–"It is an abused word used to mean almost anything by the present race of critics," he says–in his own case it is a particularly apt designation. McGrath as an architect–a designer of complete buildings–is beyond question admirably qualified to undertake important commissions of this nature, and his chief interest, self-confessed, is in planning; yet the main portion of the work he has executed up to the present time has not been buildings. He has done fabrics, floor coverings, interiors, industrial design, furniture, and even the interior of an airplane. While this is doubtless to some extent the result of a strong personal leaning, it is also a very clear indication of the broad field that lies open before the young architect today. If the architect could get away from the specialization that has characterized the profession in recent years, if he could once more set out confidently as the universal designer, if he could correlate all of his experience in handling form with his training in the matter of logically combining and expressing complicated functions, he would fill an extremely important place that no one at the present time is better qualified to occupy.

A trend certainly exists. It is not new: it might be said to have begun when William Morris found that there was no available furniture good enough to put into the house Philip Webb built for him and designed his own, thereby starting something that is only now coming to a head. This does not apply only to the designing of slick gadgets for the carriage trade. Take the small house, now the subject of so much discussion. The majority of the men now engaged in the design of small houses are architects who have been forced into it because there is no larger work to do. While a certain rise in the standard of taste and planning is perceptible as a result of this professional participation in a formerly neglected field, the small house is still in a lamentable condition. And as long as architects continue to approach the small house as an exercise in aesthetic expression rather than an economic problem it will remain that way–at least as far as the results of their efforts are concerned. Even such distinguished professionals as Neutra and Wurster in California, who are doing so much–in quite dissimilar ways–to arrive at an indigenous domestic architecture, are only scratching the surface of a problem whose roots wind through the entire economic and industrial structure of the country. The small house costs too much for the man who needs it most, and until men see this problem as basic rather than aesthetic–and the industrialists are quite as shortsighted in their approach as the architects–there will be no solution; or industry in cooperation with architects who know what they are up against will find a solution, and then there won't be any more small house architects. For such a task and others like it, men with a training like that of McGrath will be best fitted. It is no accident that he has

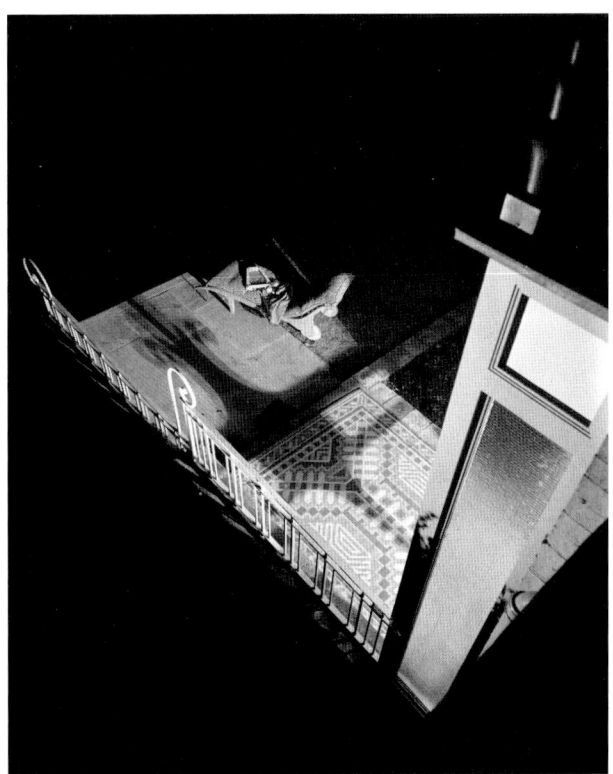

View of "Finella," an old house in Cambridge whose remodeling was McGrath's first commission. It had great influence in stimulating interest in modern design among his contemporaries.

been interesting himself in prefabrication of late.

McGrath is an Australian by birth, and his first architectural recollections are that of the Macquarie buildings designed by Francis Greenway, an English architect who was sent down for fourteen years in 1814 because he was unable to pay his debts. Greenway's buildings were fine and simple, with much of the quality of the great work of the preceding century. So the first influence on McGrath was a good one. His interests, however, were literary, not architectural, and he won the University Medal for English Verse three years in succession. He later turned to etching, wood-engraving, and book printing, but it was a study of an imaginary colonial settlement whose architecture he described and drew that prompted the then professor of English to suggest that he transfer to the department of architecture. After this change, he realized that he had finally found himself, and the literary career was abandoned. The work done in this preparatory period, however, was not wasted and later stood him in good stead. In the meantime he concentrated on architecture, finally winning a traveling fellowship, which fortunately had no restrictions, and in 1926 he arrived in London.

London did not seem very promising architecturally, nor did Oxford, and upon examining the Beaux-Arts he "was dismayed by the prospects." It is hard to realize that so short a time ago there was no modern work of any significance being done in England. The Period architects were in complete control of the situation, and the prospects for a young man with new ideas was dis-

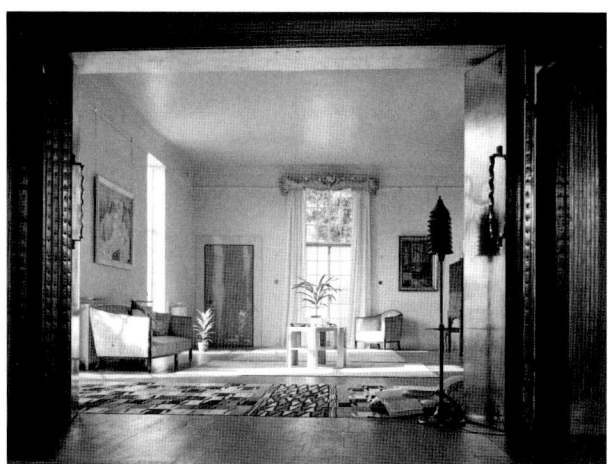

Interior views of "Finella."

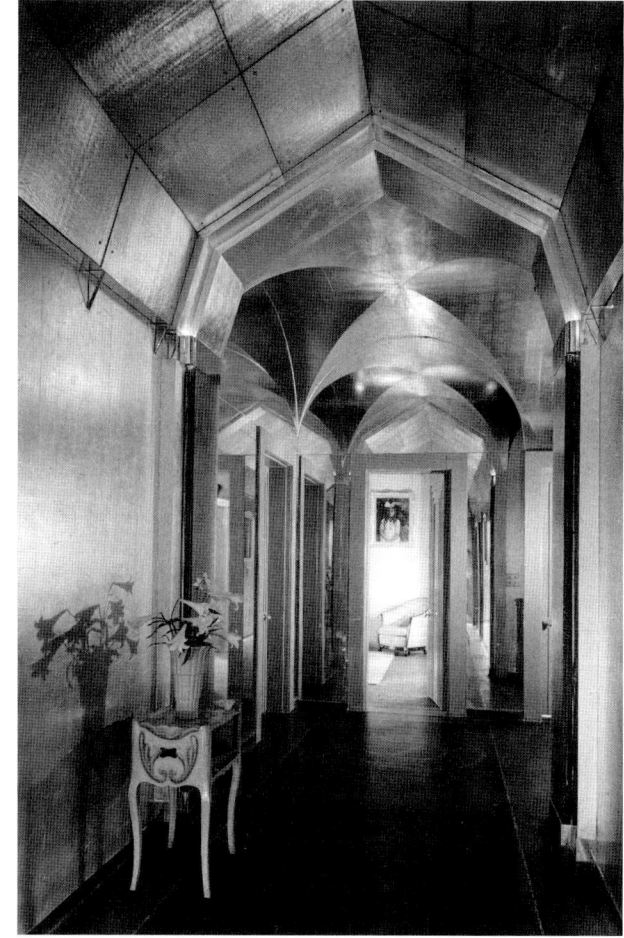

couraging in the extreme. On the verge of abandoning architecture as a profession, he met Mansfield Forbes, a remarkable personality, then Fellow of Clare College. Forbes had an extraordinary range of interests and a great gift for attracting people to him, and his rare intuition enabled him to put those who came to him on the right track. As a result of the meeting McGrath went to Clare College to do research on "Modern Entertainment Architecture" for three years. During this time he saw little of the faculty of architecture and a great deal of Forbes. Out of this stimulating friendship came his first commission, "Finella," a complete remodeling of Forbes' Victorian villa, and one of the first examples of modern interior design in England

The house was about eighty years old and in poor condition. Under McGrath's hands it underwent a complete transformation. Much glass, gold leaf, and many modern machine-made materials were introduced. The house is frankly experimental in design as well as materials. The aluminum foil, pink plaster, indirect lighting, cut-glass fountain, and so on were not intended to be the ultimate expression of any fixed ideas, but rather a searching for an atmosphere more in harmony with present-day living. Upon completion it became the natural meeting place for Forbes' large circle of friends, and in it the younger group of designers found their first encouragement. The house made something of a sensation; nothing in England had been seen that was even remotely like it. It is hard to realize in the light of today's developments in England that "Finella," which played an important part in starting off the new movement, is barely eight years old.

The "Finella" experiment had important repercussions. For one thing, it brought McGrath into contact with all of the younger men who were just starting out on similar careers, such as Wells Coates, [Serge] Chermayeff, Connell, and others. These formed the Twentieth Century Group, sponsored by Mansfield Forbes, and the first meeting took place in 1930. The object was to encourage good contemporary design, and the immediate aim was to organize an exhibition of modern art in London, something which was badly needed. The group never brought it off, but when the first exhibition was opened in 1933 many of the original members of the group were already actively at work.

Thousands of people flocked to Cambridge to see "Finella," and it was inevitable, particularly since there were so few men doing modern design, that the resulting publicity should bring more work. It did. Almost immediately afterwards McGrath was appointed Decoration Consultant to the British Broadcasting Corporation, and began work on its new studios in London. Two members of the Twentieth Century Group, Serge Chermayeff and Welles Coates, were chosen to collaborate with him. The three produced twenty-two studios for the company. All were animated by the same desires and ideals and, with the unifying and energizing influence of Forbes in the background, the success of the collaboration was inevitable. McGrath had, and still has, an overwhelming desire to make known the great possibilities of modern design. The ambition has always come before his personal aspirations. He was therefore delighted by the chance to bring in other men who shared his convictions, [remarking] with obvious pleasure that "the team spirit that produced these studios was something new in postwar English architectural design." And what pleased him most of all about the broadcasting studios was that with so many people seeing them constantly there was bound to be a strong influence and a very salutary effect.

The studios, like "Finella," were quite unlike anything ever seen before. The original practice had been to take a room and install the necessary acoustical materials, relying on entirely extraneous matter for the "architectural effect." McGrath and the others started with the acoustical requirements, organized the materials, and, by virtue of this organization, created a beautiful interior. In other words, by such a procedure the functional becomes the decorative as well, and there is no confusion as to the essential character of the room. In this work they set a precedent that has been widely followed, as in the new studios for the Columbia Broadcasting Company, and they demonstrated unmistakably that the new materials, originally conceived of as exclusively utilitarian, had definite decorative possibilities if used frankly and with an understanding of their properties. This pioneering work had a great influence on contemporary design in England; it lessened the influence of the Period architects and encouraged the young men. So strong has the movement be-

The orchestral studio in the station at Manchester. A carpeted floor is laid up in squares to facilitate placing instruments for sound control. Radiator grilles are black Bakelite tubing.

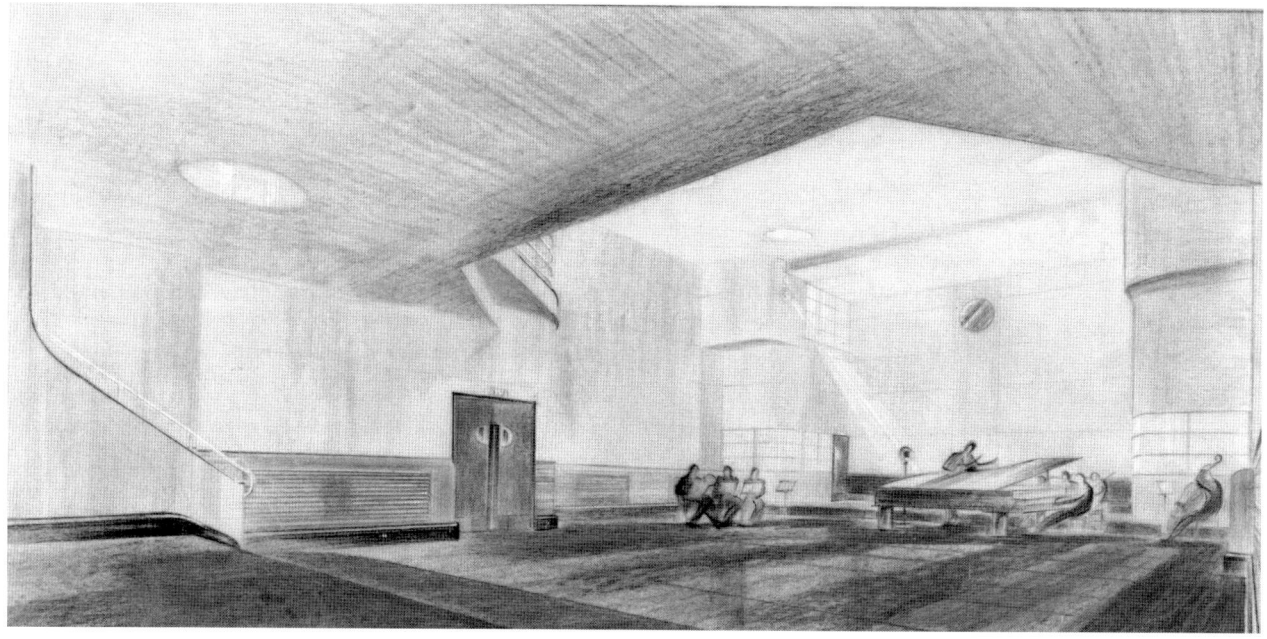

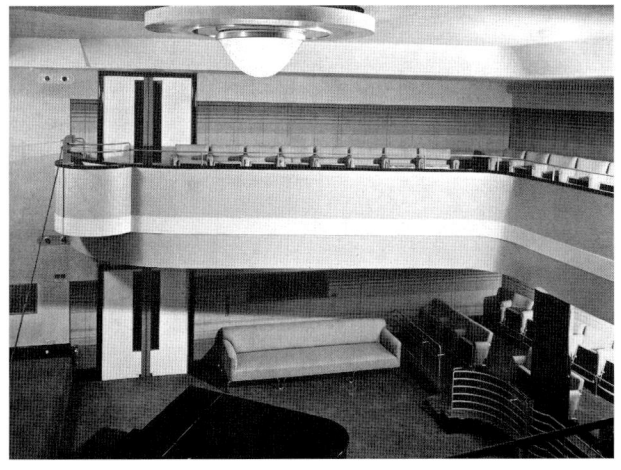

The vaudeville studio in Broadcasting House, London. One of the first studio interiors to show an intelligent and consistent use of the necessary acoustical materials for decorative effect.

come that today a majority of the work appearing in the British architectural publications is definitely modern in character.

McGrath is a mild, very agreeable person whose impatience with the slowness of the change in architecture frequently carries him away. "Why," he asks, "must our buildings always remain twenty years behind what we are capable of doing?" He knows the answer, of course, but, being keenly alive to all new developments and possessing a strongly inquisitive and forward-looking mind, he forgets that most people are not even aware of this cultural and technical lag, to say nothing of doing anything about it. His distaste for Period architecture is monumental. His list of the states of mind which distinguish the enthusiast for Period architecture omits nothing: "Stagnating conservatism, lack of creative imagination, sentimentality, respectability, snobbery, laziness." The tendency "to play safe under all circumstances" infuriates him. There is no direction to go but forward. It is not surprising, therefore, that he has done much besides design in his attempts to change the existing situation.

"Propaganda of the right sort," he has frequently remarked, "is necessary for the dissemination of fresh ideas." So, in addition to serving on many committees for the Royal Institute of British Architects, the Board of Trade's Council for Art and Industry, and others, he has frequently made use of his not inconsiderable literary gifts. *Twentieth Century Houses,* one of the best books that has yet appeared on the subject of the small house, is frankly propaganda, of a very reasoned sort, enlivened by a dry wit and a quiet but devastating irony. Another book, now in preparation, *Glass in Architecture and Decoration,* is of a more obviously technical nature, but it also has as its purpose the spreading of information on one of the most adaptable of materials in the hope that others will be encouraged to carry on further experiments.

In his own work there is certainly no indication of any attempts to play safe. He now has under construction a house of reinforced concrete, circular in form, with a pie-shaped wedge taken out of the upper floor to allow the placing of a sun deck. The advantages of such a form are not apparent, but the attempt shows a searching curiosity and the courage to find out. An even more curious project was a house he never built, "Rudderbar," designed for a woman whose main interest was aviation, and equipped with a hangar as well as a garage. It was to be a steel frame construction with a special mosaic facing, all organized for quick construction. The idea was that the aviatrix was to take off on an attempt to break the world's endurance record for solo flight, and that the house was to be then put together with the greatest possible speed so that when she finally came down she would find it finished and ready for her. The idea sounds fantastic but there is more than a grain of sense in it. It is a pity that the job never went ahead. It would have been interesting to see what happened.

McGrath's practice has been spreading steadily in the intervening years, and, in addition to private houses,

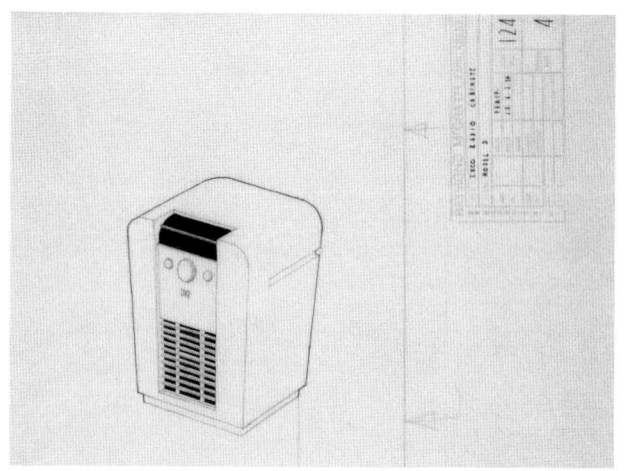

he has designed radio cabinets, motor oil equipment, oven glassware, and fabrics. He likes the variety of such commissions, and considers it "fortunate that the architect's range allows him to encompass the most minute requirements of industry." In other words, McGrath, by his initiative, has taken the position which is occupied in America by the industrial designer. This is an opportunity that has been passed up here, to the great detriment of the architectural profession, because one of the best ways to find out what present-day technical knowledge can do for the small house is to work with manufacturers and learn how and under what conditions they operate. That the architect could take care of such work is demonstrated not only by the career of Raymond McGrath but by the fact that the key men working for industrial designers today are architects.

The finish and completeness of such interiors as Fischer's Restaurant are due in large part to the broad designing experience McGrath has had. When he wants a floor or wall covering to serve a special purpose, he designs it; there is never the handicap imposed upon architects who feel that their designing ends with the building. More and more men are realizing the advantages of this control of the entire design by one individual, and it is significant that the best metal furniture, wood furniture, and similar accessories have been designed by architects who had no fear of straying from a narrow path.

With this lesson to be gained from his work, McGrath assumes an importance all out of proportion to the actual value or extent of the work itself. This is not to belittle what he has designed—quite the contrary. "Finella" today may look less fresh in spots than it did eight years ago, and better solutions of many of the problems have since been found, but McGrath's development has more than kept pace with the times so that his latest work has a simplicity and ordered quality that is impressive. He is unquestionably entitled to be considered one of the leaders of his profession in England, in spite of his comparative youth, not only because of what he has done himself, but because he inspired so many others and started so many things that have materially contributed to contemporary English architecture. His career has only started, and there is still plenty of pioneering to be done, plenty of "propaganda" as well. And not only in England. Our own young architects might look far before finding another man whose work sets so valuable an example.

opposite:
Ecko radio cabinet, a good example of the simplification of form possible in equipment of this type, which is quite architectural.

below:
Exterior drawing of Fischer's Restaurant in London.

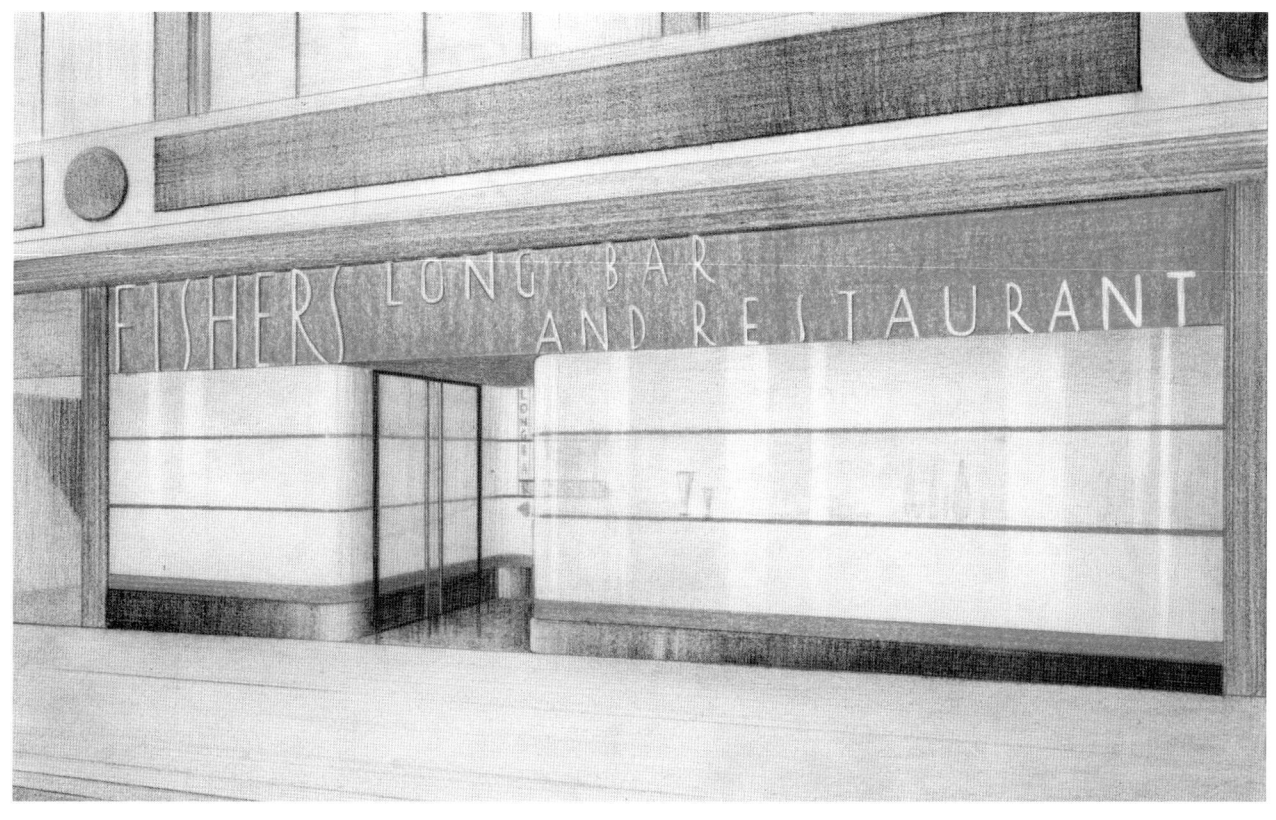

Fischer's Restaurant, a distinguished and unusual interior in which wall coverings, furnishings, and accessories were designed by the architect to create a harmonious ensemble.

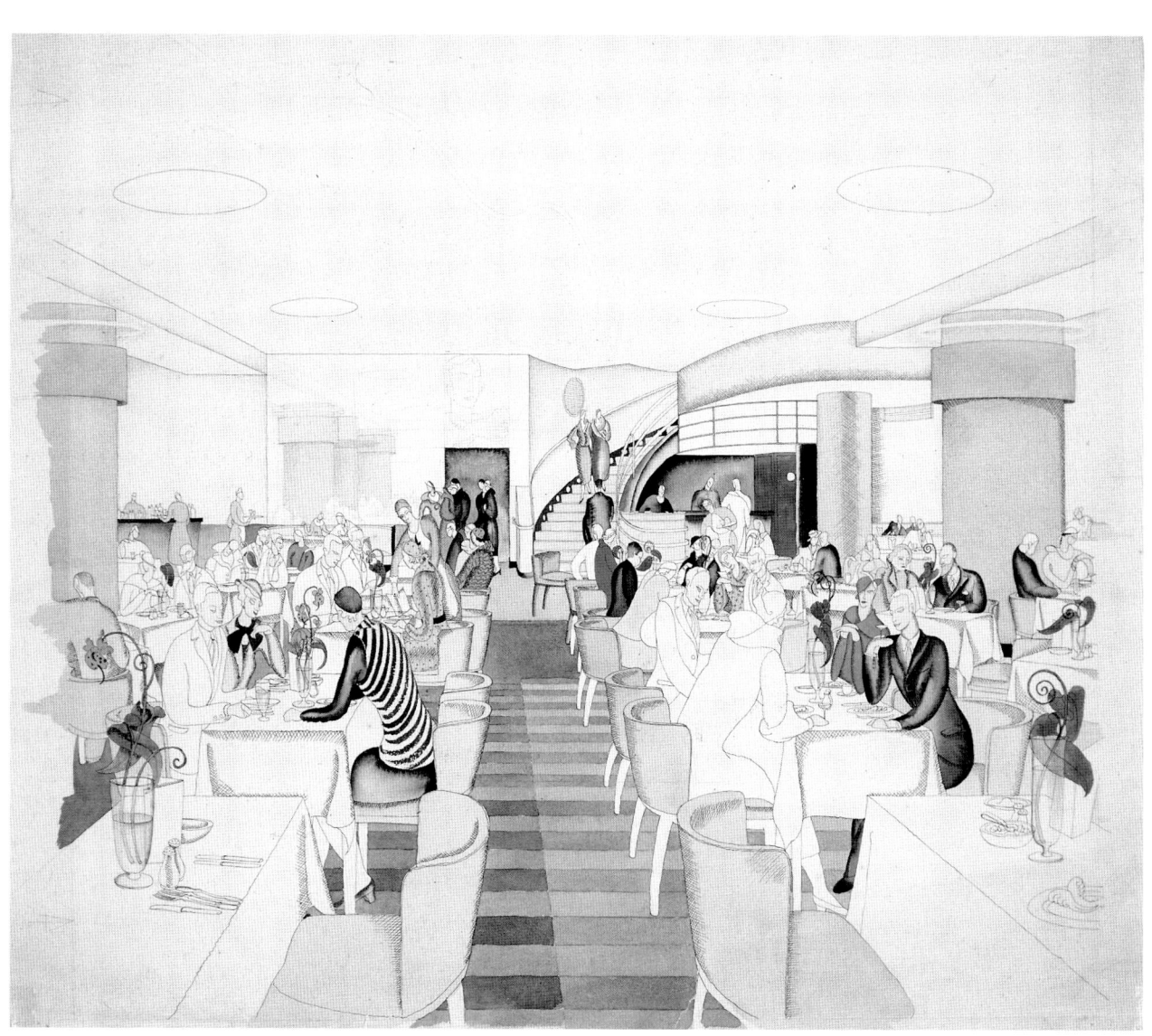

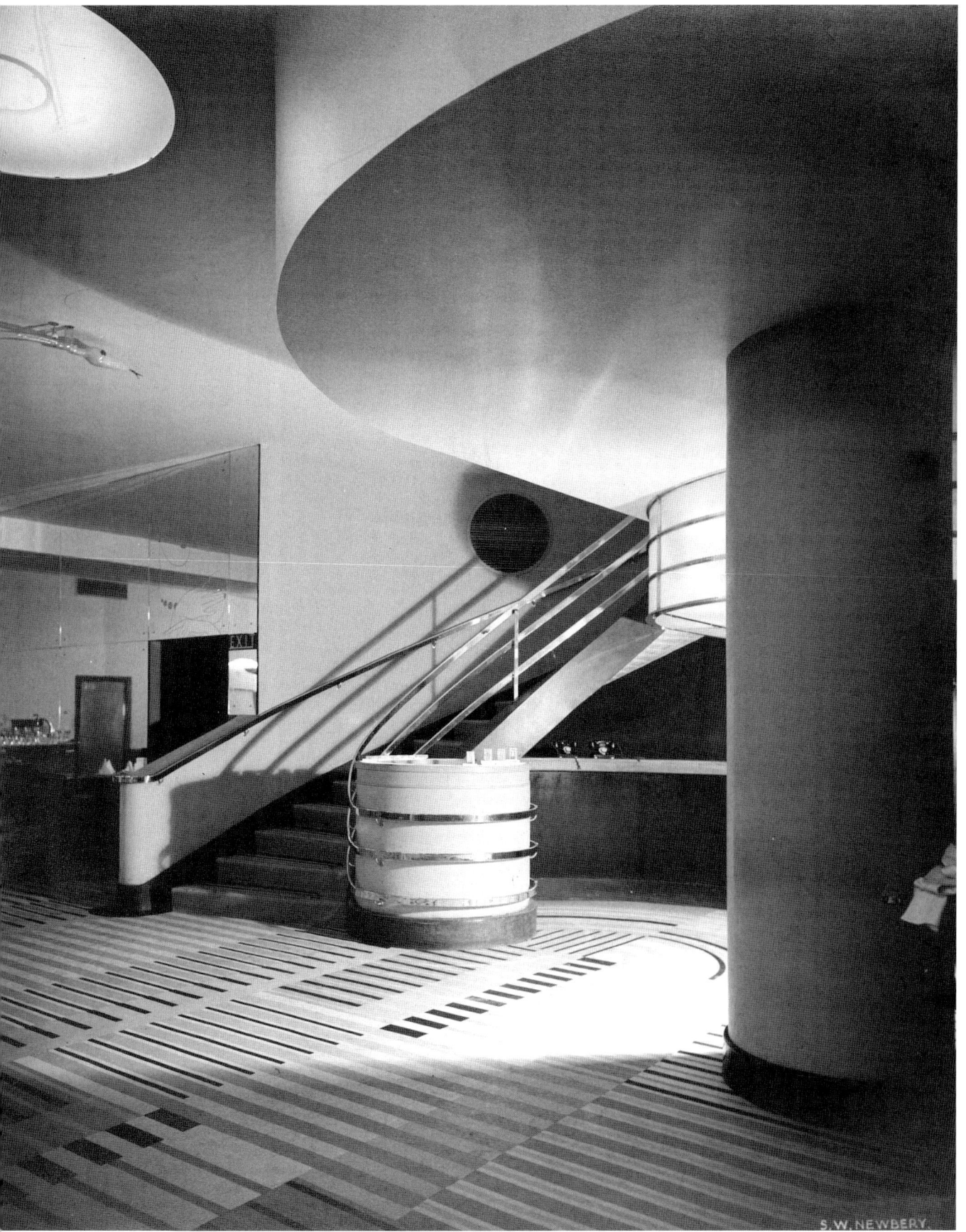

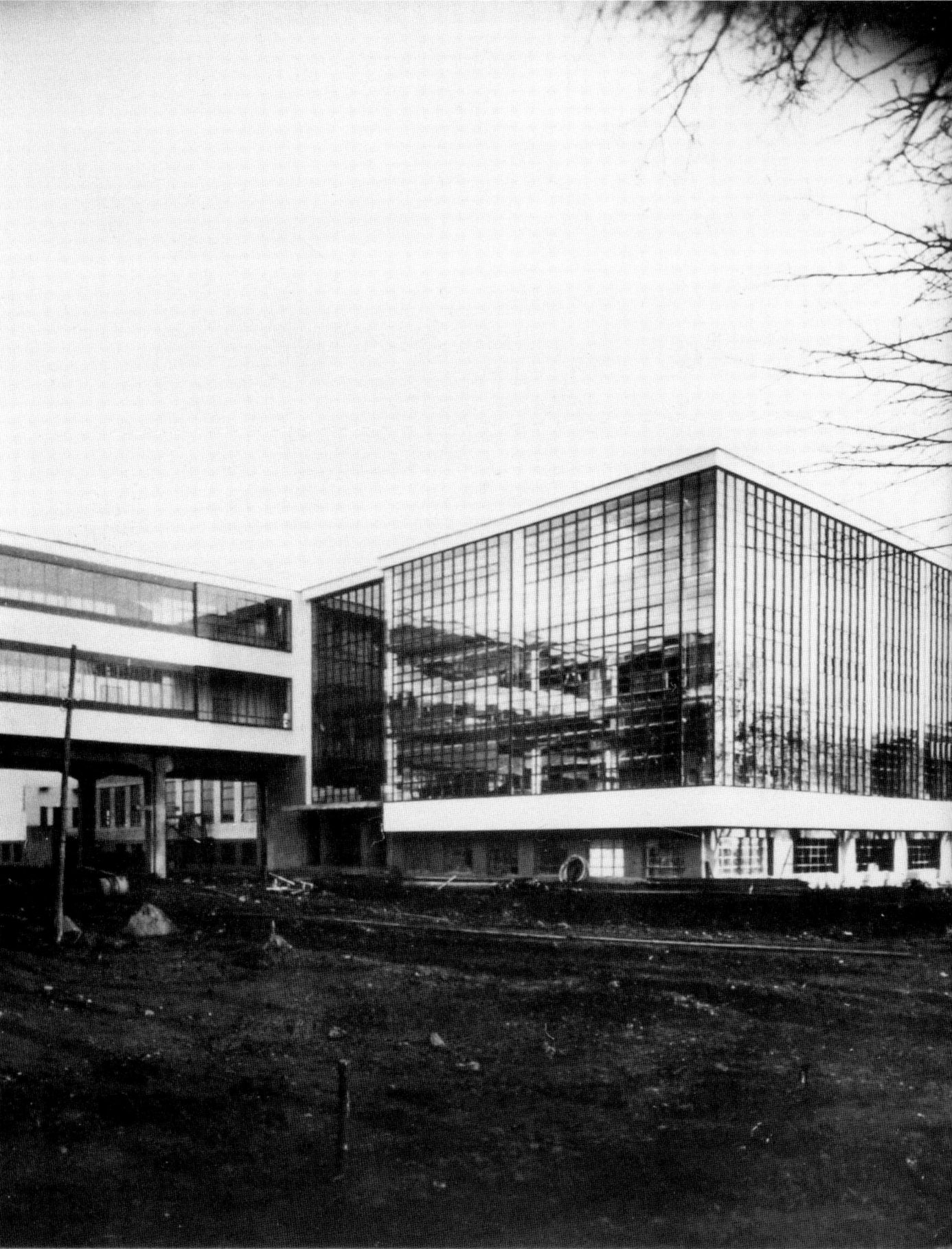

WALTER GROPIUS
GERMANY

FROM
PENCIL POINTS
AUGUST 1936

below:
The Fagus Factory, first of Gropius' pioneering works. It looks like a factory. This, in 1909, was an achievement possible only to an originator.

opposite:
The Hall of Industry at the Werkbund Exposition in Cologne. Its brilliant use of glass is notable.

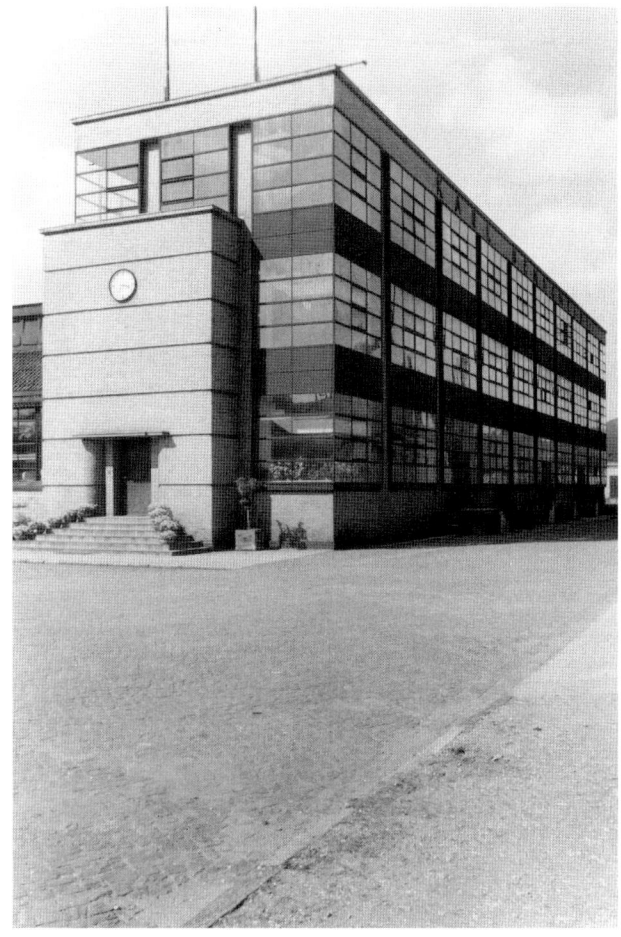

As this series progresses its title becomes increasingly inadequate. "Architect" was no accurate title for Gio Ponti, whose work in ceramic design and painting is quite as important as his buildings. Raymond McGrath, we have seen, has occupied himself almost entirely with interiors and industrial design. Others have shown equal indifference to the conventional boundaries of their profession. In the case of Walter Gropius it becomes again necessary to define a word whose meaning has shrunk during the past century to finally designate an elegant professional whose "artistic" training fitted him admirably for the task of transforming banks into Roman temples, and similarly useful activities. It is not so much that Gropius has digressed from his chosen field as that he has so broadened the concept of the architect's function. The architect is a coordinator, concerned with the economic and social aspects of building as well as the merely technical and formal problems that arise; and by "building" he means not only isolated structures, but the street, town, region, nation. The best illustration of this definition is Gropius' own career.

Born in 1883 to a Prussian family whose members included architects and builders, Gropius' choice of a profession was determined almost from birth. His formal education began at the Technische Hochschule in Berlin-Charlottenburg, where the curriculum so irked him that he left and went to Munich. Even at an early age he seems to have had definite ideas about educational methods. In 1906 he built his first buildings,

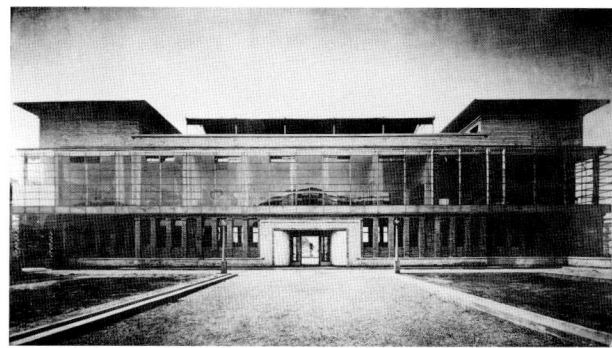

houses for workmen on his uncle's estate in Pomerania. For the next two years he traveled, working for a time in a pottery plant in Spain. His real education may be said to have begun in the office of Peter Behrens.

Behrens at this time was the greatest force in German architecture. He was one of the first to think of architecture as a problem in honest building, and Gropius freely acknowledges his debt to his master. It was here that he acquired the conviction that modern construction must be expressed in architecture and that this expression would result in unprecedented forms. This idea, in 1909, represented the first stirrings of consciousness of a new architecture in the making. It was not until after the cataclysm of 1914 that he fully realized the possibilities of this new architecture and the immensity of the task facing his generation, but by that time he had already produced two works which unmistakably revealed the quality of his thinking. The first was the well-known Fagus Factory, the second was the Hall of Machinery at the Werkbund Exposition.

Both of these buildings are great pioneering works and did much to establish Gropius' reputation. The story of how he obtained these commissions is of the greatest interest for the light it sheds on the caliber of this man whose mild, professional appearance is exceedingly deceptive. It was after he had been with Behrens for two years that Gropius got the urge to set up an office of his own, and in seeing a notice that an industrialist was planning to build a factory in Alfeld, Gropius immediately wrote to him and after a brief interview was given the commission. The Fagus building was one of the first factories which looked like a factory. It is a model of its kind.

A few years later, when the Deutsch Werkbund planned its exposition in Cologne, Gropius, as one of the younger members, was not invited to build anything. He bothered the director so much, however, that to get rid of him he was given charge of the industrial exhibition, for which he was allowed a sum so small that there was little danger, it was believed, of his disturbing anybody. But Gropius, who has never been able to see things in a small way, immediately drew up plans for an imposing hall of industry and made a tour of the Rhineland persuading industrial leaders that they should not only contribute materials for his building but give financial support. On his return he went to the burgomaster of Cologne with his plans and promises and was allowed to put up the building. This was one of Gropius' most characteristic exploits and does much to explain his phenomenal success.

It was after the war that Gropius entered on the most fruitful phase of his career. In Weimar, Henry Van de Velde, director of the Grand Ducal Art School, was preparing to retire, and he invited Gropius to take his place. Gropius accepted. His first act as director was to completely revise the curriculum and amalgamate the school with a local academy of fine arts, creating what became known as the Weimar Bauhaus. The Bauhaus gained worldwide fame after it moved to Dessau. The breach with conventional teaching methods, however, and the introduction of Gropius' fresh ideas had crystallized the form of the school before it left Weimar.

The philosophy behind the creation of the Bauhaus is of interest here because it is the philosophy of Gropius. When he became the director of the school he felt that there was a crying need for a type of training which would enable the student to gain a broad, unified view of art as something more than a collection of elaborately pigeonholed activities. The present separation of the arts and the specialized training which emphasizes this is vicious, in his opinion. Art was once a spontaneous manifestation, an integral part of the life of a people. It was when the academies came in that the decay of popular art began, leading to the present disrepute of the artist. The artist under the influence of the schools had been moving further and further from reality and had no point of contact with a developing industrial civilization. It was to develop a new type of designer familiar at the same time with the basic laws of design and with practical requirements of machine production that the Bauhaus was founded. *"A modern architectonic art,* all-embracing in its scope"—this was the goal of Gropius. It was one of the first healthy art ideas to appear in a long time.

The first period of the course lasted six months. The beginner was given elementary training in the handling of materials and tools, in geometry, drafting, and so forth. If at the end of this time the student was considered sufficiently promising he was admitted to the second course, which lasted three years and during which time he was bound as an apprentice by a written agreement with the local Trades Council. This, according to Gropius, was to discourage the entrance of amateurs who wished to get a smattering of some fashionable handicraft. Further weeding out was done before the student entered the final period, which dealt with structural instruction and consisted of alternation between manual work on actual buildings and theoretic training in the research department. At the end of this period, the length of which varied considerably, the student, if adjudged proficient, was given a Master-Builder's certificate by the Trades Council or by the Bauhaus itself.

Implicit in the idea of the Bauhaus was a revival of the old apprenticeship method which, in Gropius' estimation, is still the best kind of practical teaching. A synthetic method had to be set up because the old type of craftsmen no longer existed; so each student was given two teachers, one a trained technician, the other an artist. In this way it was hoped to avoid the dangers of the narrow, industrial outlook on the one hand and the "art for art's sake" idea on the other. The Bauhaus was never a school of arts and crafts. The point of the entire curriculum was to prepare the student for work on standardization.

In 1925 the Bauhaus moved to Dessau, and at this time the dual system of teaching was abandoned because, as Gropius had expected, it had produced a group of men in whom the viewpoints of artist and technician were successfully combined, and the best

below:
A corridor in the Bauhaus. It is in his larger work that Gropius' extreme simplicity appears to best advantage and attains a clean beauty.

right:
A view of the Bauhaus at Dessau, showing the student dormitory, and the main portion of the school in the background. Built in 1925, it was the first large truly modern building.

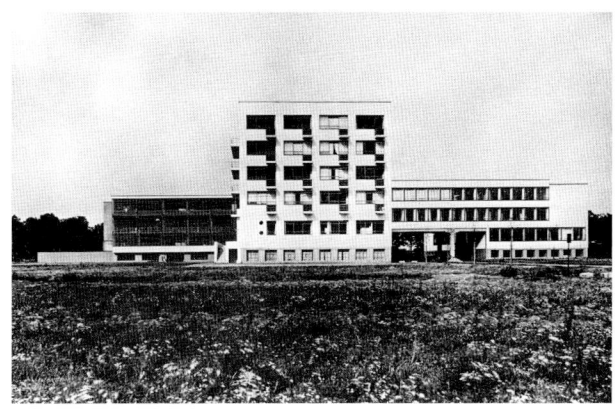

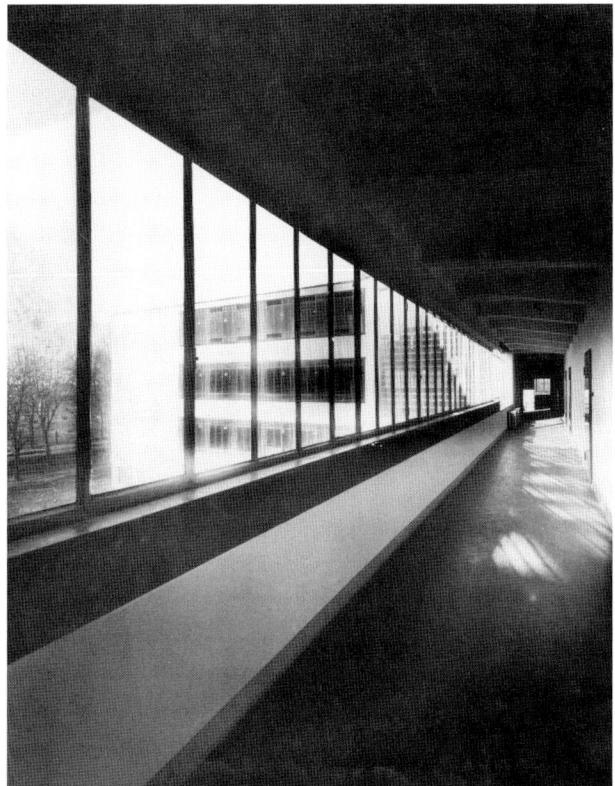

of these former students were taken into the faculty. When the Bauhaus moved, Gropius was commissioned by the town to design the new school building, several housing groups, stores, and an employment office. On this venture the entire body of students and faculty collaborated, with results that brilliantly demonstrated the essential soundness of the Bauhaus training. The school building was the greatest modern project up to that time and is the one with which Gropius is most frequently identified. Its completion marked the coming of age of a new architecture.

In 1928 Gropius resigned. He had created the Bauhaus and it was a success. German industry had begun to mass-produce Bauhaus models and to seek the school's collaboration in the design of new ones. Bauhaus students were teaching at home and abroad and occupying prominent positions in industrial concerns. The intellectual objective Gropius had set up was attained, and he saw no reason for delaying his return to private practice. Three years later the new government abolished the school. The gentlemen who held the reigns made the mistake—in their case quite understandable—of confusing art with politics.

The influence of this remarkable institution is continually increasing, and the changes in curriculum which are taking place in many of our schools of architecture are traceable to ideas Gropius put into practice in the 1920s.

On his return to private practice, Gropius automatically turned to the phase of architecture which interest-

below:
Bauhaus Building, Dessau, Werkstattenbau.

opposite:
The Sommerfeld Log House, interesting for its use of wood in a large modern residence; if not significant, it is nevertheless a most revealing piece of work and evidences Gropius' directness.

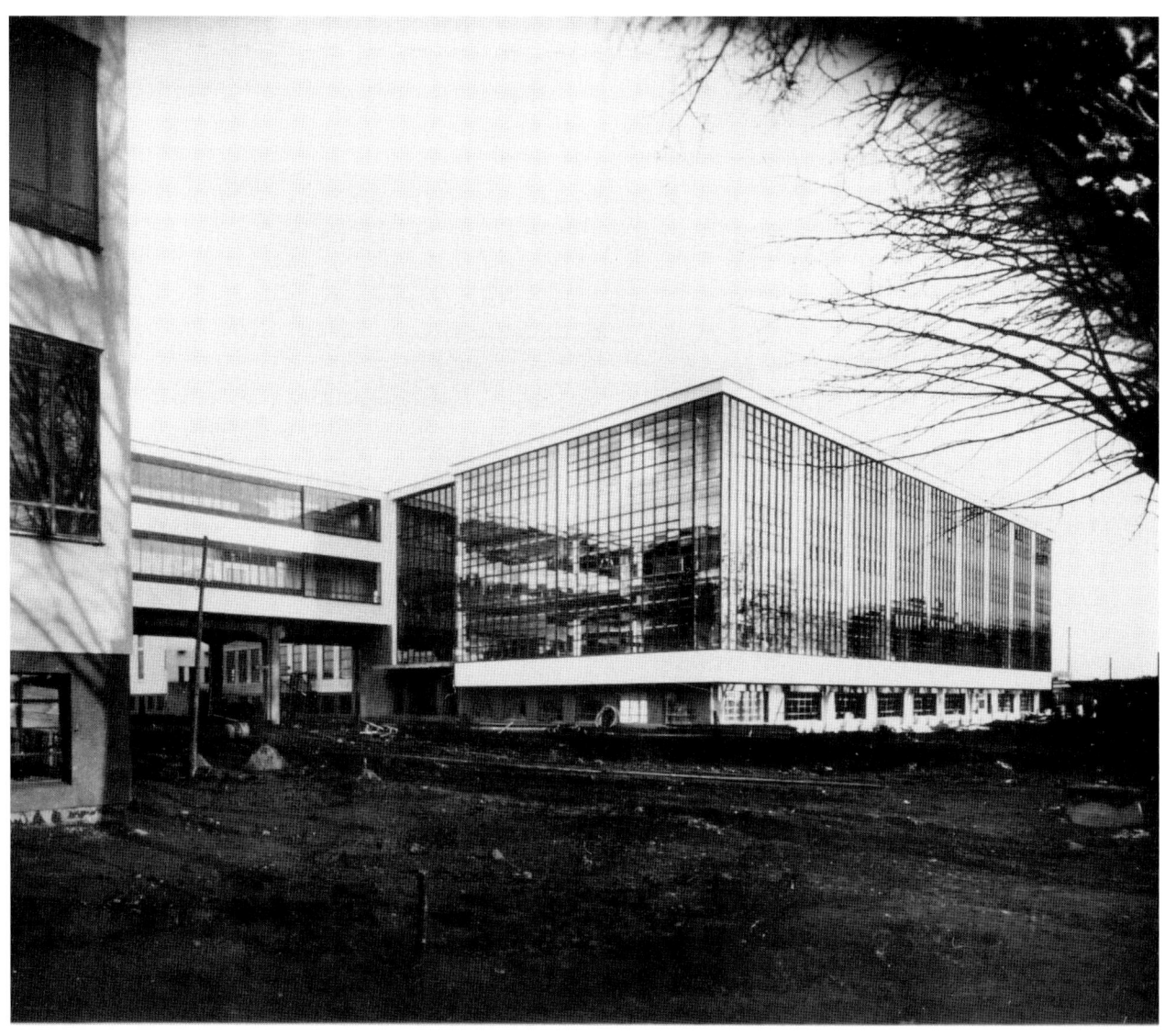

142

PORTRAITS

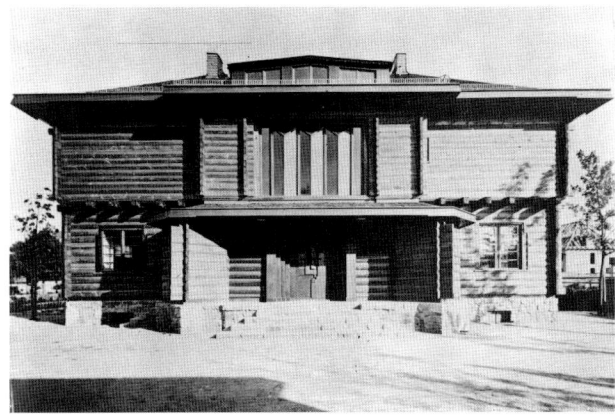

ed him most—housing. During the time he was in the Bauhaus he had taken active part in housing research and had initiated much of it. After he left he entered two competitions for the development of huge tracts of building land in Berlin and in Karlsruhe. He won both of them. Other work of a similar nature was given him at this time, of which the best known is the great Siemensstadt development. He had done some work other than large-scale housing, notably a log house for a German builder who had great tracts of timberland and saw no reason for not building his house out of his own materials. It has excellent wood character and shows the influence of Gropius' Constructivist and Neo-Expressionist associates in the Bauhaus. The owner of the house had the interesting idea of building knock-down wood houses and shipping them to America. The scheme did not turn out to be quite feasible, but this abortive attempt at prefabrication was probably due to Gropius' influence. He designed other houses, but his interest always lay in the larger aspects of housing and city planning.

The type of work Gropius did during the few busy years between leaving the Bauhaus and leaving Germany has tended to make him known as one of the strongest advocates of multifamily dwellings. To a certain extent this is true. Tenements, he claims, were in disfavor for the very good reason that the common three- to five-story walk-up type had few advantages, and he made a number of comparative studies of building heights and costs and land coverage which convinced him that where the apartment house is used eight to twelve stories would be a most desirable height. His objections to the single-family dwelling have been based on a conviction that this unit tends to produce a sprawling type of plan, whereas a combination of high apartments and single-family houses would result in a much looser and more open type of city plan. The height limits frequently imposed by European building regulations he considers irrational, and the horrible examples set by New York and Chicago not any argument against the expediency of correctly planned skyscrapers.

The tendency of some critics to consider Gropius as an advocate of soulless mechanization, a point of view based on his housing work and his experiments with the Bauhaus, is due to a complete misunderstanding of his aims. Gropius has expressed himself many times and with great clarity on this important point. "The standardization of the practical machinery of life," he has said, "implies no robotization of the individual. Were mechanization an end in itself it would be an unmitigated calamity. Its sole object, however, is to relieve the individual of physical labor so that he may develop on a higher plane." Standardization, bitterly opposed by those who saw in the end of handicrafts an approaching catastrophe, is no obstacle to the advance of civilization. In this connection Gropius likes to cite the frequently forgotten fact that in all great periods the existence of standards has been the criterion of a well-ordered and cultivated society. In the new architecture he sees a new kind of beauty no less valid than

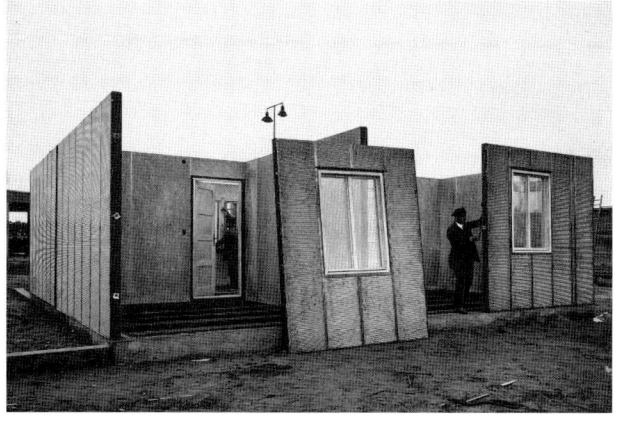

Gropius experimented with prefabricated buildings for a number of years. This photograph shows the copper house, latest of his prefabrication efforts, in its preliminary stage of assembly.

that of the past. Green cities and houses which open to admit quantities of fresh air, daylight, and sunshine have qualities in no essential way dissimilar to those of former times.

Most interesting to America is the story of Gropius and prefabrication. Since 1910 Gropius has been predicting that houses will eventually be mass-produced in factories, equipped with stock materials, and assembled on the site. In the dry assembly he sees the solution of most of the ills which beset building construction at the present time. His description of ready-made houses of solid fireproof construction delivered from stock and forming a tremendous new industry seemed fantastic to his less farsighted contemporaries, but even the small advances which have been made in this country indicate that he knew whereof he spoke. Gropius, however, for all his interest in propaganda for the new architecture, was never a man to stop with words, and in collaboration with a number of industrialists he carried out many experiments, most successful of which was his copper house. Had his activities not been disorganized by the change in government, it is likely that Germany would have taken the lead here as it had in the earlier phases of modern architecture. At the present time Gropius is in England, where his chief work has been the development of a group of better-class apartment houses located in the country a short distance from London. The concentration of a number of tenants in a few tall buildings rather than closely packed small houses makes it possible financially to leave the larger portion of the ground as a park, an arrangement he has always advocated as possessing both the advantages of city and country living. In England he is having the satisfaction of seeing his ideas adopted by a number of the younger men. Much of the outstanding work of the past few years, such as the splendid Highgate apartments by Tecton,... is directly traceable to his influence. The development at Drancy, by Beaudouin and Lods, is also an example of his principles put into practice.

Whether Gropius' future work will be done in England or Germany is a matter of conjecture. He is not against the present regime, and his departure was considered as temporary. Should the government ever realize that the shape of a roof has nothing to do with political convictions, it is entirely probable that he will return to continue a distinguished career. Like many of his generation, Gropius' importance is not restricted to his executed works. Through the Bauhaus he has had the greatest influence of any living artist, with the possible exception of Le Corbusier. Less able as a propagandist than the visionary Frenchman, more concerned with the immediate solution of practical difficulties, he has made contributions of an importance that only succeeding generations of architects will fully appreciate. Recent developments in architecture leave him completely convinced that his work was sound and timely, and the enthusiastic adoption of his ideas in England, about the only country left in Europe where architecture has no political significance, is most heartening.

For the future of architecture he has no qualms. He has always worked on basic principles, never styles, and the nature of the setbacks the new architecture has received is ample proof that there is nothing fundamentally unsound in it. When Germany repudiates modern architecture as Bolshevistic, Russia, because it is bourgeois, and Italy embraces it because it is Fascist, there is little difficulty in drawing a conclusion. The past is past, and there can be no turning back of clocks. His own statement is positive: "We have had enough and to spare of the arbitrary reproduction of historic styles. In the progress of our advance from the vagaries of mere architectural caprice to the dictates of structural logic, we have learned to see expression of our life in clear and crisply simplified forms."

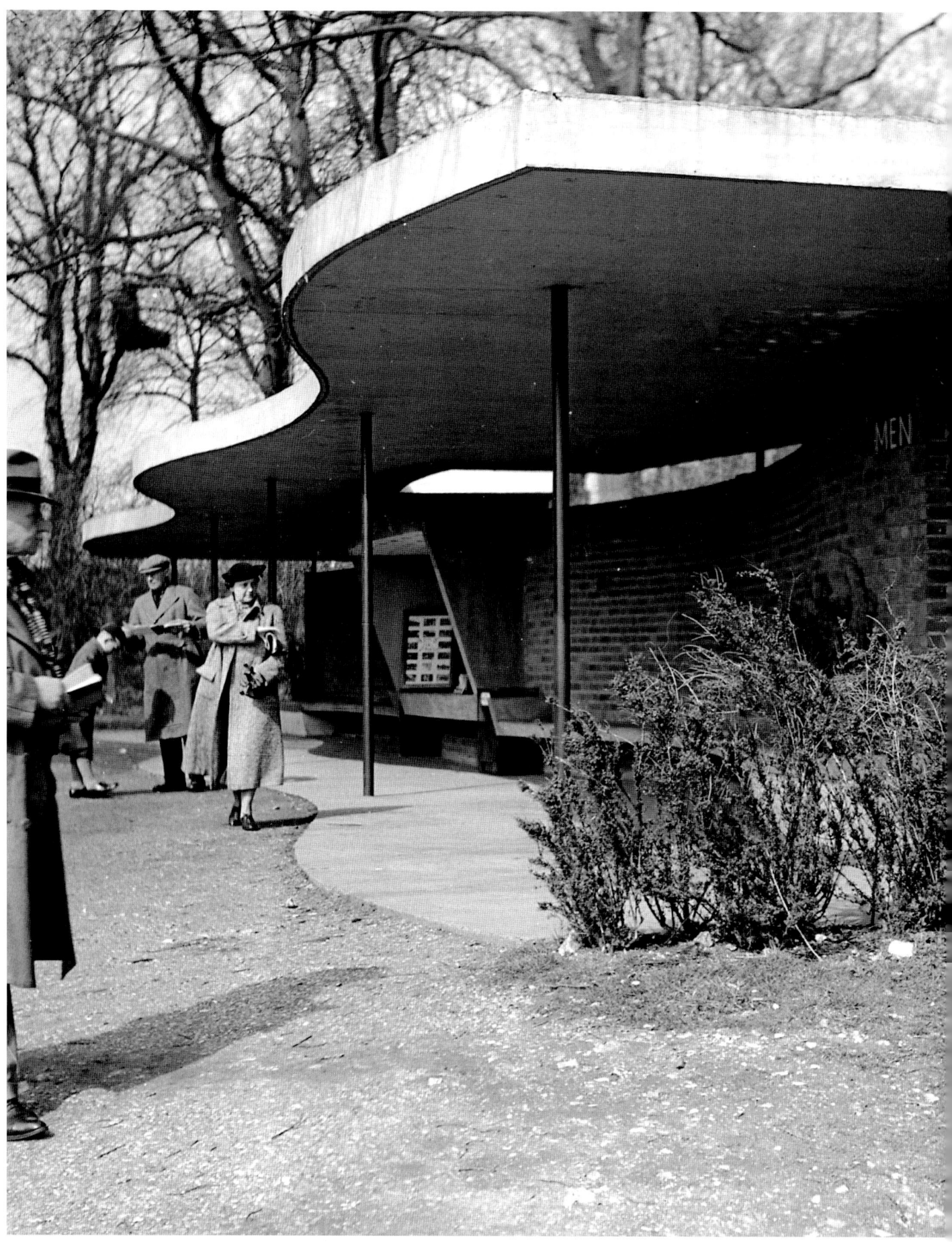

TECTON
ENGLAND

FROM
PENCIL POINTS
OCTOBER 1936

A corner of the entrance hall, Highgate Apartments.

This is the last of a series of articles on men who have succeeded in impressing their ideas upon their generation. Sometimes they did it by force of personality; sometimes it was the sheer power of an idea convincingly put on paper; sometimes it was social connections or political conniving: but whatever the means, the idea was always there. These men and their kind are creating a new architecture, and the most important single fact about them is that in spite of a wide range of temperaments, of the most bitterly opposed political convictions, they all agree on one essential point: *only architecture which takes modern techniques seriously, which uses the new tools with understanding and imagination, has any meaning in the world today.* Or tomorrow. It is also noteworthy that the great majority of these men are conscious of the social implications of modern architecture; as the corporate life becomes a more characteristic form of present-day existence the social responsibilities of the architect become greater–and also his opportunities.

While they have been primarily concerned with the thinking behind a new kind of building, the [men whose stories] have appeared in these articles have been–without exception–success stories. This in spite of the fact that Mies van der Rohe and the Brothers Luckhardt are sitting around Berlin doing virtually nothing, that Gropius is in voluntary exile, that Le Corbusier is existing on the meager proceeds of magazine articles and books. For their work has spread far beyond the confines of their own lands and has made itself felt. Of all these stories, however, none is as timely, as heartening, or as illuminating as Tecton's.

Tecton is not an architect. It is the name of a group of seven architects whose average age is under thirty. The word is Greek and means "carpenter," and so, by extension, "builder." It is a good name. We need more builders; if there had been more builders and fewer architects during the past hundred-odd years we should probably not be facing the necessity of getting out from under the accumulated scrap pile of paper architecture to resume building.

Tecton is barely four years old. It began when seven young men faced a depression and decided that their chances were better if they faced it as a group. They took a small office and worked on a cooperative basis, sharing work and fees alike. They did their own cleaning and typing. They shared all profits, but the first year there weren't any profits. When a small job finally did come in, the amount of work done on it was prodigious. With seven otherwise idle members the firm could well afford to study it down to the last scheme and the last detail, and at the very beginning a valuable habit of exhaustive research was acquired, growing into one of the most notable characteristics of the group. Each man inevitably found his special aptitude and devoted a major portion of his time to it. The result was a powerful concentration of technical knowledge, extremely usable because all were bent on achieving the same end. To correct any possible dangers of specialization, however, the group held open discussion on all projects at all

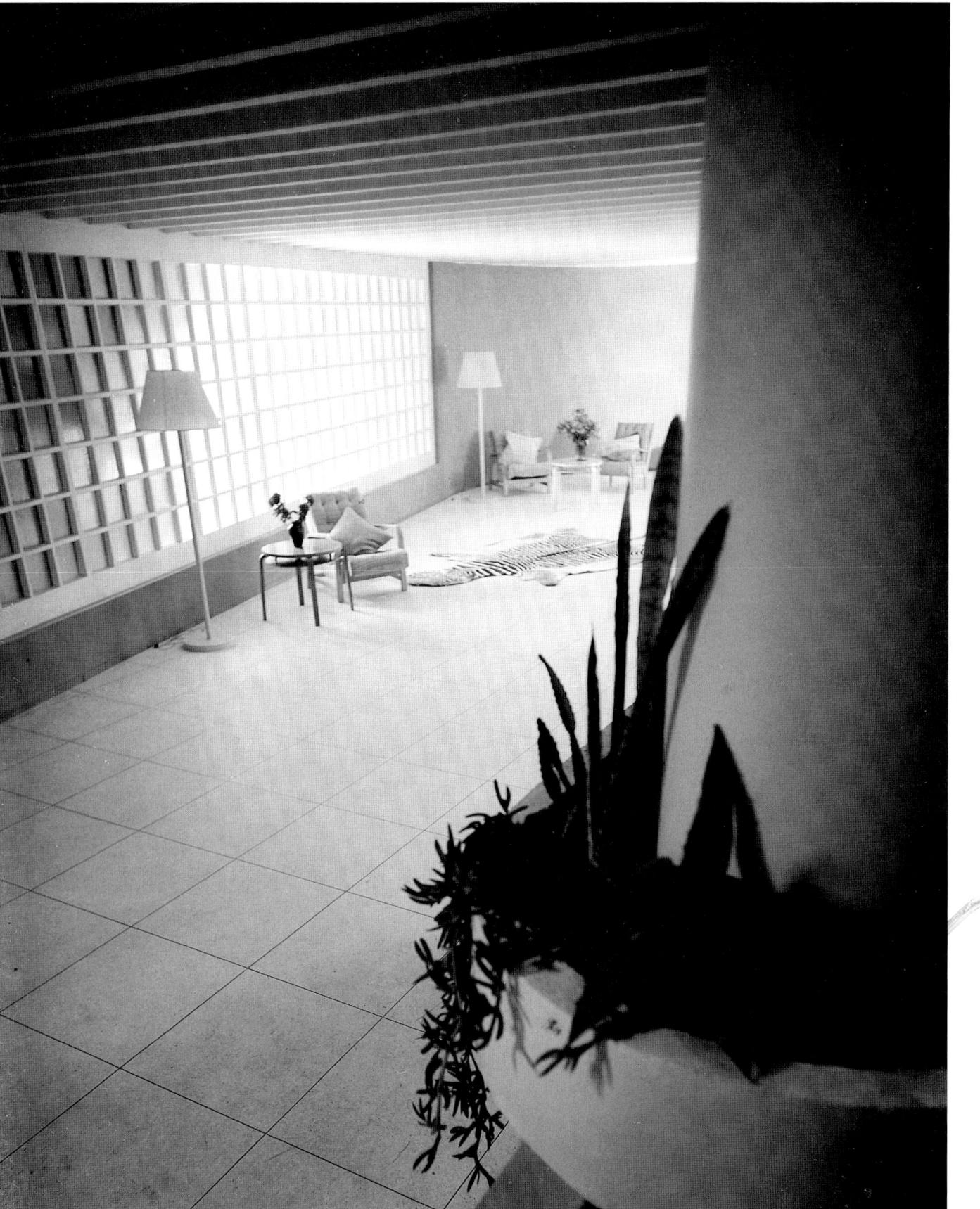

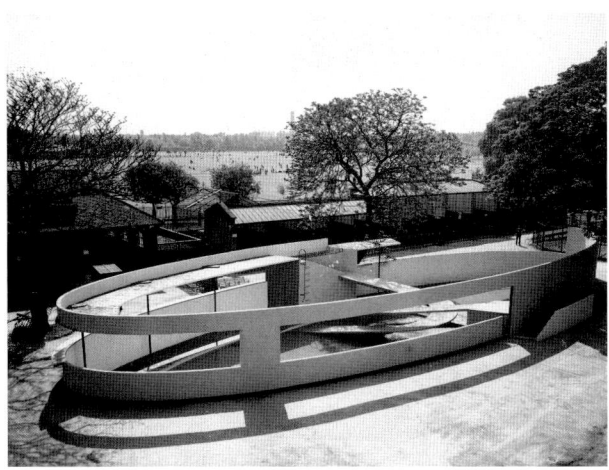

The penguin pool, one of Tecton's earliest and most brilliantly conceived works—a superlative piece of daring architectural showmanship that has attracted attention all over the world.

below, opposite: The elephant house at the London Zoo, a powerful and dramatic grouping. Note the effective use of the bathing pool as a barrier between animals and spectators.

times, and one member was assigned to a job with the responsibility of seeing that it got done. To appraise the merits of the cooperative system as practiced by Tecton, one has only to see what happened in the four years.

The second year Tecton was commissioned to do a penguin pool at the London Zoo. The pool was followed by other constructions at the zoo, work whose brilliance and unconventionality attracted much favorable attention. Since then there has been no dearth of work. Last year they entered an important competition for the design of several blocks of workingmen's flats, to be built of concrete. Their project took first prize, and not only was the solution excellent, but along with the plans they submitted a series of studies of construction methods and details of interior design, many of which were entirely new. Recently they had the satisfaction of building a large apartment house which made use of many of the ideas used in the competition.

The Penguin Pool—it deserves capitals: there is only one in the world like it—is a piece of pure constructivism. Elliptical in shape, with two delicately curved ramps of reinforced concrete, it is a delightful conception, ideally suited for showing off the rather ridiculous antics of its occupants. After this brilliant bit of showmanship there came a gorilla house—quite a different sort of problem. Gorillas in captivity are practically nonexistent, and the zoo authorities were very anxious that their very valuable pair be housed in a manner giving them every chance of survival. Extremely susceptible to colds and other infectious diseases, the gorillas

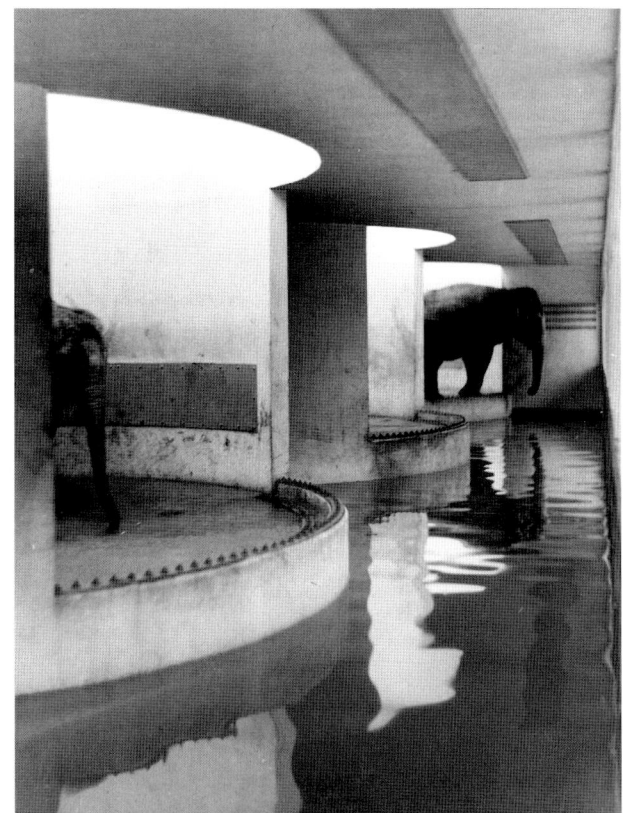

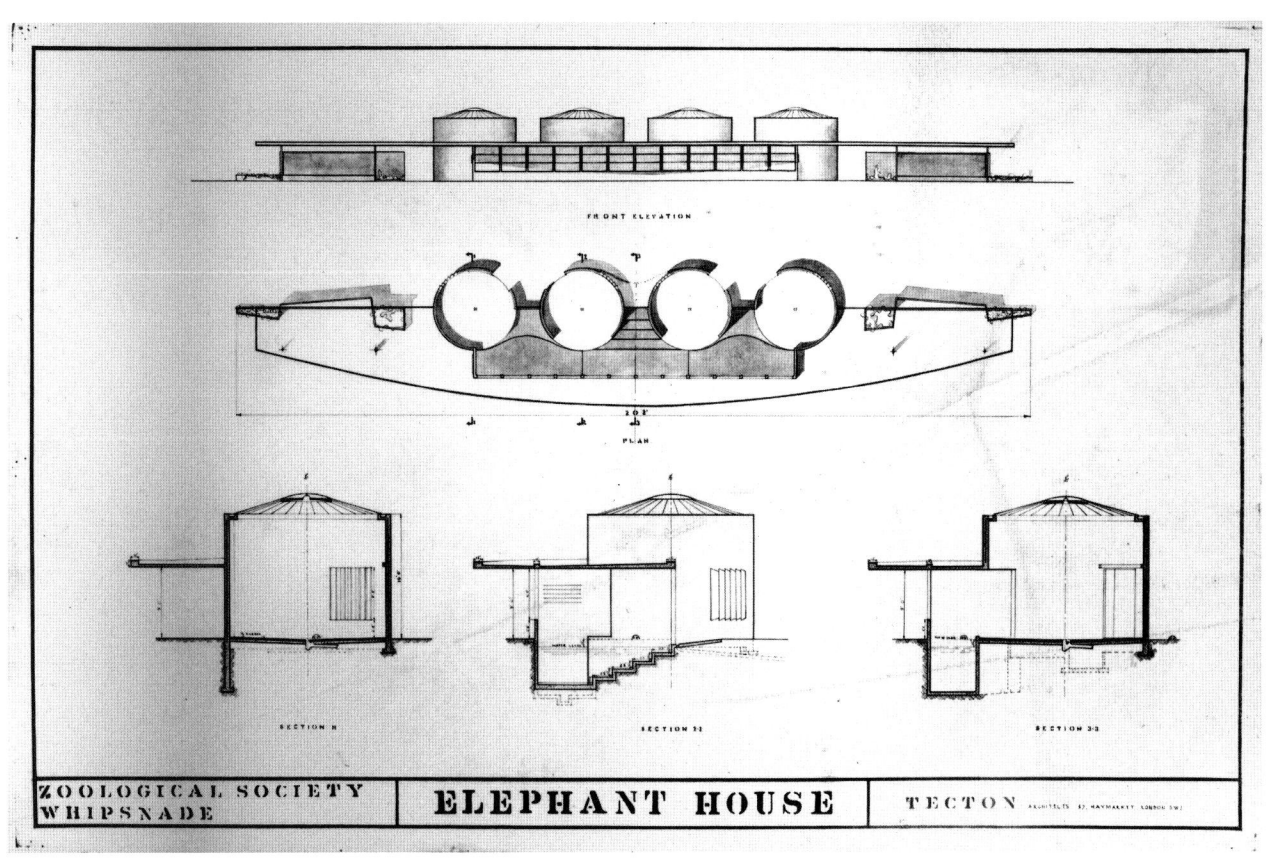

A shelter at the Whipsnade Zoo, London, similar in character to the elephant house. A tobacconist's kiosk and toilet facilities are unobtrusively provided.

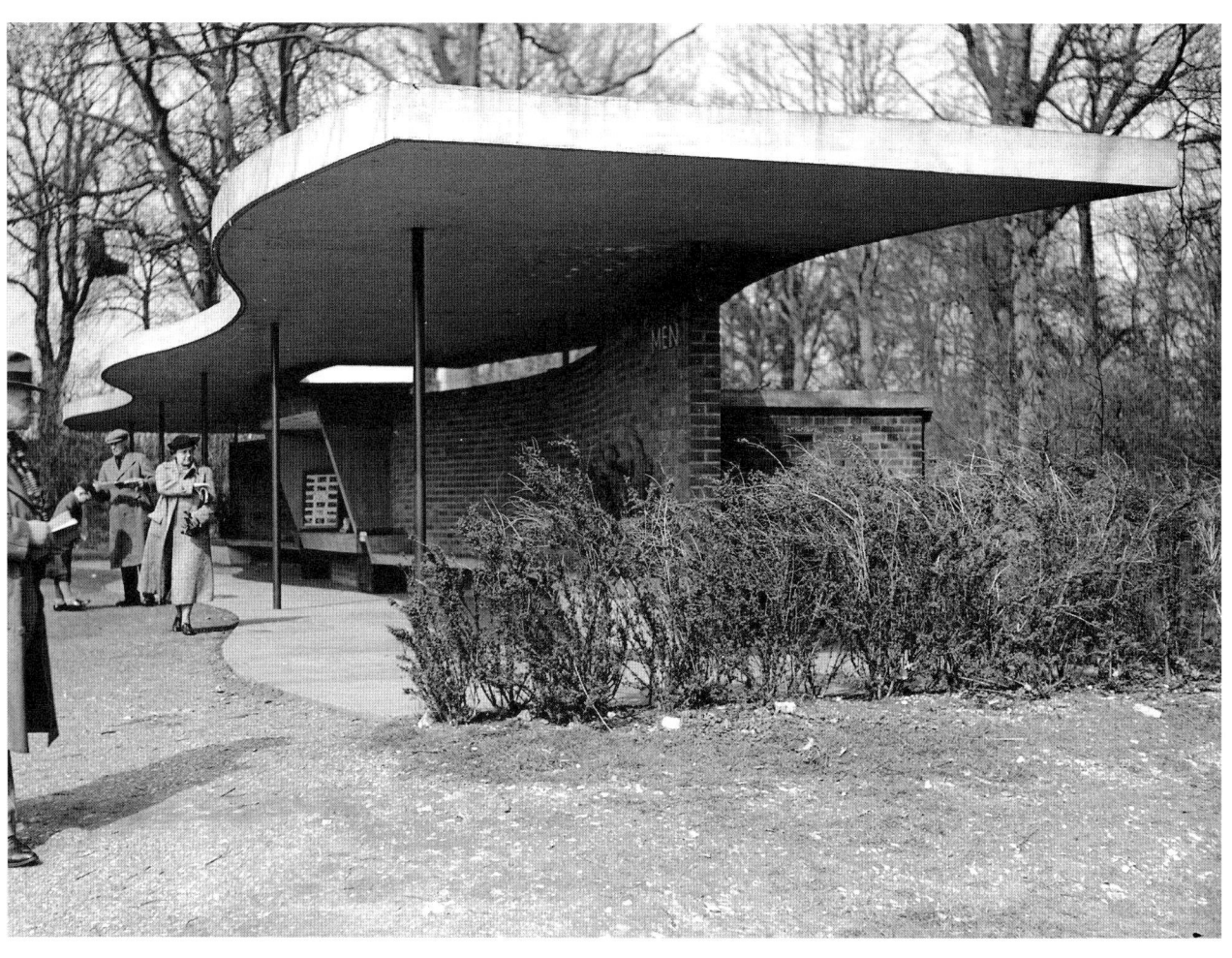

PORTRAITS

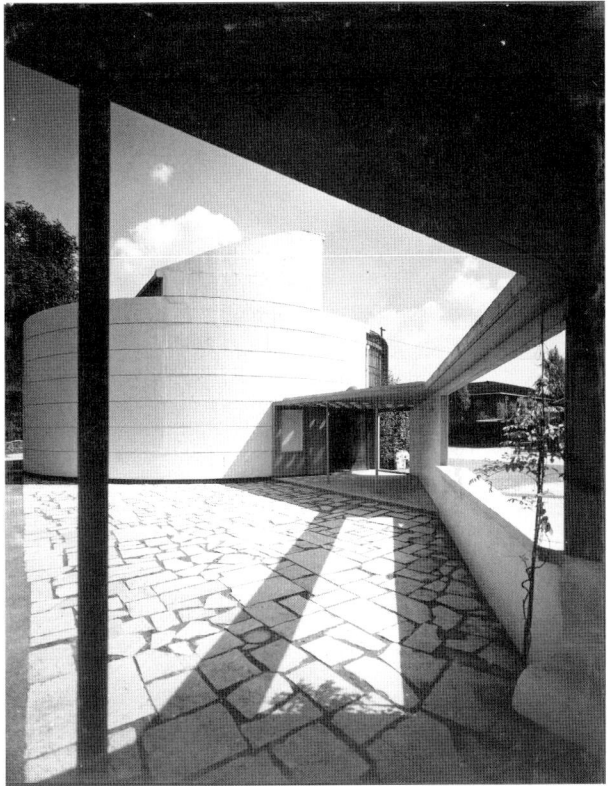

The gorilla house at the London Zoo. The building has been designed to function with the precision of a laboratory to house a pair of delicate tropical animals and keep them in good health.

were as carefully housed as though they had been the Dionnes. The house looks like no other building. Circular in form, half of it is a cage—open on the top as well as the side. Curved walls are slid around in the winter to close the cage, and the rear half is used, while the public passes through the summer cage and looks through windows at the animals within. The windows are to prevent the transmission of infectious diseases. The gorillas breathe conditioned air, are heated with radiant heat panels, and up to date have done very well indeed. The elephant house was a less delicate problem, but its solution was no less distinguished. Four Indian elephants were set in four circular cages, their bathing pool acting as a barrier between them and the public. A shelter over the windows keeps the spectators in shadow while the animals are in full light. The setting of the elephant house is particularly effective: against a dark background of trees four white drums and the strong line of the shelter stand out. So outstanding was the job that they did on housing animals that the *Architectural Record* recently ran pictures of four of their zoo buildings together with a photograph of a slum tenement, commenting of the quaintness of a world that houses its animals so well and its humans so badly. But Tecton has done pretty well on housing humans, too.

England has an interesting method of keeping up the quality of the architecture in its towns. As advisors to the local Council, a panel of architects is frequently set up, passing on the suitability of proposed buildings. When the panel is made up of conservative members, as

below:
Plan of the gorilla house. The winter entrance is through the summer cage. Note provisions for the wall of the cage to slide out of sight behind the closed half of the structure for warm weather.

opposite:
A front view of the gorilla house, showing the walls of the summer cage closed for the winter.

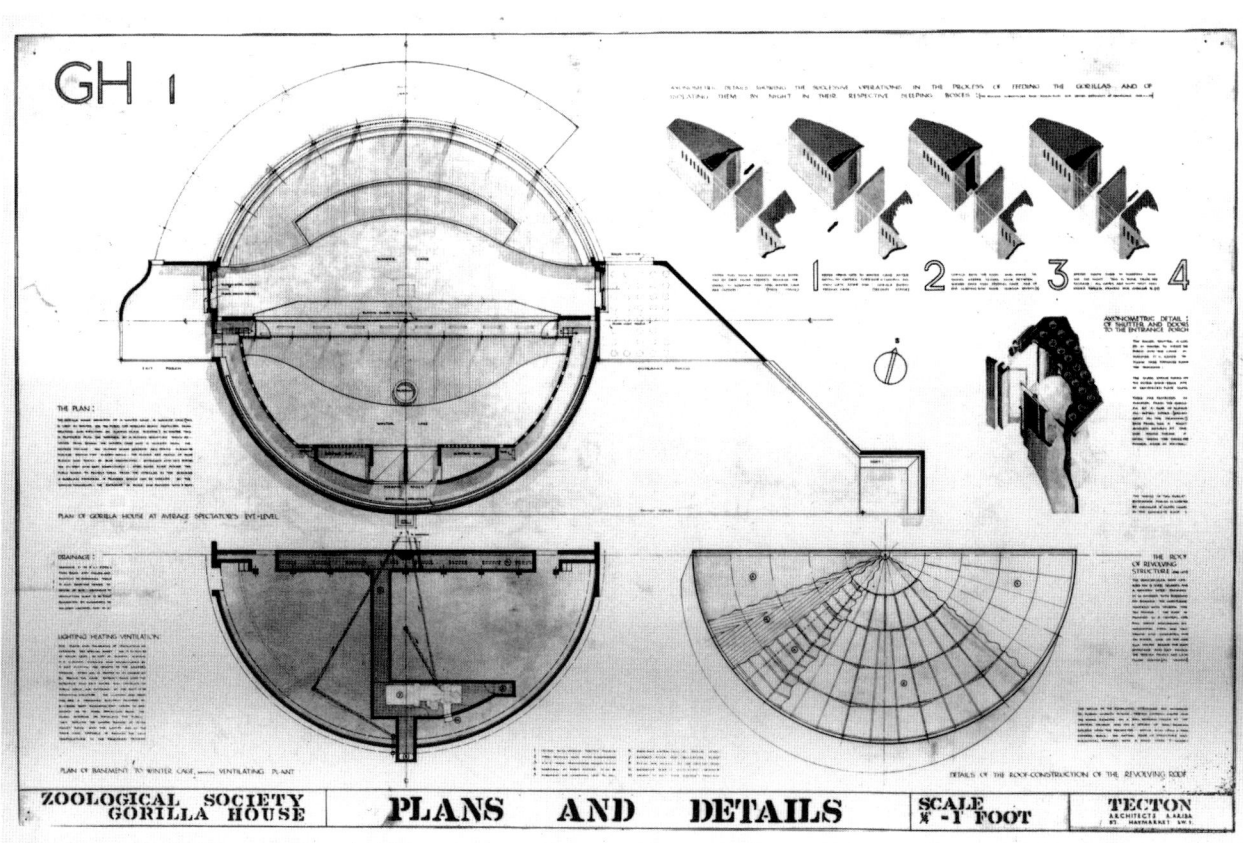

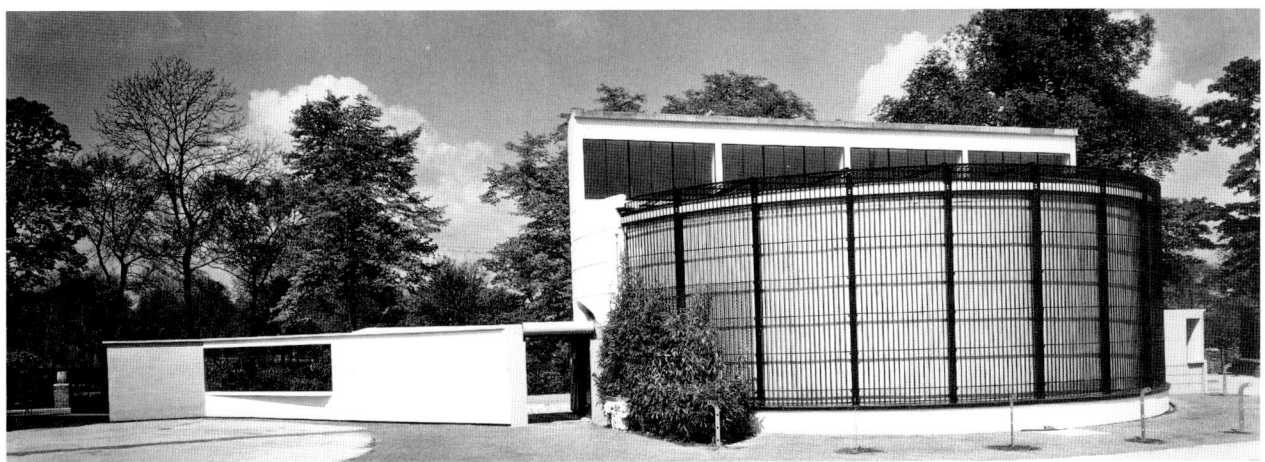

is frequently the case, and a design for a modern house is submitted, there is sometimes trouble. In 1934 Tecton designed a series of small houses for a town in Sussex. Dignified, simple in form and materials, the houses were eminently suitable for occupancy by respectable people, but the local Council thought otherwise and rejected them. The venerable gentlemen were disturbed by the evident lack of trimmings—commonly known as "architecture"—and feared that the beauty of the fake half-timber cottages in the locality would be marred by the intruders. The Advisory Panel of Architects hedged a bit when consulted, recommended certain modifications in design, and proposed that the houses be built in a "secluded, undeveloped area." Tecton didn't get much profit out of their work, but the Cuckfield Case, as it was known, did get them much useful publicity.

The Cement Marketing Company's competition for workingmen's flats was Tecton's first large-scale study of housing. For their scheme they adopted a series of strip plans, with a very simple arrangement of structural members in each building. In Tecton's project the influence of Le Corbusier was apparent, while the column arrangement recalled that of Mies van der Rohe's apartment house in Stuttgart. Although the group has never done a building that reflected other than its own point of view, its members obviously have a complete familiarity with the best of modern work and a rare understanding of its aims and underlying principles. The Tecton project combined variety of apartment layout with a rigidly standardized construction; as a result the cost per room of their design was the lowest of any submitted, although the space allotted to the various rooms was quite generous. One of the most interesting parts of their work was the system of sliding forms for concrete, used to eliminate the usual built-up forms and scaffolding. While this winning design was never built, it led directly to their biggest commission, only recently completed: the apartment house at Northfield, Highgate.

Highgate was somewhat more complicated than the competition. For one thing there was the human element to fight against. The building regulations in this suburb, which is filled with the low rows of houses so characteristic of London's outskirts, had never considered the matter of height, so when the plans for a multistoried dwelling were submitted there was a great disturbance, and the puny men, who always get frightened when a new idea appears, objected. But this time the local Council's feeble objections were brushed aside and the building was built. As soon as it was up, however, a clause was inserted into the regulations forbidding the repetition of such an unheard of venture. And what was there so bad about this high building that the Council objected to? It gave sun, air, and privacy to its occupants. It had a magnificent view of London, and made it available to most of the apartments in it. It had a roof, nine stories in the air, where recreational activities, undisturbed by traffic and street noises, were possible. And it was neither Cinema Classic, nor Jerrybuilder Tudor. It was just a building that gave its occupants more in

below:
A view of Highgate Apartments. Note the curved balconies, the open first floor, and the indication of the living room in each case with its long horizontal stretch of window with draw curtains.

opposite left:
The first floor hall shows a luxurious use of space generally given over to narrow corridors.

opposite right:
Another view of the large hall. Its sureness of handling and mastery of form command admiration.

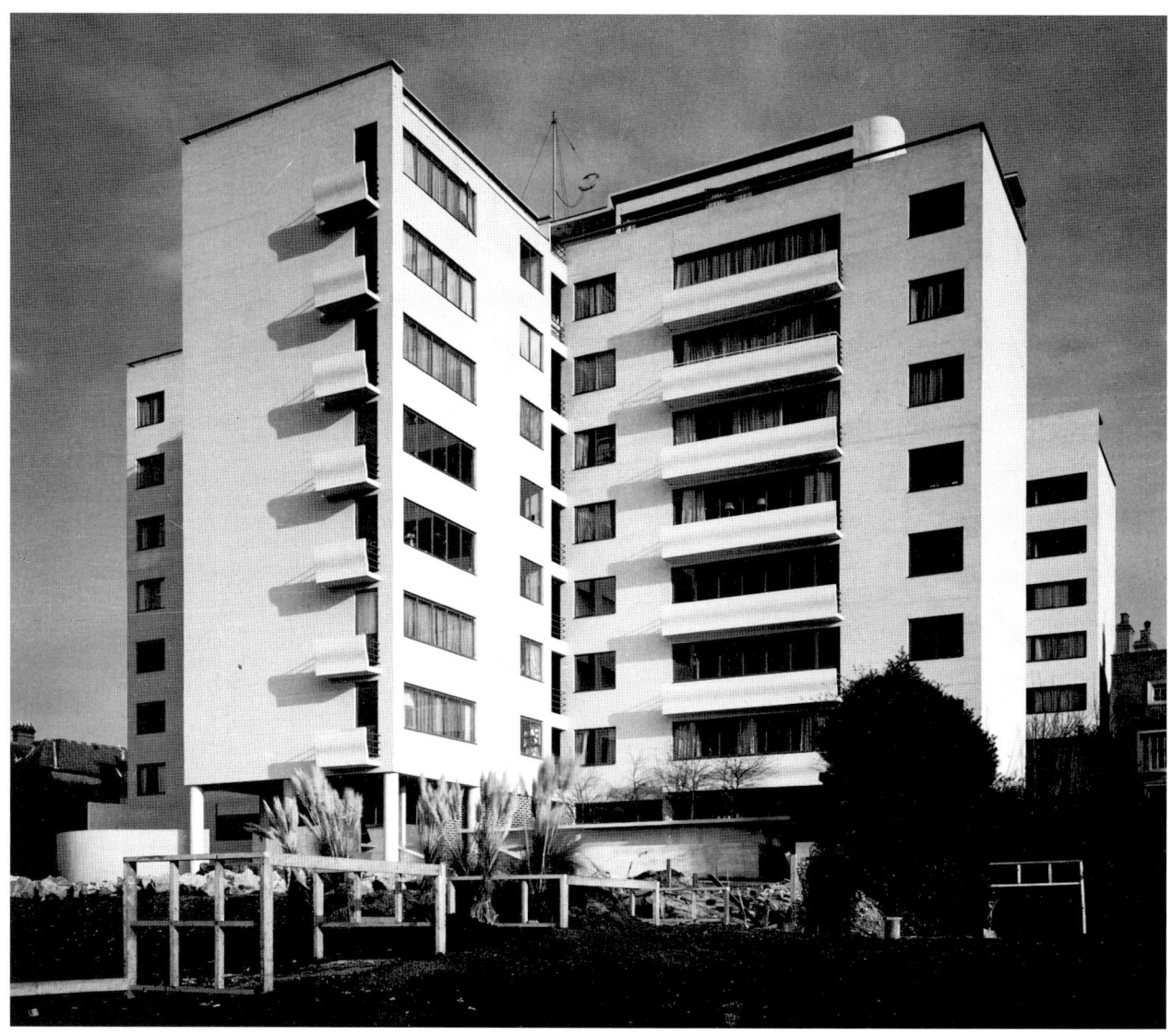

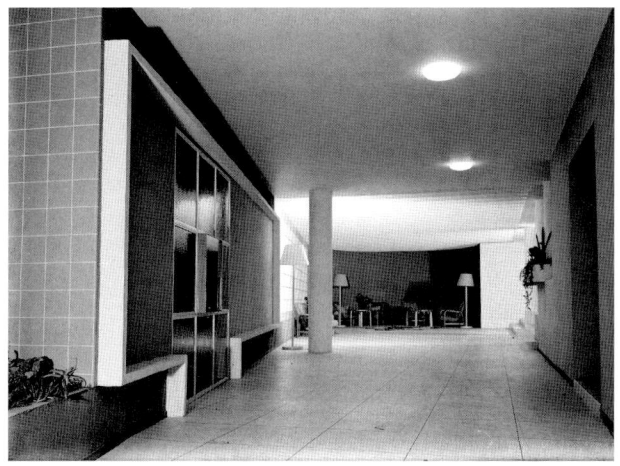 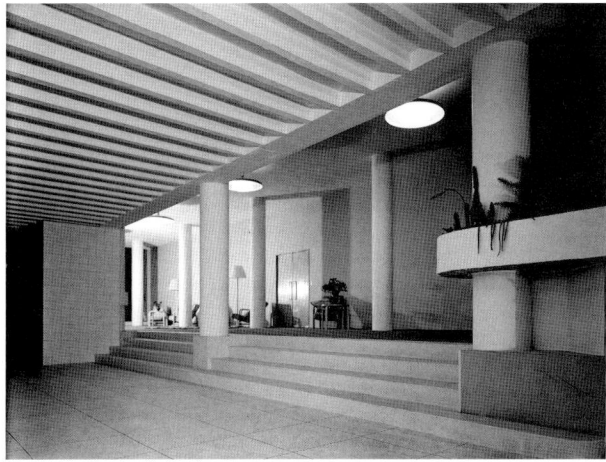

the way of amenities than any other building. So the local authorities did their level best to keep it from going up. But when completion approached it was found that not a single flat was available: they had all long since been rented by a public that knew a good thing.

Le Corbusier, who found in Highgate a realization of some of his fondest dreams, waxed eloquent on the subject, and wrote of it: "So we find in Highgate the seed of something, the seed of a vertical garden city as opposed to the horizontal extension. The building is large enough to be an example, a demonstration, a proof.... Thanks to the construction on stanchions, the ground floor is no longer that part of the building usually sacrificed, where strangled rooms crowd around access corridors. The ground floor here extends like the superb surface of a lake, absorbing easily the lines of traffic of different speed and direction.... The building at Highgate is an achievement of the first rank, and a milestone which will be useful to everybody."

The plan of Highgate is a double cruciform plan. That such a scheme has its defects the architects will be the first to confess, but granted the size of the plot and the financial limitations, it was the best that could be done. The real fault here lies not with the architects, but with the prevailing system of land planning. As in their competition project, the structural system was standardized for speed and economy; within the limits of this standardization there is every opportunity for freedom of planning. Here, due to the open-mindedness of the local building inspector, a structural system based on the intelligent use of reinforced concrete, rather than on the traditional imitation of steel framing, was used for the first time in England. The illustration shows the difference in the amount of space made available in this way.

There were many "firsts" in Highgate. Due to their background of continual research and questioning of existing methods, the members of Tecton had become skeptics of the most pronounced sort. Nothing was accepted unless it made sense. Not content with putting up a multistory building where all the houses were two or three stories, changing accepted structural methods, and abolishing the ground floor, they went on to a study of every piece of equipment—and redesigned most of it. Washbasins, waterclosets, bathtubs, casement window hardware, closets, door handles, and lighting fixtures submitted by manufacturers were rejected, redesigned, and specially built. This was not because the architects objected on aesthetic grounds, although there was ample room for complaint on this score, but because they could not see why stock equipment should not be intelligently designed for easy use, durability, and ease of cleaning. And not finding what they wanted, they designed it themselves. In America we have industrial designers doing over the commonest items of household equipment—objects that architects have been specifying for years, too lazy to even consider that improvements might be in order. England is more fortunate: with architects such as Tecton there is no need for a special profession to solve industrial design problems.

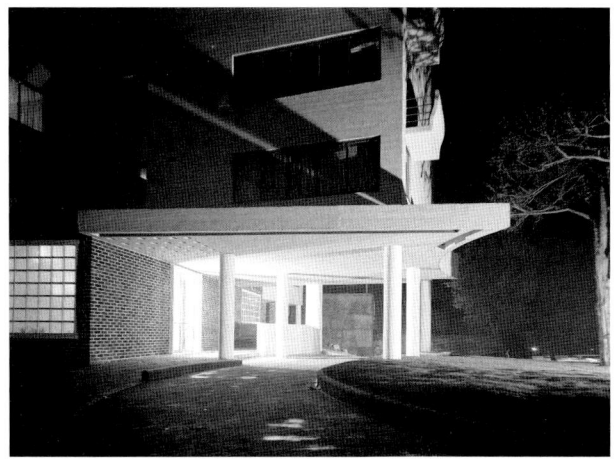 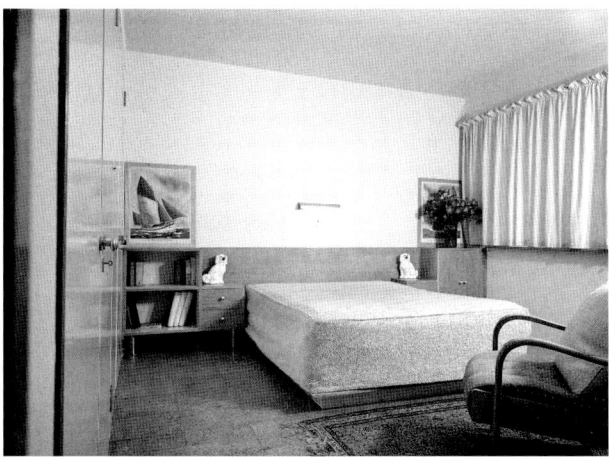

Some time before Highgate was finished, arrangements were made for the students of the Architectural Association School to pay the building a visit. When they learned of the proposed trip, the architects did a very characteristic thing. Believing that a tour of the building could not have its full value unless the students already knew what developments led to the final scheme, the members of Tecton prepared a series of diagrams which were sent to the school several days before the trip. The development of the plan was shown, details of the plans, construction, and fittings, with explanatory text containing such comments as "Any detail left to the contractors will certainly be done wrong. Better to spend a month drawing than spoil the building forever." Orientation diagrams showed how much sun entered each flat, and the text here explained why the solution, from this point of view, was not ideal. Other drawings showed briefly the development of the flat from 1800 to the present day. In short, Tecton gave its guests a complete picture of the building and the thinking and conditions that produced it. It was a nice gesture and a very intelligent one.

Today, at the ripe age of four years, Tecton can look back at solid achievement. A remarkable series of zoo buildings, brilliant in conception and craftsmanlike in execution; a difficult competition, fairly won; houses; exhibits; a list of product designs too long to enumerate; and one of the outstanding apartment buildings of the present day–this record for four years speaks well for the cooperative effort. Tecton, curiously enough, has stood up better in adversity than in success, and a few of the members have left to set themselves up in private practice. The group, however, still maintains its strong identity. Work continues to increase, and apparently the resistance of the Highgate Council has again been overcome, for there will soon be another apartment house next to the first one. Tecton can hardly have any doubts as to its future; with its sound background it is equipped for any conceivable type of design problem, whether a door knob or a town plan. The group represents the ideal of the modern architect: the coordinator of what Gropius calls "a modern architectonic art." As such, the architect will soon be able to fill the useful place in society he once occupied. Tecton has already done it. There is plenty of room for more of the same kind.

opposite left:
A night view of the entrance to Highgate, the free, spacious approach dramatically lighted.

opposite right:
A bedroom in Highgate. Simple, comfortable, pleasing in its forms and textures, the room shows how far modern design has advanced in recent years in the direction of unaffected honesty.

below:
A living room in Highgate. Plain walls are the rule. The wood furniture was designed by the well-known Finnish architect Alvar Aalto. The Oriental rug seems in harmony.

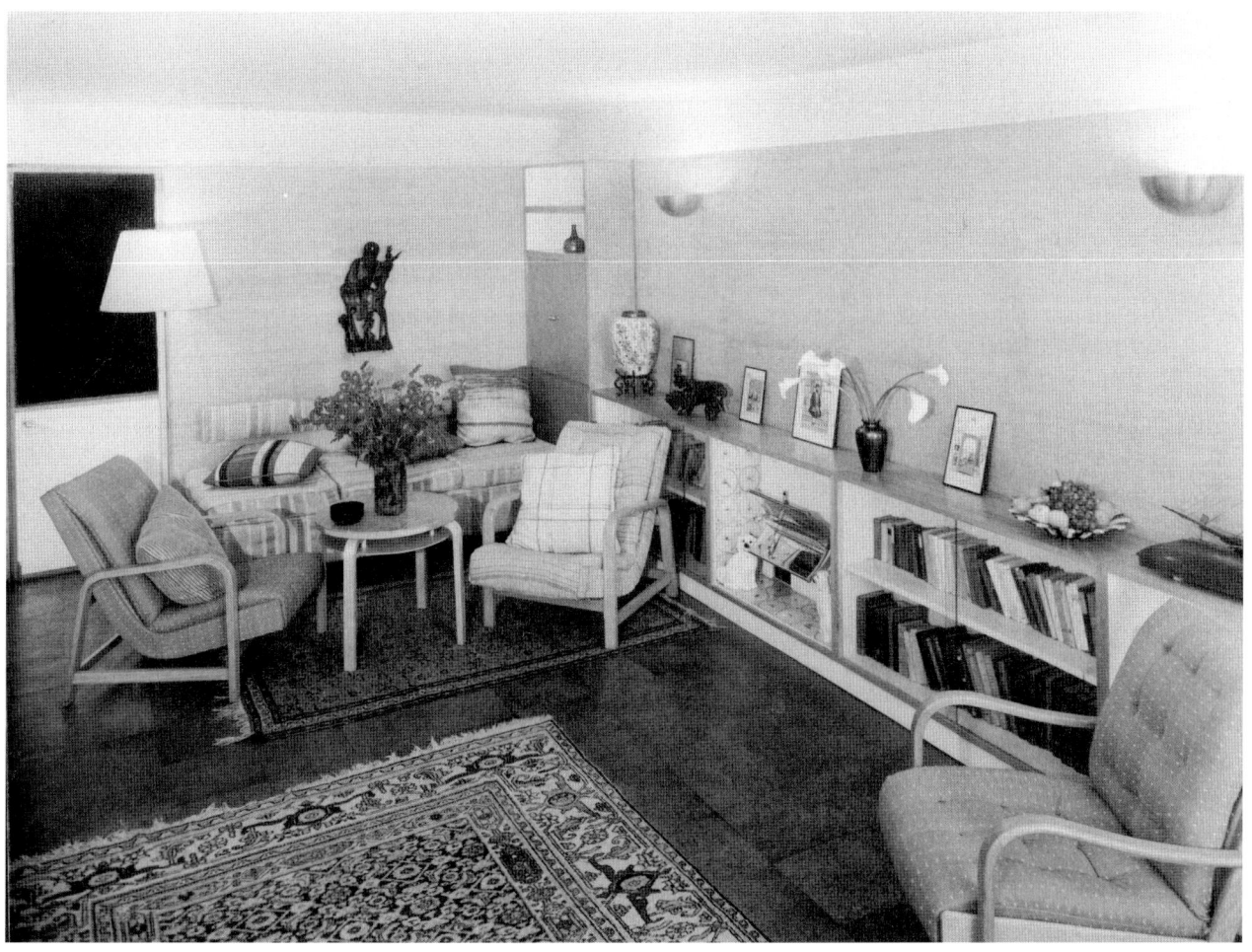

ARCHITECT BIOGRAPHIES

MARCELLO PIACENTINI

Architect and urban planner Marcello Piacentini was born in Rome in 1881 and was the son of an architect. He was influential in the architecture community through his own architectural projects, his position as the editor of the magazine *Architettura,* and his political interests. In 1907 Piacentini won his first major project, the competition to transform the town center of Bergamo, which was not realized until 1927. In 1910, Piacentini designed the Italian Pavilion for the World Exposition in Brussels, and in 1915–17 he designed the Cinema Corso, in Rome. His early work was informed by classicism in contrast to rational modernism, and during Mussolini's power he turned toward a formal monumentalism, becoming the "architect of the regime." Piacentini designed the plan for the University of Rome campus and the Administration Building (1932–35), offering symmetrical compositions and a stripped neoclassical design. Under Mussolini, Piacentini was also the general commissary for architecture for the E'42, the exhibition complex built in 1937 outside of Rome. He died in 1960 in Rome.

BENT HELWEG-MOELLER

Bent Helweg-Moeller was born in 1883 in Odense, Denmark, where he studied architecture before working for Anton Rosen from 1906–10. He practiced primarily in Copenhagen, building such projects as Heering House and the Pavilion at Tivioli Garden, as well as houses and commercial buildings. Later in his career he was in partnership with Børge Rammeskow. His archives appear to have been scattered or destroyed, and few original works remain. He died in 1956.

HANS AND VASSILI LUCKHARDT

Brothers Hans and Vassili Luckhardt were born in Berlin in 1890 and 1889, respectively. Hans attended the University of Karlsruhe, and Vassili studied at the Technische Universität Berlin, Berlin-Charlottenburg, and Dresden. From 1924 to 1934 the brothers shared their office with Alfons Anker, completing commercial and residential projects in and around Berlin such as the Telschow House, modernist housing of concrete frame and steel construction, the Reinhenhaus, as well as competition schemes for Alexanderplatz and Potsdammerplatz. They were involved in the architectural and arts community as members of the Novembergruppe, the Arbeitsrats für Kunst, and the Glass Chain.

During the period of National Socialism in Germany the Luckhardts tried to reconcile their aesthetics with the Nazi Party, and they joined the National Socialist German Workers Party, but did not receive many commissions. After World War II the Luckhardts continued to work together designing housing blocks and exhibition houses, as well as town government offices for Bavaria and Munich. Hans died in 1957. Vassili worked until his death in 1972.

GIO PONTI

Gio Ponti was born in 1891 in Milan, Italy. He matriculated at the Milan Polytechnic, but World War I interrupted his studies, and he didn't receive his architectural degree until 1921. His first design work was for the ceramic product design company Richard-Ginori, 1923–30. At the same time he started a design studio in Milan with Mino Fiocchi and Emilio Lancia, with whom he worked until 1926, when he and Lancia began a partnership that lasted until 1933. Ponti's public debut was in 1923 at the first Biannual Exhibition of the Decorative Arts in Monza, and he helped to organize the Triennial Exhibitions in Monza and Milan. In 1925 he won the Grand Prix at the Paris Expo.

Ponti's first architectural design office was with the engineers Antonio Fornaroli and Eugenio Soncini (Studio Ponti-Fornaroli-Soncini), and it was in business until 1945. Ponti and Fornaroli opened an office with Alberto Rosselli in 1952 (Studio Ponti-Fornaroli-Rosselli). Ponti combined both interests in architecture and interiors. He designed the School of Mathematics in Rome (1932–34) and the Pirelli Building in Milan (1955), as well as numerous projects around the world.

Gio Ponti founded *Domus* magazine in 1928, serving

as editor until 1941. He then began the magazine *Stile*, which he edited until 1947. He returned to *Domus* in 1947 and continued as editor until his death in 1979.

MIES VAN DER ROHE

Ludwig Mies van der Rohe was born Ludwig Mies in Aachen, Germany, in 1886. He trained with his father in the family stone-carving business until the age of nineteen, when he joined the office of Bruno Paul, Art Nouveau architect and furniture designer, in Berlin. In 1908 he began working in the studio of Peter Behrens on such projects as the AEG, in Berlin. He left Behrens' office in 1912 to start his own architectural practice in Berlin and designed numerous houses. He continued commissions with houses such as the Wolf House in Gubin (1925) and the Tugendhat House in Brno (1928-30), as well as the Barcelona Pavilion (1929). In 1930 Mies was appointed the director of the Bauhaus in Dessau until it was closed by the Nazi Party in 1933.

After World War II, Mies immigrated to the United States, where he worked at the Armour Institute of Technology (which later merged with the Lewis Institute to form the Illinois Institute of Technology). Mies designed the master plan for IIT, and almost twenty buildings within it, including Crown Hall, from 1950-56. His other significant buildings include the Farnsworth House, Plano, Illinois (1946-51); the Seagram Building, New York (1954-58); 860-880 Lake Shore Drive, Chicago (1948-51); and the National Gallery, Berlin (1962-67). Mies died in Chicago in 1969.

IVAR TENGBOM

Ivar Tengbom was born in Vireda, Sweden, in 1878. He trained in Göteborg at the Chalmers Institute of Technology, and in Stockholm at the Royal Swedish Academy of Arts, graduating in 1901. He then began working in the offices of Erik Lallerstedt, and later in partnership with Ernst Torulf, with whom he designed the church in Arvika, in 1911.

Tengbom opened an architecture office in 1912 in Stockholm, and it quickly became the largest in Sweden, employing twenty-five people. He designed the main office for the Enskilda Bank at Kungsträdgården (1912-15) and buildings such as the offices of the newspaper *Svenska Dagbladet*, the Hogalid Church, the Matchstick Palace (1928), and the Stockholm Concert Hall (1923-28), which were rationalized classical structures abandoning the more national romantic styles. He was the director of the building and urbanism department of the city of Stockholm (1924-36) and was the architect of the courthouse. Tengbom died in Sweden in 1968.

GIUSEPPE VACCARO

Giuseppe Vaccaro was born in Bologna in 1896. His best-known works, executed between the two world wars, combine classical and modern styles, such as his Post and Telegraph office building in Naples (1931-36), a curvilinear stone striped Modernist building, and the engineering school in Bologna (1929). Working with many commissions from Marcello Piacentini and through the Fascist party, he grew interested in structure and the power of concrete. After World War II, Vaccaro had to rethink the meaning of style and politics as the stripped classical Modern styles were adopted by the Nazi regime. For Vaccaro's housing in Borgo Panigale, Bologna, he turned to Italy's vernacular architecture for inspiration. In the 1930s he designed beach colonies, such as for Agip in Cesenatico, in rationalist compositions. His numerous church and urban designs explored new forms of structural experimentation. His last project was the Church of San Gregario Barbariso, in Rome (1968-71). Vaccaro died in Bologna in 1970.

EUGÈNE BEAUDOUIN

Eugène Beaudouin was born in Paris in 1898. He trained at the Ecole des Beaux-Arts before opening an office with Marcel Lods in 1925, a partnership that lasted for fifteen years. In 1928 he won the Grand Prix de Rome, and while in Rome he was commended for his measured drawings of Ispahan. In 1933 he traveled to the United States to study American urbanism. He then worked with the French garden designer J. C. N. Forestier on a plan for Havana, and on the Paris regional development plan with Henri Post.

During their partnership Beaudouin and Lods completed housing developments such as the Champ des Oiseux estate in Bagneaux and the Cité de la Muette in Drancy. The open-air school in Suresnes was a composition of smaller units, similar to his approach to housing developments. Beaudouin died in Paris in 1983.

RAYMOND McGRATH

Raymond McGrath was born in Sydney, Australia, in 1903. He graduated from Sydney University in 1926, having studied English and architecture, and moved to England for a fellowship at Clare College, Cambridge University. During McGrath's fellowship Mansfield Forbes asked him to redecorate "Finella," a Victorian house that served as the house of the college. McGrath's design explored Modernist forms, and in 1930 he set up an architecture practice in London.

McGrath's first large-scale commission was for the interiors of the Broadcasting House (BBC), in London (1933), with Wells Coates and Serge Chermayeff. McGrath also designed interiors for airplanes for Imperial Airways. During World War II, McGrath moved to Dublin and began working at the Office of Public Works, where he later began in the position of principal architect until 1968, all the while working on house commissions and projects on his own.

WALTER GROPIUS

Walter Gropius, the son of an architect, was born in Berlin in 1883. After architecture school Gropius worked at Peter Behrens' office. In 1910, Gropius started a practice in Berlin with Adolf Meyer, with whom he designed the temporary Werkbund Pavilion in 1911 and the Fagus Factory in 1913. Gropius served as a sergeant major during World War I. He replaced Henry van de Velde as master of Grand-Ducal Saxon School of Arts and Crafts in Weimar, which led to his development of the Bauhaus school in Dessau in 1919 and his directorship there through 1928, as well as the design of the school's main buildings.

During the Nazis' rise to power in Germany, Gropius fled to Britain and then to the United States, where he taught at the Harvard Graduate School of Design. He built his own house in Lincoln, Massachusetts (1932), worked with Konrad Wachsmann on prefabricated housing, and started the firm The Architects Collaborative (TAC). Gropius died in Boston in 1969.

TECTON

Tecton, a collaborative international group of architects based in London from 1931–48, included Russian architect Berthold Romanovich Lubetkin, Douglas Bailey, Anthony Chitty, Lindsay Drank, Michael Dugdale, Valentine Harding, Denys Lasdun, Godfrey Samuel, and Francis Skinner. The firm, in radical Modernist experiments, explored new uses of concrete, structure, and form with projects such as the gorilla house and the penguin pool at the London Zoo in 1934, and housing developments such as the two Highgate apartment buildings (1933–38), and the Finsbury Health Centre (1935–38). Tecton believed in designing every element of every project, including plumbing fixtures, and used both drawing and extensive model-making in their design work.

NOTES

I am most indebted to Robert A. M. Stern, dean of the Yale School of Architecture, for suggesting a new edition of Nelson's articles, and to Nina Rappaport for asking me to write this Introduction and for keeping me on my toes. Dr. Marina Sommella, Rome, one of the most knowledgeable students of Italian archival holdings of twentieth-century architecture and a former archivist at the Federal Institute of Technology (EPFL), Lausanne, gave generously of her time and knowledge, cross-checking elusive publications and searching out illustrations. Architect Emilio Terragni's passionate interest in automotive design led me onto the tracks of Tatra motorcars. The readers of my draft for Yale University Press prompted me to make improvements and avoid blunders that typically occur when a subject is as far-flung as Nelson's. Mirko Zardini, director of the Canadian Centre for Architecture, Montreal, and Italo Lupi, editor of *Abitare* magazine in Milan, as well as Elisabetta Terragni, Catherine Ingraham, Jeffrey Schnapp, and Michelangelo Sabatino, shared my enthusiasm for Nelson's pieces and made helpful suggestions.

Anyone undertaking an edition of texts on architecture will long for a quiet desk in a superb library. By appointing me Senior Mellon Fellow at the Canadian Centre for Architecture in the spring of 2006, Phyllis Lambert enabled me to dedicate a part of my residency to this project.

1. See Stanley Abercrombie, *George Nelson: The Design of Modern Design* (Cambridge: MIT Press, 1995), 27ff. Nelson published the Fairchild House in the *Architectural Forum* 78 (April 1943): 37–50, where he served as associate editor. The Fairchild House was astounding on several counts: Nelson ingeniously rethought the problem of the New York row house with a fairly narrow but deep lot, connected the front and back by fully glazed-in ramps, and brought light deep into the house while shielding interiors from the street. A drawing of the ramp (p. 45) has a more genuine Corbusian touch than the drawings he faked in order to illustrate his article on Le Corbusier. An interesting, concise, and informed publication on Nelson is Imma Forino, *George Nelson, Thinking* (Rome: Universale di architettura, 2004).

2. George Nelson and Henry Wright, *Tomorrow's House: A Complete Guide for the Home-Builder* (New York: Simon and Schuster, 1945).

3. George Nelson, "Helweg-Moeller," *Pencil Points* (February 1935).

4. *Pencil Points* (September 1935): 455.

5. It is worthwhile to take note of the several architecture competitions sponsored by General Electric, and of the entries published in *Pencil Points*. Some of the most "modern projects" in the pages of *Pencil Points* are found among these entries and in some of the advertisements, such as those proffered by General Electric in 1935.

6. John Neuhart, Marylin Neuhart, and Ray Eames, *Eames Design: The Work of the Office of Charles and Ray Eames* (New York: Abrams, 1989), 21. It is alleged that on this trip Eames saw the work of Mies van der Rohe, Walter Gropius, Le Corbusier, and Henry van de Velde "for the first time," but he obviously saw a lot more. His travel sketches are staunchly traditional and give rather hackneyed views of Bruges and other familiar destinations.

7. Pat Kirkham, *Charles and Ray Eames, Designers of the Twentieth Century* (Cambridge: MIT Press, 1993), 13, quotes "An Eames Celebration: The Several Worlds of Charles and Ray Eames," WNET-TV, New York, February 3, 1972. I cannot help noting that Eames' image of being hosed down is itself derived from the famous cold-water therapy developed by the German priest and physician Sebastian Kneipp. Eames neatly, and perhaps naively, reacted to the "purgative effect" of the Weissenhof Siedlung.

8. A reprint of the exhibition catalogue is available as Henry-Russell Hitchcock and Philip Johnson, *The International Style*, foreword by Philip Johnson (New York: Norton, 1995). See also Franz Schulze, *Philip Johnson: Life and Work* (New York: Knopf, 1994), 75–86.

9. *Der Wachsmann Report. Auskünfte eines Architekten,* ed. Michael Gruening (Berlin-East, 1985). In May 1929, Wachsmann began planning a small wooden country house for Albert Einstein in Caputh (Brandenburg), and in 1932 he won the Rome Prize of the Prussian Academy of Arts. He was living in Rome at the Villa Massimo when Nelson arrived in the city.

10. There is still no comprehensive study on the German and Austrian intellectuals and artists who hung on in Italy before the Axis was established with Mussolini and the racial laws were enacted in 1938. It is worth remembering, though, that deep into the 1930s German and Austrian intellectuals, including the art historians Rudolf Wittkower, Richard Krautheimer, and Ivoe Lany (Florentine Kunsthistorisches Institut), the architect and critic Bernard Rudofsky, the set designer, typographer, and painter Xanti Schawinsky, and many others found provisional refuge in Italy, though mostly in unremunerative conditions. See *Visionaere und Vertriebene. Oesterreichische Spuren in der Modernen Amerikanischen Architektur,* ed. M. Boeckl (Berlin, 1995). For alumni of the Bauhaus, see Gabriele Diana Grawe, *Call for Action: Mitglieder des Bauhauses in Nordamerika* (Weimar: VDG, 2002). The editors of *Quadrante,* Pier Maria Bardi and Massimo Bontempelli, reacted to the news of Hitler's ascent to power in the May 1933 issue: "It appears that bad news for rationalism is in the offing in Germany, the nation considered in the vanguard of new architecture, especially for its excellence with such masters as Gropius and Mies van der Rohe. That is in the wake of political change that has occurred with the advent of Hitler." ["Sembra che in Germania, la nazione ritenuta all'avanguardia della nuova architettura, sopratutto per l'eccellenza di maestri come Gropius e Mies Van der Rohe, spiri cattiva aria in fatto di razionalismo. Cio' in seguito ai mutamenti politici determinatisi dopo l'avvento di Hitler."]

11. Abercrombie, *George Nelson,* 6ff.

12. A. H. Granger, *Charles Follen McKim* (Boston, 1913), 87. The Rome Prize jury included William Mitchell Kendall, who, as a partner in the firm of McKim, Mead, and White, is said to have had a hand in the design of the American Academy in Rome. Nelson's entry for the prize is patterned on a clipped version of Beaux-Arts design

with competent, if dull, detailing.

13. For some intriguing parallels in public programs and resettlement and social reforms, but also significant differences between the United States and Italy, see Diane Y. Ghirardo, *Building New Communities: New Deal America and Fascist Italy* (Princeton: Princeton University Press, 1989).

14. Leland M. Roth, *McKim, Mead & White, Architects* (New York: Harper and Row, 1983), 177.

15. See Spiro Kostof, *The Third Rome, 1870-1950: Traffic and Glory* (Berkeley: University Art Museum, 1973), with individual entries on the major urban interventions. A useful survey with documentary texts is Giorgio Ciucci and Francesco Dal Co, *Architettura italiana del '900, Atlante* (Milan: Electa, 1990, 1993); Richard Etlin, *Modernism in Italian Architecture, 1890-1940* (Cambridge: MIT Press, 1991). A recent study by D. Medina Lasansky, *The Renaissance Perfected: Architecture, Spectacle, and Tourism in Fascist Italy* (University Park: Pennsylvania State University Press, 2004), esp. 1-17, is short on Rome but interesting for the Fascist creation of a topography of *italianità*. Sepp Schueller, *Das Rom Mussolinis* (Düsseldorf: Mosella, 1943). This slim volume of photographs contains many images taken in the 1930s, conveying the impression the city made on the German photographer, who lived in Rome and took thousands of photographs while the capital was transformed.

16. Italo Insolera, "La Capitale in espansione," in *Urbanistica* (Turin, 1960), 114-69; and Insolera, *Roma moderna, un secolo di storia urbanistica* (Rome, 1962).

17. The competition for the new seat of the Partito Nazionale Fascista was announced on 27 December 1933; the second stage only in 1937.

18. *Pencil Points* (January 1935): 11.

19. Quoted after *Karl Friedrich Schinkel, Reisen nach Italien,* ed. Gottfried Riemann (Berlin: Ruetten & Loening, 1979), 46 (trans. by author).

20. It is worth singling out such figures as the jurist, economist, and journalist Giuseppe Bottai (1895-1959), who left the ministry of the *corporazioni* in 1932 to take on that of the *previdenza sociale* while holding professorships in Rome and Pisa. He was the first governor of Addis Ababa, and in 1936 became minister of education *(educazione nazionale)*. Le Corbusier sought *a tout prix* to approach Mussolini through Bottai, but he failed; cf. *Dizionario biografico degli Italiani* (Rome: Fondazione Treccani, 1971), s.v. "Bottai." See also the comprehensive study by Giorgio Ciucci, *Gli architetti e il fascismo. Architetura e citta, 1922-1944* (Turin: Einaudi, 1989).

21. *Pencil Points* (May 1935): 219.

22. Ponti designed a new vestibule, courtyard, classrooms, and the *Aula magna* with a latticed ceiling of reinforced concrete. The project was completed only after the war started.

23. Witold Gombrowicz, *Polish Memories,* trans. Bill Johnston (New Haven: Yale University Press, 2004), 188-89. These memories were written for broadcast by Radio Free Europe at the end of the 1950s but never disseminated before the manuscript was published posthumously.

24. *Apollinaire on Art: Essays and Reviews, 1902-1918, by Guillaume Apollinaire,* ed. Leroy C. Breunig, trans. Susan Suleiman (New York: Viking, 1972). In little more than a decade Apollinaire wrote a variety of brief biographical sketches of artists, some only a few pages long, others encapsulated in reviews of exhibitions and occasional pieces. Gertrude Stein, *A Stein Reader,* ed. Ulla E. Dydo (Evanston, Ill.: Northwestern University Press, 1993).

25. Edward Elgar set out to portray friends with his *Enigma Variations* (1898-99), and Maurice Ravel dedicated each of his pieces forming the cycle *Le Tombeau de Couperin* to one of his friends killed during the First World War (1917). Not only are the pieces in their entirety an homage to the composer Couperin, but each component is also the memorial of an individual.

26. Much of today's rumor-mongering in the popular press, attributing verbatim statements to interviewees, and many television features, typically associated with one interviewer (Barbara Walters, Larry King, Charlie Rose, and so forth) descend from the genre of "word portraits" I'm discussing.

27. Edmund Wilson, *Axel's Castle: A Study in the Imaginative Literature of 1870-1930* (New York: Charles Scribner's Sons, 1931); Ernst Robert Curtius, *Die literarischen Wegbereiter des neuen Frankreich* (Potsdam: G. Kiepenheuer, 1920); and Curtius, *Französischer Geist im neuen Europa* (Stuttgart: DVA, 1925). These studies were stimulated by contemporary writers from cultures foreign to their interpreters, although Curtius, who was of northern German origin, grew up in bilingual Alsace, a province of France that was annexed by Germany after the Franco-Prussian war of 1870-71, only to revert to France in the interwar period, and, of course, after 1945.

28. See Giacomo Debenedetti, *Saggi critici* (Florence: Solaria, 1929). The full scope of Debenedetti's criticism has emerged only after World War II, when he held professorships at Messina and Rome, but his early writings gave every indication of a major European voice.

29. Maximilian Harden [Isidore Witkowski], 1861-1927, edited the German weekly *Die Zukunft* and published biographical sketches of contemporaries from Bismarck to Lenin, Ibsen to Lenbach. Violently opposed to Wilhelmine politics, Harden turned pacifist during the First World War and published "imaginary speeches" by the American president Woodrow Wilson that anticipated the Versailles Peace Treaty. He approved of the Peace, as did Germany's foreign minister, Walter Rathenau. Shortly after Rathenau's assassination in 1922, an attempt was made on Harden's life, leaving him seriously impaired and forcing him into exile in Switzerland.

30. Maximilian Harden, *I Meet My Contemporaries* (New York: Holt, 1925), 213. The American ambassador to France, James W. Gerard, wrote an introduction to the book. This and other translations of Harden's

essays enjoyed great popularity in the 1920s and 1930s. Interest in Harden dropped off during the Second World War. A first selection of essays was published as *Word Portraits: Character Sketches of Famous Men and Women* (Edinburgh: Blackwood, 1911). It is worth keeping in mind that some of Harden's essays were also condensed and reviewed by *Time* magazine in the July 23, 1923, and January 18, 1926, issues. The principal modern student of Harden, Uwe Weller *(Maximilian Harden und die "Zukunft"* [Bremen, 1970]) considers him to have been "the German figure most often mentioned, along with his archenemy, Kaiser Wilhelm II. He may have been the most significant political writer in twentieth-century Germany" (trans. by author). As for Lenin's embalmed body, Harden was dead right in sharing popular suspicion that the revolutionary's reputation might not outlast his embalmed body. As a matter of fact, the body is slated to be removed from its mausoleum at this time.

31. *Pencil Points* (September 1935): 453.

32. It is not surprising, then, that the drawings Le Corbusier produced while lecturing appear spontaneous, though they are premeditated and often anticipated in his published work. Several of these large-scale sheets have resurfaced and been published, such as those of his lectures in Milan (see note 82 below).

33. *Pencil Points* (August 1936): 423.

34. Walter Gropius, *Internationale Architektur* (Munich: Langen, 1925), 5: *"ein Bilderbuch moderner Baukunst."* F. R. Yerbury, *Modern European Buildings,* 1st ser. (London: Gollancz, 1928), is a compendium of images chiefly of northern and eastern European architecture. Yerbury's is the only book of its kind and time to include good pictures of three Scandinavian architects Nelson was especially interested in: Bent Hellweg-Moeller, Ivar Tengbom, and Erik Gunnar Asplund. Alberto Sartoris first published his *Gli elementi dell'architettura funzionale. Sintesi panoramica dell'architettura moderna* in 1932 (Milan, Hoepli), followed by expanded editions in 1935 and 1941.

35. Nelson also noted the affinity with William Lescaze's studios for Columbia Broadcasting Corporation (on Madison Avenue in New York) and those by McGrath for the BBC in London.

36. *Pencil Points* (June 1936): 293. The biographical connection with Nelson also led him to remark that McGrath, "at the age of 33 . . . is one of the most successful of the younger English architects" (289).

37. Donal O'Donovan, *God's Architect: A Life of Raymond McGrath* (Wicklow, Ireland: Kilbride, 1995), 95. Matters did not rest here, because McGrath had secured the services of two photographers, M. O. Dell and H. L. Wainwright, who went on to become the official photographers of the *Architectural Review* and thus cast a generation of architectural work in their mold. It is worth noting that McGrath's son, Norman, grew up to be a prominent architectural photographer. Beatriz Colomina has persuasively argued that "architecture and layout construct another architecture in the space of the page." See her *Privacy and Publicity: Modern Architecture as Mass Media* (Cambridge: MIT Press, 1994), 114.

38. *Pencil Points* (July 1935): 368.

39. Ibid., 371.

40. Ibid.

41. *Pencil Points* (November 1935): 557.

42. *Pencil Points* (January 1936): 7.

43. *Pencil Points* (March 1936): 129.

44. Ibid.

45. Ralph T. Walker, partner in Voorhees, Gmelin, and Walker of New York City, was installed as editorial advisor in February 1936. *Pencil Points* published a full-page portrait and editorial for the occasion ([March 1936]: 58ff). Walker subsequently wrote several editorials; the first, in the March 1936 issue, exalting regional and cultural differences across the United States, argued for strong ties between architects and their communities.

46. *Pencil Points* (March 1936): 113.

47. Ibid., 133.

48. Mark Twain, *A Tramp Abroad* (1880; New York: Penguin, 1997), 187: A foolish young traveler making conversation: "It's my first trip. But we've been all around—Paris and everywhere. I'm to enter Harvard next year. Studying German all the time now. Can't enter till I know German. This book's *Otto's Grammar*. It's a mighty good book to get the ich *habe gehabt haben's* out of."

49. *Pencil Points* (January 1936): 7.

50. Piacentini dedicated thirty-nine pages to Vaccaro in *L'Architettura: Rivista del Sindacato nazionale fascista architetti*, October 1932, pp. 513–52. Vaccaro also appears among the year's contributors, and his post office in Naples was to be widely featured in the leading journals.

51. An inaugural essay by Ponti in the January 1928 issue of *Domus,* entitled "La casa all'italiana," celebrates the quality of "housing" in a manner that points straight to Nelson's own design of apartments, furniture, and household equipment. Ponti wrote: "The Italian house is straightforward, ready to accommodate furniture and works of art. . . . Its design does not simply respond to material necessities, it is not made to be a 'machine à habiter.' What is considered its 'comfort' isn't simply the match of objects and needs. . . . This 'comfort' consists in something higher, for it aims to lend us, by means of architecture, a measure for our thoughts, a simplicity to our sound customs, and by its largesse a confident and communal sense of life." (trans. by author). Ponti went on to envision a comfortable house that breathes an air of peace.

52. Abercrombie, *George Nelson,* preface by Ettore Sottsass, Jr., viii.

53. Sheldon Cheney, *The New World Architecture* (London: Longman's, Green, 1930), 40.

54. Ibid.

55. Ibid., 360.

56. Gio Ponti participated in 1927 in an exhibit of modern decorative art at Macy's in New York. He was thus somewhat known in the United States. See Robert A. M. Stern and Thomas Mellins, *New York 1930* (New York: Rizzoli, 1988).

57. *Pencil Points* (April 1935): 4. On Ponti's interiors see Marianne Lamonaca, "Tradition as Transformation: Gio Ponti's Program for the Modern Italian Home, 1928–1933," in *Studies in the Decorative Arts* (Fall/Winter 1997-98): 52–82.

58. *Casabella* (1933): 18. The editor of *Casabella,* Giuseppe Pagano, already had published an article on Luckhardt and Anker in July 1932, following up in August with Mendelsohn and in September with Dudok.

59. *Pencil Points* (March 1935): 129.

60. Ibid., 116.

61. The issue of competitions surfaces in articles, notes, and letters to the editor in numerous issues of *Pencil Points.* See esp. H. Van Buren Magonigle (February 1935): 63ff.

62. *Pencil Points* (February 1935): 11.

63. Ibid., 12.

64. Ibid., 9.

65. *Internationale Architektur,* ed. Walter Gropius (Munich: Langen, 1925 [compiled summer 1924]), Bauhausbuecher 1.

66. For Walter Curt Behrendt, *Der Sieg des neuen Baustils* (The victory of the new building style), see the translation published in the series Texts & Documents (Los Angeles: Getty Research Institute, 2000), trans. Harry Francis Mallgrave. In his Introduction, Detlef Mertins draws a richly detailed picture of the issues and controversies surrounding Behrendt's arguments and his role as a critic of modern German architecture.

67. Gustav Adolf Platz, *Die Baukunst der neuesten Zeit* (Berlin: Propylaeen, 1930). Yerbury, *Modern European Buildings*. While including a considerable variety of works of engineering, Platz concentrates mainly on "das deutsche Sprachgebiet und die Sphaere seiner unmittelbaren Beziehungen" (12), but this restriction cannot but be chauvinistic and is further undermined by the exclusion of Scandinavia.

68. Raymond McGrath, *Twentieth Century Houses* (London: Faber and Faber, [1934]). McGrath's range of examples is the widest and most original. It is detailed in the documentation of every project and sensitive to finer differences in kind and quality. McGrath takes for granted that the twentieth-century home sprang from the reforms of William Morris, Charles F. A. Voysey, and Charles Rennie Mackintosh. His analysis centers on the creation of individual dwellings with all their appurtenances. He evaluates his examples well beyond the criteria of functionalism and industrialization, considering instead livability, details, and atmosphere.

69. Yerbury, *Modern European Buildings,* 6.

70. *Pencil Points* (October 1936): 538.

71. Ibid., 531.

72. Abercrombie observed as much when he characterized Nelson's attitude as a teacher at Columbia University during the war: "The patterns that Hitchcock and Johnson had identified as constituting the International Style had become patterns Nelson disliked, and he disliked them *because* they were patterns, repeated by rote" (29).

73. *Occidente, Sintesi dell'attivita letteraria nel mondo* (Rome), 12 issues, 1932–35. The range of contributors and subjects is worthy of the journal's title, including Aldous Huxley, D. H. Lawrence, James Joyce, Virginia Woolf, Joseph Conrad, William Faulkner, John Dos Passos, Jean Cocteau, Luigi Pirandello, Italo Svevo, Giuseppe Bottai, and even German-language authors whose work could no longer be published in Germany. As with most of these ventures, Massimo Bontempelli, then coeditor of *Quadrante,* also appeared in the pages of *Occidente.*

74. Bela Balazs' "Le forbici poetiche," *Occidente* 9 (1935): 46–47, argues that cinematographic "montage can not only suggest associations, but also produce them" in an interior vision that alternates between conscious and subconscious (47). Accordingly, plates from Max Ernst's *Une semaine de bonté* appear in the same issue.

75. Hitchcock, *Modern Architecture,* 148.

76. *Pencil Points* (July 1936): 377.

77. *Pencil Points* (August 1936): 432.

78. Ibid.

79. As he admitted to John Dixon in an interview reported in Abercrombie, *George Nelson,* 14ff.

80. Le Corbusier and Pierre Jeanneret, *Oeuvre complète de 1929-1934* (Zurich: Les Editions d'Architecture, 1934), 202: "Le Corbusier was constantly surrounded by members of the new generation. and he was delighted to find among them so much intelligence and such sound information" (trans. by author). One is tempted to think that the eager questioning of a George Nelson may have contributed to the master's condescending recognition of talent among the young.

81. See Giorgio Ciucci, "A Roma con Bottai," in *Rassegna* [I clienti di Le Corbusier] 2, no. 3 (1980): 66–71, with bibliography and an analysis of Le Corbusier's attempts to secure a commission from the Italian government. He failed, and in his Roman lecture in October 1937 resigned himself to defeat across the board: *"Si potrebbe quasi dire: ovunque siamo sconfitti: Francia, Russia, Germania, Italia"* (p. 71).

82. *Quadrante* 13 (May 1934): 5–26. The journal's coeditor, Pier Maria Bardi, introduced Le Corbusier, and his lectures were published on the basis of stenographic transcription. While Le Corbusier rehearsed the premises of his theory, as he was fond of doing, his drawings did not actually include the suggestive juxtaposition between the Campo Santo in Pisa and his project for the Palace of the Soviets that Nelson imitated in his sketches. Le Corbusier moved on to Milan, where he gave essentially the same lecture on June 19, 1934, at the *Circolo filologico*. His lecture notes

in the Fondation Le Corbusier, Paris, did refer to the cycle of life, symbolically represented by the sun, lungs, and the "harmonie biologique," including air conditioning! See Archivio Bottoni, *Le Corbusier, Urbanisme* (Milan: Mazzotta, 1983). Six large drawings are reproduced in color.

83. *Quadrante* 13 (May 1934): 23: *"Interpretazione di Le Corbusier"* by an "anonymous psychologist."

84. *Pencil Points* (September 1935): 479–85. The same issue also carries an obituary for Van Buren Magonigle (1867–1935).

85. Ibid.

86. Schulze, *Philip Johnson,* 123–25.

87. This rather lame slogan ran below the flag of *Pencil Points* until February 1936, when it was quietly dropped. A month later the new cover struck a fresh note, and advertisers likewise came forward with striking designs: Alcoa inserted a full-page image of the grand entrance to an International Building Congress (Budapest) in blazing 1937 style, highlighted by silver overprinting to celebrate the use of aluminum.

88. The new cover graphics were, lo and behold, by Ralph Walker.

89. The managing editor, Kenneth Reid, responded to a barrage of reader's letters in the July 1936 issue with an article titled "Design > Architecture." "Since the April issue of *Pencil Points* appeared, with its strikingly different cover, we have been asked by a number of people if the prominence given to the word DESIGN signified any impending change in our editorial policy" (375). Reid, of course, calmed his readership, but the change in graphic design did signal some moves beyond graphics. An obvious hypothesis would suggest that the new architecture presented almost every month in Nelson's articles did not leave *Pencil Points* and its readership immune. As the chief recurrent feature in the journal, apart from the staid periodic presentation of Colonial New England houses, Nelson's articles must have led in a different editorial direction. The passing of such old grumps as H. van Buren Magonigle in 1935, and competition with the *Architectural Forum,* certainly paved the way to the evolution of *Pencil Points* into *Progressive Architecture;* see P/A, 50th Anniversary Issue (June 1970): 130ff, especially Suzanne Stephens, "Architectural Journalism Analyzed: Reflections on a Half Century," 133–39.

90. Hitchcock, *Modern Architecture,* 205.

91. Letter by C. Magi Spinetti, published in *Quadrante* 8 (December 1933): 47. "Il pensiero e la vita spirituale sono fluttuazioni astratte di ogni momento ma la impronta e' la loro rivelazione, la fotografia che mette in luce certi lineamenti che all'occhio e col movimento sfuggono." I have freely translated this sentence into English.

INDEX

References to illustrations appear in *italics*.

Aalto, Alvar, 159
Ahlberg, Haakon, 97
Alexanderplatz (Berlin), 53, *54*, 161
Algiers, 70-71, 74-75, *75*
American Academy (Rome), 5, *5*, 7, 11, 30
Anker, Alfons, 49, 161
Apollinaire, Guillaume, 9, 166n24
architects: biographies of, 161-63; English, 126; German, 7; Italian, 6, 11, 14-15, 19, 31, 35; Jewish, 3, 16; lives and lifestyles of, 12-15; "word portraits" of, 10
Architects Collaborative, The (TAC), 163
Architectural Forum (journal), 25, *26*
Architectural Record (journal), 25
architecture, modern, 32, 118, 148; American critics of, 17; books and journals on, 7, 15-18, *17;* German, 83, 139; Italian, 71; as "modern architectonic art," 140, 158; national identity and, 19-20; Nazi condemnation of, 16, 88; politics and, 145; totalitarian views of, 21; as way of living, 12
Architettura (magazine), 30, 161
Architettura d'oggi (journal), 16
Armée du Salut (Le Corbusier), *73*, 74
art, modern, 16, 129
"art for art's sake," 91, 140
Arvika Church (Sweden), *96*, 97, 162
Axel's Castle (Wilson), 9

Bailey, Douglas, 163
Banca d'Italia [Bank of Italy] (Rome), 20, 32
Barcelona Exposition (1929), 91, *91*, 162
Barman, Christian, 104
Barocco (Baroque) style, 108
Bauhaus, 19, 20, 50, 88, 91, 139-43, *141-42;* closed by Nazis, 162; in Dessau, 50, 88, 139-42, *141*, 162, 163; furniture design of, 17; machine production and, 77, *141;* montage illustration and, 25; philosophy of, 77; in Weimar, 139, 140
Bauhaus Bücher, 11
Beaudouin, Eugène, 13-14, 116-25, 145; biography, 162-63; open-air school (Suresnes), *114*, 118, *119*, 120, *120*, *122*, 163
Beaux-Arts, 50, 67, 91; Ecole des Beaux-Arts (Paris), 96, 116-17, 162; in England, 127; proclaimed dead, 91, 116
Behrendt, Walter Curt, 18
Behrens, Peter, 53, 82, 83-84, 139, 162, 163
Berenson, Bernard, 2
Berlin, 15, 16, 82, 143; Building Exposition, 88; Columbus Haus, 84; Luckhardt brothers' designs, *46*, 48-49, *49*, *51-55;* Telschow House, 161

Biennial Exposition (Venice), 60
Bocquillon, 123
Bologna, 110, 113, 162
Bontempelli, Massimo, 7, 165n10
Brasini, Armando, 31
Brescia, Italy, *28*, *34*, 35, *36*
Broadcasting House, BBC (London), *131*, 163
Brochner, Georg, 40
building materials, 51, 53, 128; glass, 74, 76; reinforced concrete, 157

Cancellotti, Gino, 36
Capitoline Hill (Rome), 6, 31
cars, 7, *7*, 18, 35; Czech-made, 18, *18*, 54; Luckhardts and, 53-54
Casa all'italiana, La (Ponti), 16, 63
Casabella (journal), 7, *8*, 16, 63, 167n58
Cecchi, Emilio, 7
Cederwall, Gustaf, 102
ceramic designs, 58-59, *59*, *60*, *62*, 63, *63*, 138
Cheney, Sheldon, 15
Chermayeff, Serge, 129, 163
Chicago, 143
Chicago Tribune building, 31
Chitty, Anthony, 163
Church of Christ the King (Rome), 33, 37, *37*
CIAM (Congrès International d'Architecture Moderne), 2
Cinema Corso (Rome), 20
Città universitaria [University City] (Rome), 6, 16, 63-64, *65-66*, 161
City Building (Stockholm), 102-3, *104*, 105
city planning, 53, 54, 72
Coates, Welles, 129, 163
Cologne, 139
Colosseum (Rome), 6
Columbus Haus (Berlin), 53, 84
communism, 10, 88, 122
Concert Hall, Stockholm, 97, *99*, 162
Connell, Amyas, 129
Constructivism, 143
Copenhagen, 40, 43-44, *45*
Corbusier, Le (Charles-Édouard Jeanneret), 12, 14, 19, 70-79, 108, 148; Algiers and, 70-71, 74-75, *75;* Armée du Salut, *73*, 74; on Highgate Apartments, 156; influence of, 145, 155; international focus of, 17; lectures, 11, 21, 72, 166n32, 168n82; Maison Suisse, 76, *79;* Palace of the Soviets (Moscow), 76, *76-78;* Paris envisioned by, 53; pavilion for Paris Exposition (1925), 70, *70;* as pioneer, 48; publicity and, 82; *Quadrante* illustrations, 21, *21*
Corriere della Sera (newspaper), 63
Coughlin, Rev. Charles E., 21

Cret, Paul P., 21
Curtius, Ernst Robert, 9, 10, 166n27

Das Werk (journal), 23, *23*
Debenedetti, Giacomo, 9, 166n28
Denmark, 40, 43, 60, 161
department stores, 44
Dessau, Bauhaus in, 50, 88, 139-42, *141*, 162, 163
Deutsche Werkbund, 86, 88, 139, 163
Domus (journal), 7, 14, 63, 161-62
Dugdale, Michael, 163

Eames, Charles, 3, 165nn6-7
Egypt, 117
Elemeni dell'architettura funzionale, Gli (Sartoris), 16
elephant house (London Zoo), 150, *151*, 153
Empire style, 86
Engelbrekt Church (Sweden), 96
England, 12, 127-28, 144-45, 157
Enskilda Bank (Stockholm), 97, *98*, 162
Esselte Building (Stockholm), *105*
Ethiopia, 6, 7, 20

Fagus Factory, *138*, 139
fascism, Italian, 8, 32, 108, 162; modern architecture embraced by, 21, 145; symbolism in architecture, *110*, 111, *112*, 113
Film Guild Cinema (New York), 16
"Finella" House (Cambridge, England), *124*, *127*, *128*, 132, 163
Finsbury Health Centre, 163
Fischer's Restaurant (London), 132, *133-35*
Florence, American émigrés in, 2
Florence, city of, 36
Forbes, Mansfield, 128, 129
Forester, J. C. N., 162
Fornaroli, Antonio, 161
Foro Italico (Rome), 6
Forum (Rome), 33
France, 13, 70, 96, 118, 166n27
Französischer Geist im neuen Europa (Curtius), 9
furniture design, 26, *27*, 50, 126, 132; Luckhardts and, 53-54; Mies van der Rohe and, *88*

garden city, 157
Gate, Simon, 102
Germany, 2, 10, 12, 19, 82; Axis alliance with Italy, 9, 165n10; Jewish architects' flight from, 3; Nazi regime, 20, 54, 145
Gershwin, George, 18
Ghelardini, Armando, 20
Glass in Architecture and Decoration (McGrath), 131

INDEX

171

Gombrowicz, Witold, 7, 9
Goncourt brothers, 9
Goodhue, Bertram, 83
gorilla house (London Zoo), 150, 153, *153–55,* 163
Gothenburg, Sweden, 94, 97
Gothic style, 108
Greece, 117
green cities, 144
Greenway, Francis, 127
Gropius, Walter, 11, 16, 19, 138–45, 158; Bauhaus and, 50, 88, 139–43, *141–42,* 145; biography, 163; emigration from Germany, 91, 163; Hall of Industry (Cologne), *136,* 138, 139, *139; Internationale Architektur* and, 18; Nazis and, 17, 49, 163; as pioneer, 48; prefabrication and, 143, 144, *144,* 163; workers' housing and, 15

Hall of Industry (Cologne), *136,* 138, 139, *139*
Harden, Maximilian, 10, 166nn29–30
Harding, Valentine, 163
Heering, Peter, 41, 43
Heering's Gaard, *38,* 41, *42, 43*
Helweg-Moeller, Bengt, 19, 40–45, 60, 161
Hemingway, Ernest, 2
Henrot, 123
Herbé, Paul, 117, 123
Highgate Apartments (London), 19, 145, *149,* 155–58, *156–59,* 163
Hitchcock, Henry-Russell, 3, 15, 19, 20, 168n72
Hitler, Adolf, 16, 49, 88, 165n10
Hogalid Church (Stockholm), *95,* 98, *100, 101,* 162
housing: apartments in Milan, *67;* Beaudouin and, 118, 121–22; International Style and, 50; Mies van der Rohe and, 88, *90,* 155; multifamily dwellings, 143; as "problem of civilization," 14; public housing in Germany, 16; for workers, 15; for zoo animals, 19, 150, *150–55,* 153. *See also* Highgate Apartments (London)
Hubbe House Project, *85, 86*
Hult, Robert, 102

industrial design, 132, *132,* 138, 157
Internationale Architektur (journal), 18
internationalism, 17
International Style, 18, 19, 168n72; Le Corbusier and, 76; MoMA show (1932), 15, 18; Piacentini and, 32; Tengbom and, 102, *104,* 105; typography and, 25
International Style, The (catalogue and exhibition), 15
Isherwood, Christopher, 2
Italo-Ethiopian war, 6, 7

Italy, 3, 12, 20, 117; Axis alliance with Germany, 9, 165n10; Fascist regime, 30, 32, 108, 145, 162

James, Henry, 5
Johnson, Philip, 3, 21, 168n72

Kiesler, Frederick, 16
Kocher, A. Lawrence, 25
Kreuger, Ivar, 100

Lallerstedt, Erik, 152
Largo Argentina (Rome), 6
Lasdun, Denys, 163
League of Nations, 20, 110
Lenin, V. I., 10, 166n30
Libera, Adalberto, 16
Lingeri, Pietro, 16
Literarischen Wegbereiter des neuen Frankreich, Die (Curtius), 9
Lods, Marcel, 118, 123, 145, 163
London, 19, 127, 144; Broadcasting House, BBC, *131,* 163; Highgate Apartments, 19, 145, *149,* 155–58, *156–59,* 163; London Zoo, 19, 150, *150–55,* 153, 163
Lubetkin, Berthold Romanovich, 163
Luckhardt, Hans, 16–17, 48–55, 148, 161
Luckhardt, Vassili, 16–17, 18, 48–55, 148, 161
Lugo (Italy), town square, *112*

Macquarie buildings, 127
Magonigle, Harold Van Buren, 17, 21
Maison Suisse, 76, *79*
Malaparte, Curzio, 7
Malinowsky, 40
Malmsten, Carl, 102
McGrath, Raymond, 11, 14, 126–32, 138, 167–68n68, 167n36; biography, 163; "Finella" house (Cambridge, England), *124, 127, 128,* 128–29, 132, 163; Fischer's Restaurant (London), 132, *133–35; Twentieth Century Houses,* 19
McKim, Mead, and White, 5
Mendelsohn, Erich, 3, 14, 17; Columbus Haus, 53, 84; flight from Nazis, 49, 91; Ufa-Palast, 15, *17*
Mies van der Rohe, Ludwig, 2, 10–11, 16, 21, 82–91, 148; apartment house (Stuttgart), *90,* 155; Barcelona Exposition (1929) and, 91, *91;* Bauhaus and, 88–89, 91; biography, 162; on death of Beaux-Arts, 91, 116; Glass Skyscraper, *83,* 84, *84;* interviewed by Nelson, 14; Nazis and, 49; Tugendhat House (Brno), 82, *85–87,* 86, 91
Milan, 16, 60, 66, 71, 161; apartment houses in, *67;* "Eiffel Tower" of, *56, 64;* Pirelli Building, 161

Milles, Carl, 97, 102
Ministry of Corporations (Rome), *109,* 110
Modern Architecture: Romanticism and Reintegration (Hitchcock), 15
Moravia, Alberto, 7
Morris, William, 126, 168n68
Moscow, 76, *76–78*
Museum of Modern Art (MoMA), 3, 18, 21
Mussolini, Benito ("the Duce"), 5, 6, 9, 35; approval of modern architecture, 108; architectural legacy of, 13; expansionist war and, 7; Piacentini and, 161; Vaccaro and, 113

Naples, Italy, 36, *106, 110–11,* 113
nationalism, 108
Nazism, 3, 48, 50, 161; Bauhaus shut down by, 162; modern architecture condemned by, 16, 88
Neilsson, Jais, 40
Nelson, George: at *Architectural Forum,* 26; education, 3, 5; furniture design of, 26, *27;* Gropius and, 20–21; interior designs of, 2; International Style and, 168n72; journalistic portraits by, 9–11; on lives and lifestyles, 12–15; *Pencil Points* articles, 23, 25–26; photography and, 11; portrait, 2, *2;* prizes and awards, 5; in Rome, 5, 7, 16; *Tomorrow's House,* 4; "word portraits" by, 21
Neo-Expressionism, 143
neo-Renaissance style, 5
Netherlands, 19
Neutra, Richard, 13–14, 17, 126
Newport, R.I., 5
New World Architecture (Cheney), 15, *17*
New York, city of, 5, 16, 21, 143
"New York Skyscraper" (Brescia, Italy), *28, 36*
Nitti, Francesco, 7

Occidente (journal), 20, *20*
Oeuvre complète (Le Corbusier), 21
orchestral studio (Manchester, England), *130*
Ospedale Maggiore (Milan), banners for, 60, *61*
Ostberg, Ragnar, 40
Oud, 48

Pagano, Giuseppe, 16
Palace of the Soviets (Moscow), 76, *76–78,* 168n82
Palazzo delle Esposizioni (Rome), 5, *6*
Palazzo del Littorio (Rome), 113, *113*
Palazzo Venezia (Rome), 6
Panama Pacific Exposition (1915), 31
Paris, 18, 163; American émigrés in, 2;

demolition of city center, 71; Drancy suburb, 121, 145; Ecole des Beaux-Arts, 96, 116–17, 162; Exposition (1925), 41, *41* 59, 70, *70;* World Exhibition (1937), 20
Paris Prize, 5
Paul, Bruno, 83, 162
Pencil Points (journal), 13, 17, 21, 168nn87–89; advertisements in, *25;* cover designs, *22;* evolution into *Progressive Architecture,* 26; Nelson's articles, 23, 25–26; public competitions in, 18; on rise of totalitarianism, 20; typography in, 23, 25
penguin pool (London Zoo), 19, 150, *150,* 163
Period architects, 127, 129, 131
Persia, 117
photography, 11, 16
Piacentini, Marcello, 6, 7, 14, 18, 30–37, 110; biography, 161; buildings designed by, 20; as editor of *Architettura d'oggi,* 16; Fascist regime and, 30, 32
Pirandello, Luigi, 7
Pisa, city of, 76
Platz, Gustav Adolf, 18
Ponti, Gio, 6, 58–60, 63–64, 66–67; biography, 161–62; *Casa all'italiana, La,* 16; ceramic designs, 58–59, *59, 60, 62,* 63, *63,* 138; as editor of *Domus,* 7, 14, 63, 161–62; International Style and, 19, *58, 59;* School of Mathematics (Rome) designs, 63–64, *65–66*
Post, Henri, 163
Post Office (Brescia, Italy), *34,* 35
Post Office (Naples, Italy), *106, 110–11,* 113
prefabrication, 19, 51, 118; Gropius and, 143, 144, *144,* 163; McGrath and, 127
Progressive Architecture (journal), 26
propaganda, 131, 132, 144, 145
Propylaeen series, 18
Proust, Marcel, 9

Quadrante (journal), 7, 16; cover designs, 23, *24;* on Hitler's rise to power, 165n10; Le Corbusier illustrations, 21, *21;* on typography, 25–26

Rammeskow, Børge, 161
Reich, Lilly, 86, *89*
Reid, Kenneth, 26, 168n89
Renaissance style, 36, 37, 58, 74, 83, 97
Rome, ancient, 16, 108
Rome, city of, 5, 70, 117; Church of Christ the King, 33, 37, *37;* Institute Mathematica, 161; Ministry of Corporations, *109,* 110; Palazzo del Littorio, 113, *113;* Piacentini's work in, 30–32; reformed, 5–7, *6–8,* 9
Rome Prize, 5
Rosen, Anton, 161

Rosselli, Alberto, 161
"Rudderbar" house (unbuilt), 131
Russia, 21, 32, 71, 74, 145

Saarinen, Eliel, 26, 31
Samuel, Godfrey, 163
Sant'Elia, Antonio, 108
Sartoris, Alberto, 11, 16, 19
Scandinavia, 2, 12, 40
Schindler, Rudolf, 17
Schinkel, Karl Friedrich, 7
"Sette note per i Luckhardt" (Venturi), 16
Sherman Fairchild House, 2, *3,* 165n1
Sieg des neuen Baustils (journal), 18
Skinner, Francis, 163
skyscrapers, 53, *83, 84,* 143
Sommerfeld Log House, 142, *143*
Soncini, Eugenio, 161
Sottsass, Ettore, Jr., 15
Soviet Union, 20
standardization, 140, 143
Stein, Gertrude, 2, 9
Steinberg, Saul, 3
Stille (magazine), 162
Stockholm, 94, 96–97; City Building, 102–3, *104,* 105; Concert Hall, 97, *99,* 162; Enskilda Bank, 97, *98,* 162; Esselte Building, *105;* Hogalid Church, 162; Swedish Match Company Building, 100, 102, *102, 103;* Town Hall, 94, 96
Stuttgart, Germany, 3, 88, *90,* 155
Suresnes (France), open-air school in, *114,* 118, *119,* 120, *120, 122,* 163
sventramenti, 6
Sweden, 40, 94, 162
Swedish Match Company Building, 100, 102, *102, 103*

Taine, Hippolyte, 9
Taut, Bruno, 50, 91
Taut, Max, 50, 91
tea shop (Copenhagen), *44,* 45
Tecton studio, 13, 19, 148–58; animal houses at London Zoo, 19, 150, *150–55,* 153; biography, 163; Highgate Apartments (London), 19, 145, *149,* 155–58, *156–59,* 163
Telschow House (Berlin), 161
tenements, 143
Tengbom, Ivar, 94–105; Arvika Church, *96,* 97; biography, 162; Concert Hall, Stockholm, 97, *99;* Enskilda Bank, 97, *98;* Hogalid Church, *95,* 98, *100, 101;* Swedish Match Company Building, 100, 102, *102,* 103
Terragni, Giuseppe, 16
Tomorrow's House: A Complete Guide for

the Home-Builder (Nelson and Wright), *4*
Torulf, Ernst, 96, 162
totalitarianism, 2, 9, 20
"Tower of the Revolution," 33
"Triumph of Death, The" (Pointi), *62*
Tugendhat House (Brno, Czechoslovakia), 2, 15, 82, *87,* 91, 162
Twentieth Century Group, 129
Twentieth Century Houses (McGrath), 19, *19,* 131
typography, 25

Ufa-Palast (Berlin), 15, 17
United States, 16, 167n45; Beaudouin in, 13, 162; Gropius in, 163; Mies van der Rohe in, 88; reception of modern architecture in, 15, 16

Vaccaro, Giuseppe, 13, 14, 109–13; biography, 162; Ministry of Corporations (Rome), *109,* 110; Palazzo del Littorio (Rome), 113, *113;* Post Office (Naples), *106, 110–11,* 113
Valéry, Paul, 9
Van der Velde, Henry, 139, 163
Vatican City, 6, 117
Venice, 7, 60
Venturi, Lionello, 16
Via Barberini (Rome), 6
Via delle Botteghe Oscure (Rome), 6
Via dell'Impero (Rome), 6, *7,* 33
Villa Aurelia (Rome), 5
Villa Borghese (Rome), 7, 9

Wachsmann, Konrad, 3, 163
Walker, Ralph, 13, 167n45
Webb, Philip, 126
Weissenhof Siedlung (Stuttgart), 3
Das Werk (journal), 23, *23*
Werkbund Exposition (Cologne), *136,* 138, 139, *139*
Wilson, Edmund, 9
World War I, 161, 163, 166n25, 166n29
World War II, 161, 162, 163, 166n28
Wright, Frank Lloyd, 15, 26, 82
Wurster, William, 126

Yale University, 3, 5
Yerbury, F. R., 11, 18, 19, 166–67n34

zoo animals, housing of, 19, 150, *150–55,* 153

ILLUSTRATION CREDITS

Numbers indicate page number; t = top, b = bottom, l = left, c = center, r = right.

Akademie der Künste, 46, 51, 52, 53l, 53r, 54, 55; Alinari/Art Resource, NY, 28, 33, 36, 37r, 64 (Gio Ponti Archives—S. Licitra, Milano), 106, 110l, 110r, 111; American Academy in Rome, Photo Archive, 5; © Archivio Vaccaro, ii, 109, 112, 113; Art Resource, 138, 141r (Photo Credits: Foto Marburg); Avery Architectural and Fine Arts Library, Columbia University, 20, 24; CNAC/MNAM/Dist. Réunion des Musées Nationaux/Art Resource, NY, 136, 142 (Photo Credits: Lucia Moholy); Collection Centre Canadien d'Architecture/Canadian Centre for Architecture, Montreal, 1, 4, 25; Collection of Hannah Purdy, 96, 98, 101, 103r, 104, 105; Die Neue Sammlung—State Museum of Applied Arts | Design in the Pinakothek der Moderne, Munich, Germany, © Die Neue Sammlung State Museum of Applied Arts and Design, Munich, and photographer: Rainer Viertlboeck, 7; © Fondation le Corbusier, 68, 70, 73t, 73b, 74, 75l, 75r, 76, 77, 78, 79t, 79b; ©Gio Ponti Archives—S. Licitra, Milan, 56, 58l, 58r, 59t, 59b, 60l, 60r, 61l, 61r, 62t, 62l, 62r, 63, 65t, 65c, 65b, 66t, 66b, 67; Digital Image © The Museum of Modern Art/Licensed by SCALA/Art Resource, NY, 80, 83, 84, 85, 86l, 86r, 87l, 87r, 88l, 88r, 89, 91; Jacqueline Nelson, 2; © President and Fellows of Harvard College, Busch-Reisinger Museum, Gift of Walter Gropius, 139, 141l, 143, 144; RIBA Library Drawings Collection, 134, 151, 154; RIBA Library Photographs Collection, vi, 34, 37l, 38, 41, 42, 43, 44 (artist: Francis Rowland Yerbury), 49l, 49r, 90, 92, 95, 99, 100, 102, 103l, 114, 119, 120, 122, 127 (Dell & Wainwright), 128t (Dell & Wainwright), 128b (Dell & Wainwright), 131, 135, 146 (Bryan & Norman Westwood), 149 (Dell & Wainwright), 150l, 150r, 152 (Bryan & Norman Westwood), 153, 155, 156, 157l (Dell & Wainwright), 157r (Dell & Wainwright), 158l (Dell & Wainwright), 158r (Dell & Wainwright), 159; Victoria and Albert Museum, London /Raymond McGrath, 124, 130, 132, 133.